The Phnom Penh Airlift

D1713952

To all "pig pilots,"
whose efforts gave over a million people
an extra year of life

The Phnom Penh Airlift

Confessions of a Pig Pilot in the Early 1970s

by

Charles W. Heckman

McFarland & Company, Inc., Publishers
Jefferson, North Carolina, and London

British Library Cataloguing-in-Publication data are available

Library of Congress Cataloguing-in-Publication Data

Heckman, Charles W., 1941–
     The Phnom Penh airlift : confessions of a pig pilot in the early
1970s / by Charles W. Heckman.
     p. cm.
     [Includes index.]
     ISBN 0-89950-491-4 (sewn softcover : 50# alk. paper) ∞
     1. Cambodia – History – Civil War, 1970–1975.   2. Airlift, Military –
United States – History – 20th century.   3. Cambodia – History – Civil
War, 1970–1975 – Personal narratives, American.   4. Heckman, Charles
W., 1941–   . I. Title.
DS554.8.H42   1990
959.704'348 – dc20   89-43650
                                                                                            CIP

Manufactured in the United States of America

McFarland & Company, Inc., Publishers
Box 611, Jefferson, North Carolina 28640

Foreword

Charlie Heckman and I first met in Vientiane, Laos, in the fall of 1970. We were in a new hire Air America pilot class for the C-123K. Unfortunately, the class was furloughed, and we never flew for that colorful organization. Since flying was in an extended slump back in the States, we decided to remain in Southeast Asia.

Charlie found employment as a DC-3 captain for Xieng Khouang Airlines, operated by Laotian General Vang Pao. I managed to convince Air America to retain me as a helicopter systems ground school instructor. During the next three years, Charlie and I occasionally ran across each other in Vientiane, and exchanged experiences. I discovered that Charlie had another intense interest besides flying — biology! While in Vientiane, Charlie completed the requirements for a master of science degree in biology and based his field work on the life of a Lao rice paddy. I considered this to be a quite commendable activity and somewhat amusing as the average expatriate pilot in Southeast Asia did not spend his spare time in this manner.

As the events in Southeast Asia moved into the 1970s, a war-weary U.S. Government began disengaging itself from its commitments in that area. The efforts in Laos were among the first to be sacrificed. Air America began losing contracts and entered a phase of terminal shrinking. By the middle of 1973, I could see that my position with Air America probably would not exist past the end of the year.

As I searched for employment options, I heard through the pilot grapevine that an airlift was underway in Cambodia using mainly DC-3s. A quick trip to Oakland, California, in December of 1973 provided me with a DC-3 type rating. Soon afterward, I resigned from Air America and entered Cambodia in February 1974 purely on speculation that I would be able to find employment as a pilot. After several inquiries, I landed a job with Tri-9 Airlines. It was not my vast multi-engine experience they were interested in, however. (Other than a DC-3 type rating, my multi-engine experience was minimal). Tri-9 had purchased a Lao registered DC-3, and to meet Cambodian requirements, they needed pilots with a Laotian license to crew it. Fortunately, I had the foresight to acquire a Lao license while living in Vientiane and was hired on the basis that I held the right piece of paper. I discovered, to my pleasure, that the captain hired to fly the aircraft was none other than Charlie Heckman. The DC-3 involved was XW-TFB, General Vang Pao's former aircraft.

In Cambodia, Tri-9 often leased their airplanes and crews to local businessmen who wanted to operate an airline. Consequently, the aircraft had a variety of names and paint schemes on them over the years. Eventually, the company operated the DC-3s under its own subsidiary name of Golden Eagle Airlines. The company painted XW-TFB and another U.S. registered DC-3 according to this motif. A black profile was painted on the stepped nose to resemble the head of an eagle, the fuselage was white, and the vertical stabilizer had a spray of diverging yellow stripes representing tail feathers. It was, without a doubt, the most "macho" paint scheme in Cambodia.

During my six months as a copilot, I had plenty to learn about operating a DC-3 off the short and narrow strips of Cambodia. They were a collection of blocked off sections of blacktop highway, old sand bars, and laterite strips that dated back to World War II. When my time came to check out as captain, Charlie's knowledge and patient instruction gave me the skill to be successful.

Cambodia was a beautiful and fascinating area to fly over. Much of the flying was done along the shore of Lake Ton Le Sap which changes its area by one third through the cycle of seasons and is populated by air breathing fish. On the north shore was the village of Siem Reap. Flying over the north edge of Siem Reap, one could see the magnificent Ankor Wat temple which marked the height of ancient Cambodian civilization. The exhilaration of this experience was tempered by the chilling observation that Cambodian culture was proceeding along a path of self destruction.

Charlie and I spent many pleasant evenings together in Phnom Penh. At Charlie's insistence, we eschewed the pedi-cab transporation and walked everywhere we went, often to a Korean restaurant away from the center of town. After dinner, we wandered through the streets visiting shops where silver coins of French, Spanish and Japanese origin could be found.

Even though the war had created a deterioration of the physical and social environment of Phnom Penh, enough remnants of the French influence remained to remind one of past happier times. Tree-lined boulevards still existed and poinciana trees lined the road into town from the airport. The Le Phnom Hotel (formerly the Royale) was still functioning, although hot water and electricity were lamentably unpredictable. It had the expected high ceilings with slow rotating fans and a staff that spoke fluent French dressed in starched white blouses. In the rear, bougainvillea and jasmine climbed the walls next to a small swimming pool. Adjacent to this was an excellent French restaurant where evening would find a mixture of pilots, journalists, embassy staff members and local businessmen, each with his own opinion on what was going wrong in the conduct of the war and how to correct it. One could imagine Michener or Maugham sitting quietly in a corner listening and taking notes.

The profits to be made around the periphery of the Cambodian War attracted a variety of colorful characters. It drew opportunistic businessmen who were quite comforable with the graft and corruption of the Cambodian government and the easy access to U.S. dollars. Pilots and mechanics of American, Chinese, Thai, Lao, Philippine, French and British origin appeared on the scene. Moving among such a mix of characters in a tropical wartime atmosphere of faded French colonialism made one feel like a character out of a B-grade adventure movie.

Several weeks after I checked out as a captain, Charlie left Cambodia to pursue a Ph.D. in biology in Germany. I continued flying until February 1975. By this time, daily rocketing of Pochentong Airport and the resulting destruction of several aircraft made continued airline operations untenable. Tri-9 decided to cease operating and evacuate Phnom Penh.

On February 8, 1975, I, my copilot and our wives, along with two spare engines, lifted off Pochentong Airport in XW-TFB bound for Singapore. For nearly five hours we flew south over the Gulf of Thailand until we touched down at Changi International Airport. Thus ended my year of living dangerously, flying over a beautiful but sad little country that was destined to become "The Killing Fields."

Bennett P. Crawford
Wichita, Kansas

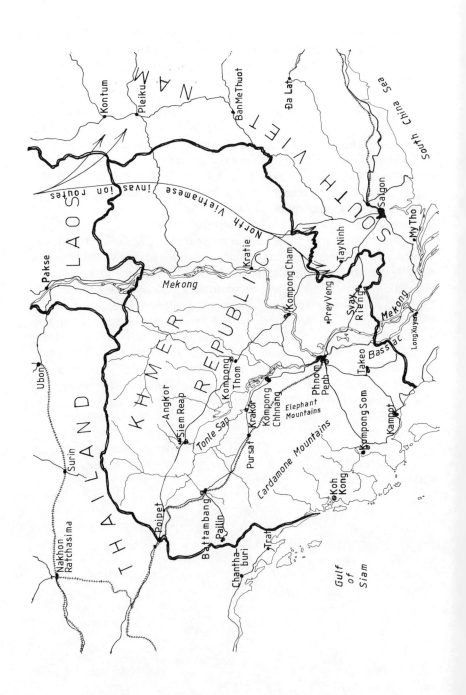

Preface

This book was written in 1975–76 while I was doing my doctoral research on the ecology of rice fields in Thailand. It was intended to be a firsthand, eyewitness account of the events that were still fresh in my memory, and it included much critique on the general organization of the efforts to save the Khmer Republic. Obviously, the airlift had been keeping the small nation from being taken over by North Vietnam and its cruel indigenous allies, the Khmer Rouge. Its successful operation, unfortunately, was impeded by the greed of a few shippers, a corrupt bureaucracy, and the mercurial dilettantism of the American aid mission, whose directors seemed more interested in saving face in defeat than in giving our Southeast Asian allies a chance to survive.

In spite of the ultimate failure of America's war effort in Southeast Asia, the airlift gave one to two million people more than one extra year of life and probably gave many others the chance to escape or send family members out of the country before the eclipse of civilization following the victory of the Khmer Rouge. A few years earlier, the United States government had been willing to give out billions of dollars and sacrifice tens of thousands of American lives to "win the minds and hearts" of the people of Southeast Asia, but at the time of the airlift, America was in the process of abandoning its allies to their fate, and only a handful of pilots from many different nations were keeping the lifelines between the main cities of the Khmer Republic open.

The story of the airlift is the prelude to a tragedy of historic dimensions. The Khmers were without a doubt the people who suffered most, but the South Vietnamese who had actively supported their own government or worked with the Americans, as well as various ethnic groups in Laos, particularly the Meos, faced long terms in "re-education" centers, which were usually nothing but forced labor camps, or they were threatened with outright extermination. After the armed conflicts following America's

Opposite: Blockaded capitals supplied with food and other necessities during the United States' involvement in the Indochina War.

ix

withdrawal subsided, the economy of the region under communist control deteriorated dramatically, and refugees have streamed from the region without interruption. Back in the United States, the Americans who had fought in the war faced a more subtle form of persecution in the form of job discrimination, denial of benefits by the Veterans Administration, and various forms of subtle vilification in the press. In view of the shabby performance of its own government, it is not surprising that American society preferred to ignore the horrors it left behind. For many years, there was little interest in factual reports on what had gone on during America's involvement in the war in France's former Indo-China colonies.

There has recently been an increased interest in firsthand reports on all aspects of the war, and perhaps some lessons can finally be learned, not only about the military failure but also about the senseless bureaucratic system that has been sapping America's strength. I therefore felt that the time was right for the publication of my manuscript.

Obviously, the United States is still living with the consequences of its Southeast Asian fiasco. It is therefore absolutely essential for the American people to start facing the facts and critically examining all available information to understand what went wrong. Only in this way, can future failures on such a colossal scale be avoided.

Charles W. Heckman
Hamburg, Germany

Introduction

The general principles of fortification and siege are as old as the art of war. The engineering and tactical aspects are continually modified, but the principles remain. A weaker army occupies a fortified position from which a larger one cannot dislodge it. By cutting off supplies from the outside, the besiegers try to starve the besieged into surrender. The decisive factor is then whether the allies of the besieged can succeed in getting enough supplies through the blockade to keep the defenders alive and in condition to maintain their defense. The loss of time and resources by the besiegers sometimes gives the opposing forces the opportunity to gather a large enough army to win the ultimate victory, whereas the rapid capture of the strongpoint permits the victorious attackers to move on to other conquests.

The advent of aviation has added a new dimension to the ancient art. Instead of fighting their way through with a supply train, the relieving forces can simply fly over the blocking positions of the besiegers.

The 20th century has seen some epic airlifts. The "hump" operation over the Himalayas to supply the Chinese Army in Yunnan was perhaps the first attempt on a large scale. The bureaucratic blockade of Berlin by Stalin during "peacetime" was overcome by an airlift. An unsuccessful and rather ineffective air supply operation was organized to supply the French outposts at Dien Bien Phu in 1954, and a decade later, air supply of isolated strongpoints in Vietnam became a standard procedure during America's well financed participation in the Indo-China war.

The 1970s saw another great airlift to supply a national capital and many provincial capitals for almost five years. Because the Americans were no longer as freespending as they had been during the 1960s, this airlift was organized as a low-budget operation. Unfortunately, the organizers were in many cases "low-budget" as well, and the operation took on some aspects of a comic opera with a tragic ending.

The events that led up to the war in Cambodia are numerous, but the Khmers themselves were simply caught between two hostile giants and could do little to influence these events. Whatever they did attempt invariably proved unwise.

1

While the American government was becoming more and more involved in the civil war in Vietnam, Norodom Sihanouk allowed his country to be used as a base for the North Vietnamese forces in exchange for huge handouts from the communist bloc. The eastern part of Cambodia came under direct Vietnamese communist domination, while Phnom Penh was built into one of the most beautiful capitals in Southeast Asia.

In 1970, the United States outbid Russia for the minds and hearts of Sihanouk's ministers, and while the prince was away on a tour, his own government deposed him and switched sides. The new chief of state, Lon Nol, found that it was not an easy job to expel the communists, who were already in control of a large part of the country. Although it was greatly enlarged by the recruitment of highly enthusiastic young men and women who often had to supply their own weapons in order to enlist, the Khmer Army was gradually driven from many parts of the country. One by one, the highways between Phnom Penh and the provincial capitals were choked off.

As the new government came to power, changing the name of the country from Cambodia to the Khmer Republic, Air Cambodge, the national airline, did not have a single domestic flight. Almost overnight, airfields opened for commercial operations in all parts of the country. The airlift provided the only reliable means of transportation to the province capitals that the government still controlled. The Khmer leadership realized that air was vital to the survival of the country, and private companies were officially invited to operate domestic flights. The foreign companies were not allowed to do business as such but were required by the government to operate under contract with Khmer firms, ostensibly to keep the profits in the country.

The first to accept the invitation were some carriers with operations in Laos. Continental Air Services, a company with American government contracts, opened for business in Phnom Penh under the colors of a local firm, Khmer Akas (Khmer Airlines). Jimmy L., the owner of Lao Air Charter, set up Cambodia Air Commercial (CACO).

Other companies soon arrived to fill the rapidly growing demand for air transport. The Tri-9 corporation took over the domestic routes that were assigned to Air Cambodge. Stan Booker, a wheeler-dealer type in the aviation business, brought in some aircraft and contracted them to several local firms.

Continental Air Services gave up their operations rather quickly. Its profits had not been comparable to those the management was used to making in Laos, where the company was under direct contract with the United States government. Furthermore, they were receiving payment in Khmer riels, which were worthless outside the country and were losing value at an alarming rate within. The company departed shortly after one of its DC-3s crashed near Kampot on the southern coast, killing everyone on board.

My own experience in the Khmer Republic began in 1971, when I traveled in the country for three days. While flying for a commercial aviation company in Laos, I kept track of events in Phnom Penh. In September 1973, I moved to Phnom Penh and participated in the airlift as a DC-3 captain.

This account, which I began writing shortly before the communists took over the country and completed at the end of 1976, includes not only my own account of the events I witnessed but also the impressions and the conclusions I had drawn at the time from my experiences. It is my hope that this recounting of events will be of value to historians after time has diminished the urge to forget America's Indo-China fiasco, and objective analyses and investigations of the failure become possible.

Chapter 1

Some archaeologists believe that the site of the world's first agricultural civilization is Southeast Asia. In any event, it is certain that the ebb and flow of human migration from all parts of the earth have passed across this fertile corner of Asia.

The bewildering array of races, languages, religions, and cultures attests to these past migrations. The latest additions to the potpourri, the abandoned children of the American GIs, black and white, have grown to adulthood among other recent arrivals from China and India, with descendants of the conquerors who founded the great kingdoms of Thailand, Vietnam, Burma, and Laos, as well as with the people who were there as far back as history records, namely, the Khmers, the Mons, the Chams, and the Malays.

Besides the major groups, Southeast Asia is inhabited by a countless number of smaller ethnic groups, many confined to isolated mountain regions. Some of these people speak languages, the origins of which are unknown. Perhaps it was an ancestor of one of these long isolated tribes who first learned to prepare a plot of land, plant seeds, and harvest the crop.

My first experience with Southeast Asia came at a time of intense but short-lived interest in the region by the government of the United States. I served as an Air Force pilot from 1964 through 1968, first flying C-130 transports for 18 months from Okinawa to bases in friendly countries of continental Southeast Asia and the Philippines, then flying for almost 2 years as a forward air controller over South and North Vietnam, Laos, and occasionally Thailand.

At that time, Cambodia was a country that we strictly avoided. Our C-130s flew either north of it over Laos or south over the sea en route to Thailand from points east. It was the only country in the region east of Burma we did not cross. The pilot of a C-123, who had graduated from my alma mater a year before me, had been shot down and killed while flying over a piece of territory claimed by both South Vietnam and Cambodia. His death prompted the United States government to change the maps, giving the disputed land to Cambodia.

4

The story was told in Air Force circles that the A-1 aircraft used to shoot down the C-123 had been given to France by the United States. As the war in Vietnam heated up, the United States government asked for the return of the aircraft. Instead, de Gaulle turned them over to Prince Sihanouk (translates "Roaring Lion").

My final two months of military service were spent flying O-2 observation aircraft over the Ho Chi Minh Trail in southern Laos. My unit flew out of Pleiku Air Base, and to save time and fuel, we sometimes crossed a narrow strip of Cambodia in northeastern Ratanakiri Province wedged between Laos and Vietnam. The Ho Chi Minh Trail led into this strip of land, where we could see parking areas in which war materials were undoubtedly stored under the forest cover. At the time, eastern Cambodia was famous as a sanctuary for the North Vietnamese.

To acquire all of the advantages of war without facing the dangers, the world political leaders have learned to limit armed conflict to specific geographical areas and formulate rules similar to those used in professional sports. According to our rules, the Cambodian border was an imaginary line behind which the North Vietnamese could remain unmolested. They could cross the line at any time, kill as many South Vietnamese and Americans as they could find, and if they could make it back across the line, they could thumb their noses in safety at their pursuers. The rules, of course, were not all one-sided. The Russians tolerated American air superiority over Laos and did not supply the North Vietnamese with the equipment required to seriously challenge it.

The chief opponents in Southeast Asia were the Soviet Union and the United States. The Chinese government apparently hoped that neither side would achieve complete victory and thereby establish a powerful base to the south. The conflict presented many interesting twists and turns. No one seemed concerned about the fate of the millions who happened to be caught between the opposing sides.

In 1969 the coup d'état that deposed Prince Sihanouk opened the way for the Khmer Army to turn on the hordes of North Vietnamese who had been enjoying Khmer hospitality for so long. The inexperienced Khmers were resoundingly thrashed, and only direct South Vietnamese and American intervention prevented total disaster.

In October 1970 I returned as a civilian to Southeast Asia to work as a pilot in Vientiane, Laos. During a few days off, I visited some old friends in Vietnam, and on my way back to Vientiane, I stopped in Phnom Penh.

My flight was the first one to land after a major communist attack on the airport. The MIG-17s that the Khmers had been using to bomb the Viet Cong had all been destroyed. One of the reminders of the past friendship with the communist bloc was thereby removed. Many DC-3s and other old airplanes had also become wreckage. The Caravelle, which had been the pride of Royal Air Cambodge, rested in its hangar with the roof collapsed over it. All of this damage was the work of a few communist sappers, attesting to the laxity of the Khmer guards. Under the conditions that prevailed near the end of 1970, an attack on the airport should have been expected, if not by the Khmers, certainly by their new American mentors. Apparently, no one was prepared.

As I entered the terminal over the heaps of broken glass that were once windows, I noted that most of my fellow passengers were reporters. They held all kinds of press identification cards in their hands to show the immigration police. They were a motley-looking entourage, which did not surprise me considering the quality of reporting that I was used to reading. I recognized several of them later in the restaurants near the Monorom Hotel where I stayed. During the three days that I spent in Phnom Penh, I saw them sitting at the bar, looking worse and worse every time I passed the hotel. One was interviewing the same English-speaking Khmer every time I stopped in the restaurant to eat. Was he the source of all the news that America and Europe would receive about the war?

During my 22 months as an Air Force pilot in forward combat zones of Vietnam, I had seen only one or two freelance reporters. Apparently journalists with comfortable jobs don't venture forth in search of news anymore. Perhaps that explains why freelance reporters made up the bulk of those missing or captured.

Not being a reporter, I walked around and tried to see as much of the city as I could. I found that the local currency, the riel, was not popular with shopkeepers. It was not accepted at all in the hotel. The official exchange rate at the time was 54 riels to the dollar, but in practice, it varied between 80 and 90 to 1.

Many office buildings were surrounded by concertina wire, and even the post office had a guard to check its customers for weapons. Posters, showing the Khmer Army driving out grisly-looking North Vietnamese invaders, hung everywhere. Among the many units of new recruits marching in the streets, spirits seemed very high. The soldiers, including girls, carried a variety of old weapons. There were more volunteers than could be accepted, and there were rumors that recruits would have to supply their own weapons to be accepted. In spite of the *élan*, I had a sense of foreboding. Could these new, inexperienced troops with their untried leaders match the North Vietnamese communists who had been fighting continuously for more than 20 years?

My flight to Vientiane was cancelled, and no other flights were expected for several days. To make it back before my leave time expired, I decided to travel overland from Battambang. I met some Filipino mechanics, whom I knew from Laos, and they reserved me a place aboard one of their company's DC-3s bound for Battambang.

XW-TFB, a DC-3 belonging to Tri-9 Airways International and painted in the colors of Golden Eagle Airlines, being flown by the author over the Khmer Republic (photo by Bill Ernst, courtesy of Charley Pennington).

The Sankha Hotel in Battambang was considerably cheaper than the hotels in Phnom Penh, but the manager expected to be paid in dollars, too. That evening I had a conversation with some of the people who were setting up a trucking operation between Thailand and the Khmer Republic. One was Thai; the others, Khmer. One of the Khmers, an employee of Tela Khmer (Khmer Oil) in Phnom Penh, showed remarkable optimism about the war. He said the Khmers believed the problem in South Vietnam to be that the communists were indistinguishable from the rest of the population. It was impossible to tell who the enemy was. In Cambodia, the Khmer population was united against the communists, and the people were distinct in looks, language, religion and culture. The Vietnamese enemy could therefore be recognized wherever he appeared, and a long guerrilla war would be impossible.

I did not share his optimism and suggested that the war would be long and hard. I warned him that the Vietnamese had had years of fighting experience and had been equipped with massive amounts of modern weaponry by the Russians.

The Khmers seemed quite different from the other people I had met in Southeast Asia. They seemed physically tougher, more open, and rather outgoing, but they lacked intellectual depth and cunning. Their physical appearance is very distinct. Most Khmers have very dark skin, somewhat curly hair, roundish eyes and rather thick lips. My first impression was that they were a rather likeable people. Their country looked rather neat, but it lacked industry. The population was sparce and well dispersed throughout the countryside.

The next morning I boarded a train pulled by a shiny steam locomotive donated by the People's Republic of China to Prince Sihanouk's government. A flatcar loaded with sandbags was pushed ahead of it to prematurely detonate mines. The railroad line was open to the Thai border, where it met the Thai National Railroad at the border post of Poipet. The tracks were not the same gauge, so passengers had to walk across the border to change trains. I took a small bus to Aranya Prathet, where I boarded a bus to return to Vientiane.

Chapter 2

The news that I heard of the military actions during the next two years bore out my worst fears. At first, things seemed to go well. The Khmers' sudden change of sides had apparently taken the Vietnamese communists by surprise. The government forces quickly captured the majority of province capitals and about three quarters of the country. The Khmer commander at Kratie in the Northeast wavered, however, and in his absence a subordinate turned the garrison over to the communists, who suddenly espoused the cause of the deposed prince to rally support. Much of eastern Cambodia remained in the hands of the Viet Cong, who had long occupied it. They had grown so complacent in many of their base areas, however, that they were rather easily rooted out by well supported government drives.

Just before the coup, the Khmer Army had been well supplied with arms by a ship, supposedly bound for South Vietnam but hijacked and diverted to the port of Sihanoukville, later renamed Kompong Som. The communists first tried to fight conventional battles and suffered severe losses. They had to evacuate many of their safe areas, and Highway 1 was opened for its entire length from Phnom Penh to Saigon.

The optimism engendered by the initial successes led to overambitious campaigns. The Khmer Army launched a vigorous series of operations to keep the other major highways open. Most did not go very well, but one of them, called Operation Chenla IV, named for an ancient Khmer kingdom, ended in complete disaster and marked the end of the offensive operations.

The hatreds bred by war are often diverted from the enemy, and in the Khmer Republic, a very ugly anti–Vietnamese pogrom began, which wiped out or expelled the noncommunist Vietnamese population of the country. During French colonial times, the Annamese, as the people from Central Vietnam had been called, were encouraged to migrate throughout all of Indochina. They were employed as minor government officials, office workers, and soldiers in preference to Khmers and Laos. The political unity established within the entire region made it easy for farmers and fishermen from

Vietnam to settle in unoccupied Cambodian territory. The fishing industry on the great lake of the Tonle Sap was chiefly in the hands of the Vietnamese settlers. These people had formed the backbone of the rural economy in many parts of Cambodia.

The jealousy of the Khmers was undoubtedly the underlying cause of the savagery against the more industrious Vietnamese. Word of mass killings reached South Vietnam as large numbers of refugees streamed toward Saigon. The Khmer government justified the killings by claiming that it could not risk having communist sympathizers in the country.

The main result, however, was the alienation of the Khmers' best natural ally, South Vietnam. The Vietnamese have a close-knit society, and the slaughter of noncommunist kin prompted the soldiers in some South Vietnamese military units operating in Cambodia to kill Khmer villagers in reprisal. Fire fights were reported between Vietnamese and Khmer soldiers, and it became evident that joint military operations by the two countries would prove counterproductive.

To understand why the cooperation that seemed so vital for both countries never developed, it is necessary to review the historical development of Southeast Asia. Briefly stated, the southward migration of the Thai and Lao people in the west and the Vietnamese in the east had gradually eliminated a large kingdom of a people called the Chams and reduced the formerly extensive kingdom of the Khmers to a tiny enclave. Cambodia was saved from complete extinction in 1863, when King Norodom made his country a French protectorate. A year earlier, France had annexed Saigon and the Mekong Delta as a colony, Cochin China, which had been nominally the king's territory.

Prince Sihanouk has often been outspoken in denouncing this "betrayal" of his country by King Norodom, and he named a street in Phnom Penh after Prince Sisowath, who spoke out for the independence of Cambodia before the French National Assembly in 1907 and thereby removed himself from contention for the throne. Sihanouk himself has often claimed that he was picked by the French to rule his country because they thought that he could easily be controlled.

In this regard, Sihanouk has either fully misunderstood or deliberately misstated the situation. While the Vietnamese might well resent the French conquest of their expanding empire, the Khmers were saved by the French and spared the fate of the Chams, whose kingdom had been fully extinguished by the Vietnamese.

Prince Sihanouk personally led Cambodia despotically after the withdrawal of the French from Indochina. It is necessary to study his personality and actions to understand Cambodian politics during the Vietnam War. It is easy to learn his views because of his prolific writing. In one of his books, *My War with the CIA*, coauthored by an Australian communist, he condemned the CIA for trying to overthrow him for many years but readily admitted allowing the Vietnamese communist forces to use his land as a base for their activities.

The deterioration of his relationship with the United States during the 1950s led to a complete break in 1962, when the employees of the United States Agency for International Development (USAID) were given 24 hours to leave the country. Since they had no time to dispose of their personal property, some of them were so enraged that they burned their automobiles in the streets rather than let some Cambodian officials have them for nothing. Although the mutual alienation of Sihanouk and the American diplomats in his country is attributed by him to abstractions, such as "imperialism", it is clear from the prince's book that there was very strong personal animosity between the prince and the American ambassador at the time, Robert McClintock.

Certainly, it would have taken a man capable of great diplomacy to deal with the prince who represented an anachronism, living in the style of an oriental despot with a harem while making grand pronouncements about the modernization of his land. Ambassador McClintock obviously lacked the necessary qualities, and his needling of the prince seems to have been a key factor in destroying Khmer-American relations. In his book, Sihanouk related an incident that took place during the dedication of a maternity hospital donated by the United States. The ambassador asked the prince, a polygamist, what he, as an expert at making babies, thought of the facility. Sihanouk bore a grudge for many years, and he was not a man who could separate personal feelings from matters of state. This failure of diplomacy bore fruit for the Vietnamese communists, who were allowed to entrench themselves in Cambodian territory so securely that they could no longer be rooted out by joint American-Vietnamese-Khmer clearing operations after Cambodia changed sides in the war.

Robert McClintock seems to have established his niche in history by making short quips to infuriate people. During the heated discussions between the French and Americans on possible methods of saving the embattled French stronghold of Dien Bien Phu by using American B-29s, diplomat McClintock flippantly remarked, "War is too serious a business to be left entirely to generals," a statement quoted from Georges Clemenceau. This witticism provoked one of the American generals to rebuke him angrily. In spite of his habit of putting out small emotional fires by dousing them with gasoline, he rose steadily through the ranks in the foreign service until he reached a position where he could do some real harm.

While giving vital support to the Vietnamese communists, Prince Sihanouk waged a relentless and ruthless campaign against the Cambodian communist forces. To repay the prince for his help, the Viet Cong gave no aid to their Khmer comrades, and the Cambodian communist party remained small and ineffective. Its leadership, however, was enhanced by a few dedicated and efficient Khmer officials, who had been hounded out of office by the prince and his cronies for being too diligent or honest. Ieng Sary was the most prominent émigré to the communists.

Distrust between the Khmers and Vietnamese communists began to increase, and the prince reportedly made a secret agreement with the United States to allow B-52 raids and other air strikes on his territory. Because of the sensitivity of the issue and the desire of Sihanouk to maintain the guise of neutrality, it was understood that the moves against the communists would remain absolutely secret.

Unfortunately for Sihanouk, security within the massive American bureaucracy is normally as tight as a sieve. Sympathy for the Viet Cong and antipathy by many Federal employees toward Nixon guaranteed an immediate release of the details of Sihanouk's agreement to the leading newspapers. The prince was so shocked that he refused further cooperation with the Americans. His ministers were more willing to openly cooperate in the fight against the communists, and while he was away on a tour of France, they overthrew him.

It is ironic that Prince Sihanouk was finally eliminated, not because he made his country a major base for the North Vietnamese Army but because he secretly began to make concessions to the United States. The disaffected American civil servant who was so determined to undo his country's foreign policy by releasing details of a secret agreement sent the most prominent Cambodian of all into the camp of the Khmer Rouge, who had long been his bitter foes.

To complete the background of the airlift, something must be said about the military situation. The Khmers were unfortunate to have allied themselves with the United States at the time they did. Like most of the people in Southeast Asia, they underestimated the strength of the anti–Vietnam War movements and the war weariness of the Americans in general. They had no idea that any debacle involving the president of the United States could actually be so serious as to remove almost the entire top layer of the American executive branch and drastically alter many longstanding policies. The Khmers were totally ignorant about the psychological processes at work within America, and they foolishly trusted the promises and secret assurances of the officials from Washington who committed themselves to give all the support necessary to overcome the enemy.

The Khmers, like the South Vietnamese, would be entirely dependent on the United States for all things military, just as the North Vietnamese depended entirely on the Soviet Union for everything they needed to continue fighting, except people. The ultimate responsibility for all military actions on the allied side therefore rested with the joint chiefs-of-staff in collaboration with their civilian superiors in the defense department. It is fashionable to excuse American generals from their responsibility for failures on the grounds that their allies refused to cooperate properly. In practice, if not in theory, the United States was running the military show in Southeast Asia, and just as in World War II, leadership meant gaining the cooperation of the allies. American officials were undeniably interfering in the internal affairs of South Vietnam, Laos, and the Khmer Republic, but when necessary steps were not taken, the responsible Americans would invariably pass the buck by saying that they could not interfere in the internal affairs of sovereign states. It may be all too human to want credit for successes and to blame others for failure, but where the opportunity for this was as great as it was in Southeast Asia, this practice became a form of institutionalized self-deception.

The greatest failure of the allied side was in the overall strategy, which ignored time-tested geopolitical considerations. Holding the high ground is a principle of warfare that has always been important and is usually decisive. Geographically, Laos is the heart of Southeast Asia. The communists took and held the mountain range in eastern Laos throughout the war. The South Vietnamese disaster at Tchepone in eastern Laos in 1971 assured the communists of their ultimate victory. Although the North Vietnamese nearly always avoided a set-piece battle, they made an exception at Tchepone, putting a tremendous effort into the counterattack to rout the South Vietnamese. This shows that the North Vietnamese leaders knew that control of Eastern Laos was essential to winning the war.

With eastern Laos under control, two routes of invasion were open into South Vietnam: one across the Demilitarized Zone (DMZ) and eastward from the mountains into the narrow coastal strip north of Danang; the other through the Central Highlands. Both paths of invasion were attractive, but the route south from the DMZ was narrow, and the way through the highlands was long and rough. The alternative of a direct attack on Saigon was extremely desirable, and that one required the control of eastern Cambodia.

The communists did not have the strength to attack along all three routes, but it was essential for them to keep the roads open, thereby forcing the South Vietnamese to disperse their resources. The interpretation of allied intelligence was so poor that the enemy, moving along their excellent road system, could mass for a surprise attack from any of the three directions.

The American leadership decided early in the war to compensate for poor strategy with massive firepower. Technology would create new geopolitical realities, and the communists would be so intimidated that they would rush to the negotiating table. "Reconnaissance by fire" would keep the enemy at "arm's length." which would "save lives." This saved enemy lives as well and protracted the conflict. The enemy knew by the sound of the fire where the allies were moving, and they could evade the sweeps and usually pick and choose the battlefield.

Eventually, the allies would not engage the enemy at all when not assured of massive fire support, and ground interdiction of the supply lines was never seriously attempted. After the United States Congress cut off the funds for air support in the summer of 1973, massive fire support was no longer available, and many Americans predicted immediate disaster for the allies. In Cambodia, nevertheless, little happened for several months. When forced into a strictly defensive posture, the Khmers proved to be quite stubborn. The Khmer Air Force had been given some T-28s and Helio Stallions to provide air support for their ground forces. Their pilots, unfortunately, were not chosen on the basis of ability, and they had received the minimum possible training. As relatives of well-to-do government officials, the young men placed in the cockpits of the tiny bombers were not too well disposed to taking personal risks. Their American mentors had taught them the method of reconnaissance and bombing from high altitude to avoid the risk of ground fire. This definitely cut down their losses and also greatly limited their accuracy. The enormous number of bomb craters in the middle of empty rice fields was irrefutable evidence that the American bombing had been equally inaccurate.

Now that there was a massive influx of American supplies going directly into the hands of the Khmers, corruption began to develop on a massive scale, just as it had elsewhere in Southeast Asia. This, more than any other factor, sapped the strength of the vital supply effort. The failure to control this corruption was the greatest manifestation of weakness by the allies.

Chapter 3

In September 1973, I arrived in Phnom Penh aboard the Royal Air Lao Electra from Vientiane. I had been hired by a new company, Southeast Asia Air Transport (SEAAT), as a DC-3 captain. The SEAAT aircraft and crews were to fly under the colors of Air Cambodge, the national airline of the Khmer Republic. Mid-September was a period of confusion for the company as the managers tried to accumulate the vast array of permits necessary to operate. Even though it was no secret that the country now depended on the airlift for survival, the bureaucratic mafia was so entrenched that every routine paper required an interminable waiting period unless bribes were paid.

My own first requirement was a Khmer authorization to fly in the country. Although I was to fly a United States registered aircraft, I brought both my United States and Lao pilot licenses to the Khmer Director of Civil Aviation (DCA). That was my first mistake.

The Khmer DCA required pilots to pass a written test. It consisted of ten questions copied from an American flight study guide. This served no other purpose than to give the DCA employees an excuse to "put the squeeze" on anyone who failed. When the test was first instituted, all pilots already flying in the country had been required to take it. Several failed. Rather than take it again, they told their companies to fix it up for them. The next day, they were flying again, and the DCA officials were a little richer. The loss to their companies would have been enormous if they had been grounded for a few days to wait for a retest.

Although I passed the test, I was given an authorization to fly only Lao registered DC-3s. To most people, a DC-3 is a DC-3, but not to the greedy DCA employees. To add one word to the document required several weeks, unless the company was willing to pay extra. Since the DC-3s were not yet authorized either, there was no hurry and nothing was paid.

The Americans who managed the company were notorious sharps, and they lived up to their reputations. I was told on arrival that I would go on the payroll after I received my authorization. That meant that the loss caused by delays in processing my papers would be mine. My authorization

15

Private enterprise thrived on the streets of Phnom Penh in the mid-1970s (photo courtesy of Bill Ernst).

for Lao DC-3s was ready in six days, so I made sure that I was on the payroll before I initiated getting it amended.

SEAAT housed us in a rented surburban villa just outside Phnom Penh. The managers were obviously building a large organization, and they talked as if they anticipated some big developments. When I arrived, there were already ten pilots on the payroll, plus a chief pilot. Several others were on leave. Two were on sick leave in local hospitals with typhoid fever, which was epidemic in Phnom Penh at the time.

September is near the end of the rainy season and the flooded sections of the city, inhabited by thousands of refugees, provided the necessary environment for the spread of epidemics. Public sanitation in the Khmer Republic was worse than anything I had encountered previously in Southeast Asia. The city was dirtier than any other I had seen there. The sidewalks were black and sticky, and the strong smell of human excrement baking in the sun filled the air whenever the wind blew from the northeast, which was almost six months each year. In a small hospital, where we visited one of the sick pilots, an average of six Khmer typhoid victims was brought in daily. The death rate was five out of six. Both pilots who had contracted typhoid had previously been vaccinated against the disease, and that probably saved their lives. They were both extremely ill for several weeks.

While a large number of penniless refugees flooded into the city, a sizeable portion of the population was doing very well. Phnom Penh had the highest per capita Mercedes population that I have ever seen. Most of them belonged to army officers and government officials, and some owners had an extra one that they rented out. The SEAAT management had leased several of these. The salaries of the civil servants were never particularly high, and the raging inflation made them almost negligible. The Khmer officials turned to various methods of white collar crime to maintain their high living standards.

In all fairness, I have to state that I did meet some honest and hard-working Khmer officers. They were all out in remote provinces trying to hold their country together. The Khmer soldiers at some of these isolated locations fought with great bravery under the worst possible conditions. In the capital, I neither met nor heard of competent officers or civil servants. The Phnom Penh elite apparently farmed out all of the good people in order to have a clear field to pursue their illegal endeavors, the nature of which I was soon to become acutely aware.

The consumer-oriented society, so much discussed in America, flourished in Phnom Penh during the war. The best restaurants were full of uniformed military men and civilians sitting for hours eating and drinking. Many traveled in military vehicles, while others flaunted their well-maintained Mercedes. To demonstrate the superiority of the United States, the American embassy staff traveled in American cars much larger than the Mercedes, but they were only rarely seen outside of the fortified compounds.

It quickly became evident that everyone was working for his own benefit. Personal profit was much more important than the common good, and almost all of the Khmers I talked to had an almost childlike faith that the United States would stand by them, come what may. They were so convinced that American prestige would require the United States to take every necessary measure to win that they did nothing positive to help their nation survive. They did not seem to realize that the supply effort they were weakening by their demands for graft might break down and bring disaster on all of them.

In mid–October, our DC-3s were still waiting for the permits to fly to Bangkok for the Federal Aviation Agency's airworthiness inspection. The other SEAAT DC-3 captain, a retired Thai Air Force pilot named Sangob Suvannisang, had had little to do since arriving in Phnom Penh. Our chief pilot arranged for us to fly a DC-3 belonging to another company until our own aircraft were ready. We had prepared for our first flight, and the aircraft had been loaded with cargo. I had already received my authorization to fly United States registered aircraft, and the DC-3 I was to fly was registered in the United States. Everything was in order, we thought. When we handed in the flight plan, the Khmer tower clerk said that he could not approve it. The chief pilot told us to wait outside because it was a sensitive matter. He made it a policy to keep us away from the Khmer officials and

The best photographer among the pilots, Bill Ernst, talking with some Khmer rangers taking a break in a Phnom Penh city park (photo courtesy of Bill Ernst).

had gone so far as to forbid the pilots from going to the Directorate of Civil Aviation office for anything after taking the test.

After a considerable period of time, the representative of the company we were to fly for, a young Chinese-Khmer, informed us regretfully that the flight had been cancelled. The official reason was that the letter requesting our authorizations had come from Air Cambodge, and the aircraft we were attempting to fly was leased by another company, Khemera Air Transport. The real reason, as we were told by the company representative, was that our chief pilot would not pay a large bribe that the tower authorities required before they would overlook the little discrepancy they had found.

The Khmer officials were strange people to deal with. They knew absolutely nothing about aviation, but they were good at picking out the slightest inconsistency on an official form. Relations with them started off very badly and deteriorated from there. They outwardly gave the impression of being very stupid. After getting to know them better, it became obvious that they really were. I had previously dealt with Thai, Vietnamese, Lao and Chinese officials and businessmen and found them all to be generally equal or superior to Americans in intelligence. In fact, in business dealings with these people, Americans invariably came out second best. It took me some time to adjust to the fact that a group of people in Southeast Asia could really be so stupid.

Although the Khmer officials seemed short on brains, they were rather proud and stubborn. This was a disastrous combination. To this brand of crook, not only the amount of money was important, but the way it was given assumed certain aesthetic qualities. In general, bribery was handled by the cargo shippers, most of whom were Chinese with Khmer names. The Chinese have a reputation for paying generously for the privilege of doing business. As a result, they seemed to be particularly attractive targets for the money-hungry Khmer authorities. At times, the insatiable greed of the airport officials caused the cancellation of flights, when, according to the shippers, the bribes demanded exceeded the profit to be made from the trip.

On October 21 the SEAAT management spent the day rounding up the vast number of signatures required before the DC-3s would be allowed to fly to Bangkok. We planned to depart early on the morning of the 22nd, but we found that we still lacked some signatures on some of the papers. The Khmers at the airport created delay after delay. We had moved from the suburban villa to the downtown Sokhalay Hotel a few days earlier, and we waited there for the car to come and pick us up. We were walking around in the vicinity of the hotel in the late afternoon after wearing out a few chairs in the lobby when the car suddenly arrived. We didn't see it, and the driver didn't see us. It was already the last minute because the airport closed each day at 6:00 P.M. sharp, so Cedric Warren, one of the vice-presidents of SEAAT, decided to take one of the aircraft and fly it there himself, leaving the other one for us to fly the next day. On take-off, as he reached a speed of about 60 knots, both of his engines quit. He restarted them and tried to take off again, but the same thing happened. He never found out why.

On October 23 we finally took off for Bangkok to have the inspection performed. Sangob Suvannisang and I flew one DC-3, Cedric Warren flew the other with David Chester as his copilot. The Federal Aviation Agency (FAA) inspector had arrived in Bangkok, and he was treated in a manner befitting a federal inspector. He was supplied with such a liberal number of drinks at his hotel that he was quickly able to sign the airworthiness certificates, even though there were a few items on the aircraft that did not meet FAA standards, such as fixed baffles instead of movable cowl flaps. His only comment was that there were no red lines painted on the instruments. After all, an inspector always has to find something that requires corrective action, otherwise someone might doubt that he is doing a good job. A SEAAT mechanic and I painted the instruments before we took off for Phnom Penh.

While the papers were being attended to, I was able to take an FAA written examination. When I handed it in, the inspector asked to see a document that I had left in Phnom Penh. Cedric Warren decided that I would ferry the SEAAT Dornier Do-28A to Bangkok for its airworthiness inspection the next day, and I could bring the document with me. We were just able to make it back to Phnom Penh with our DC-3 before curfew because Sangob knew the ins and outs of the Thai airport regulations.

On October 26 I returned with the Dornier and the SEAAT vice president. The FAA examiner told me that he had made a mistake, and the document was not required for American citizens after all. I was not too upset because I had had the opportunity to fly an interesting aircraft. This one had previously been owned by Continental Air Services in Vientiane, Laos. Several years earlier it had been parked next to an Air America machine that had not been tied down. A sudden wind storm blew this airplane against the Dornier, cracking the wooden wing spar. Air America shipped the wounded German aircraft to its maintenance shop in Tainan, Taiwan, and replaced the wood spar, unfortunately with teakwood. The Dornier was now so heavy that it could no longer carry a profitable load. It remained in Continental's maintenance area for four or five years before it was sold to two mechanics who made it airworthy again. They offered it for sale in the Bangkok newspapers for $10,000, but it could have been had for less. The price SEAAT paid for it was rumored to be about $20,000, at least on paper, but I do not know with certainty.

The SEAAT vice-president remained in Bangkok, and I flew the Dornier back alone. About half way back, the engines began running so roughly that I considered landing at one of the fields en route. First, the left engine started backfiring. I pulled the power all the way to idle and was considering shutting it down when the right engine began running roughly, too. The aircraft flew poorly on one engine, so I began alternately reducing power on each engine while running the other one up to maximum power. I judged the problem to be badly fouled spark plugs, so I used various defouling procedures involving the mixture control. In this way, I kept both engines running until I reached Phnom Penh. The mechanics spent the next few days washing a thick, gummy substance off the spark plugs. Apparently, the fuel tank preservative had never been washed out. I had noticed that the DC-3s also had a sticky substance in the fuel while we were preflighting them prior to leaving for Bangkok. The fuel was sent for analysis, but the substance could not be identified. It was also probably a tank preservative.

The Dornier's technical problems were minor compared to those created by the bureaucracy. Cedric, the SEAAT vice-president, and I had gone to Phnom Penh Airport early in the morning on October 26, hoping to get an early start for Bangkok in the Dornier. Cedric took the deck of authorization papers with him back to town to try to fill up the vast number of signature blocks. He personally traveled from office to office getting the various officials to sign. None of the people were in their offices and finding them was like a scavenger hunt. He even got General Fernandez, the loser of Chenla IV, out of bed during his afternoon nap. The procedures were made so difficult so money could be demanded for timely service. At about 5 P.M. Cedric finally returned to the airport with all of the required forms. We had to be off the ground by 5:30 because of the airport curfew.

While Cedric warmed up the engines, I rushed in to file the flight plan. I then jumped in the company car and rode out to the runway where I leaped into the cockpit as Cedric lined the plane up for take-off. We got off the ground with only about 1½ minutes to spare.

The next day I was prepared to leave for Phnom Penh, but the FAA inspector overslept and then insisted on going to the military side of the Bangkok Airport to eat a big breakfast before signing the papers. He didn't have enough time to look at the aircraft, but he pored over the books and had a long conversation with Cedric, who told him all about the dirty tricks used by various competitors of SEAAT, chiefly Stan Booker, who was alleged to have said that he would rather steal a nickel than earn a dollar.

After my planned take-off time had long passed, the papers were finally signed. The Dornier was loaded with spare parts, and I headed to the car hired by the president of SEAAT to pick up the aircraft log books. There was no car. We searched for almost an hour before we found it parked in a lot far from where we had seen it last. The driver had needed a nap. Cedric departed for the railroad station, and I left for the aircraft parking ramp.

Unfortunately, we had arrived in Bangkok so late the previous evening that the office of the World Travel Service, which generally handled the airport formalities for Air Cambodge, was already closed. As I prepared for take-off, the office was closed for lunch. It seemed that our aircraft had never been signed in, so there was no place for me to sign out. The airman spoke almost no English, and if I had not been able to speak Thai, I might have been there for days. I explained the situation, and the airmen called the customs officer who supplied our manifest and assured them that everything had been in order when we arrived. The airmen then decided that it would be permissible for me to sign in on the proper page and then sign out again. I went to the aircraft and started the engines, but when I called ground control I was told to return to the terminal building. When I arrived, the airman told me that everything was in order but ground control had been late in receiving the word that my flight had been cleared.

The Dornier was parked some distance from the terminal, and it was already too late for me to make it to Phnom Penh before the curfew. I unloaded all of the spare parts I was supposed to take with me and stored them in the Thai-Am maintenance office. I scheduled myself for an early morning departure, and the next afternoon I landed in Phnom Penh.

After its arrival the Dornier never flew again. Air Cambodge would not agree to painting its name on such a funny looking machine. It was a good short take-off and landing (STOL) aircraft, and it could have brought small loads almost anywhere in the country, but the Air Cambodge employees knew only how to snicker at it.

During the period from September 15, when we had been scheduled to begin commercial DC-3 operations, and October 29, when we actually did, food had become scarce in the city. A communist offensive had cut some of the last road links, and the inflation began to accelerate. Our dollars bought more and more riels, while the riels bought less and less. The SEAAT management was very perturbed by the fact that even a contract with the national airline had not prevented them from losing a month and a half of flying time, chiefly because of the greed and stupidity of some of the Khmer authorities. There were hints that managers of competing companies were paying bribes to delay issuance of our authorizations.

Chapter 4

My first commercial flight in the country was aboard N82AC with Bill Ernst as my copilot. He had been an army enlisted man in Vietnam, learned to fly, and used his GI Bill benefits to get his commercial license. He had flown only light aircraft and hoped to gain experience on DC-3s and larger aircraft.

We flew four trips to Kompong Chhnang that day, while Captain Sangob and his copilot flew to Kompong Thom. The wet southwest monsoon had just ended, and after the six months of rain comes a season when the visibility is almost unlimited. From the air, the scenery in parts of Southeast Asia is among the most beautiful on the planet.

The plain below us was still flooded, and where the war had not yet made refugees out of the farmers, its rice fields were deep green. In every direction from Phnom Penh, richly colored and impressive landscapes could be seen. To the north and east of the city flows part of one of the world's great river systems. Four branches form a great confluence at Phnom Penh. From the north flows the Mekong, nearly overflowing its banks at the end of the rainy season. Some of the water comes from the Himalayas in Tibet, where the Mekong and Yangtze arise and flow parallel only a few kilometers apart horizontally but separated by high mountains. The rapidly flowing water carries trees, assorted debris and enormous quantities of mud. When the water reaches Phnom Penh, it may take any of three paths. The Mekong departs to the east, carrying with it the greatest amount of water on its rush to the South China Sea. The Bassac, the first branch of the Mekong Delta, flows to the southeast. The water may flow back into the Mekong many miles downstream through one of the many anastomosing channels. To the northwest flows the Tonle Sap. This river swells into a great lake that occupies much of the country's surface area and provides it with one of the largest single sources of freshwater fish in the world. The water flows from the Mekong into the Tonle Sap during the late rainy season and early dry season, then reverses direction as the water level in the rivers falls. The Tonle Sap is one of the only rivers in the world that reverses direction every six months.

To the north and east beyond the rivers are vast expanses of rice fields, and in the distance, north of the great bend of the Mekong to the east, the forests and plantations around Kompong Cham are visible.

To the south stretch the highways to Kampot and Kompong Som. Great mountains arise, and beyond them lie the turquoise waters in the bays and inlets along the southern coast. Travelling to the southwest was perhaps the most scenic route. The vast Elephant Mountain Range with its rainforest cover crosses the route to the sea and to Thailand. Eastward lies Vietnam and the great green and brown Mekong Delta.

Our trip to Kompong Chhnang took us to the west northwest. We circled to 3000 feet over Phnom Penh's Pochentong Airport, then headed toward our destination. Ahead and to our left were the northernmost mountains in the Elephant Range. Among them rises the highest peak in the range to almost 6000 feet, the highest point in the country. Lying to the north of the mountains is the Great Lake.

In 1973 the shores of the Tonle Sap River leading into the Great Lake were lined with buildings. Temples and markets, as well as private homes, stood astride the highway paralleling the river, showing no signs of war damage. The American bombing that had ended in August had been directed mainly at rice fields and water buffaloes, marking open fields with vast numbers of craters. The United States Air Force seemed to use ordnance similarly to the way the Chinese use firecrackers at New Year's. If they make enough bangs and flashes, the communists, like evil spirits, will be scared away. Enemy property should not be damaged, however.

The Khmers went to the other extreme. They seemed to have no regard for their fellow citizens. The artillery units around the capital fired at everything and anybody within range. Like the United States Air Force, they did not seem to do much damage to the enemy, but they systematically leveled all of the buildings along the river and created a steady flow of refugees into the already overcrowded capital. I knew that the country would never again be as beautiful as it was that October, at least in my lifetime.

At Kompong Chhnang we found a newly surfaced gravel runway. I was warned not to land on the end because of the holes and ruts. I landed long and found that the rest of the runway was also a little bouncy, but not too bad. As time went on, the furrows deepened and the bumps became harder. After the trips there, hydraulic fluid usually seeped from around the strut seals.

On our first day of business, we learned that the cargo shippers we were dealing with were crooks. They liked to overload the aircraft after telling the pilot that the cargo weighed exactly the 3200 kilos permitted by their contract. When an aircraft arrived, cargo was loaded until the pilot got suspicious. A long argument would then ensue about how much had to be taken off. Overloads on the DC-3 damage the aircraft, overwork the engines, and are very dangerous in emergencies, especially in case of engine failure on take-off.

Most of the shippers were Chinese; none were Khmer. We were to be confronted with some formidably clever forms of deception. One group of the four groups of shippers we dealt with proved to be the greatest problem for our operation. One of the bosses was thin and sneaky-looking; the other was fat and always wore a camouflaged hat. A particularly nasty teenaged relative assisted them in their crimes. Their cargo was always baskets of fresh fish, sometimes accompanied by sacks of peas, peanuts and sweet potatoes. By looking at the compression of the aircraft tires, I could usually make a good estimate of how heavy the aircraft was. After the aircraft was fully loaded, the tires always looked too flat, so I would remove several 60 kilogram sacks until the tire compression looked almost right. Each time, the shippers would argue vehemently about my procedures, but whenever I weighed the cargo after landing at Phnom Penh, we were nevertheless 100 to 200 kilograms overweight. If we had taken the sacks I had thrown off, we would have been dangerously overweight. SEAAT showed very little interest in solving this problem.

On November 5 we had been loaded for our third of four scheduled trips from Kompong Chhnang to Phnom Penh. The cargo looked a little heavy, but I was trying to stay ahead of schedule, so I prepared for take-off. As we made our 180° turn to line up with the runway for take-off, I noticed that we needed more power than usual to turn. We were right on the runway centerline as I added power for take-off. Suddenly, the left wheel broke through the runway surface and sank into the ground almost to the axle, causing the left wing to dip almost to the ground. I quickly shut down the left engine to keep the prop from hitting the ground.

The runway surface was supported by a rock layer only about 18 inches thick. Below was sand softened by six months of heavy rain. The left axle rested on the ground and the tire was tightly wedged between large rocks. Digging out the rocks blocking the front wheel failed to free the aircraft.

The Khmer Air Force maintenance team arrived with a tow truck and tried to pull the aircraft backwards. The truck tires just spun on the soft surface and the aircraft would not budge. I told the mechanics to stop before they damaged the aircraft. We had to unload the cargo. Some of the passengers tried to help dig the aircraft out, but their efforts were counterproductive. One started putting the rocks back in front of the tire, so I asked them not to help. A farmer arrived with a hoe, and he turned out to be the only helper with any sense. The farmer and I did most of the digging because the Khmer Air Force personnel considered physical work beneath their dignity.

Finally, a tug arrived with a large piece of aluminum planking and a Khmer Air Force man who knew what to do. We put the planking under the wheel to distribute the weight, and the tug pulled the aircraft right out.

At Phnom Penh we weighed the cargo and passengers and discovered that we had carried over 3800 kilos plus the weight of a great deal of ice that had melted away. The extra 600 kilos had helped us break through the runway and lose one revenue trip for the day. I protested to Air Cambodge and our chief pilot and asked for something to be done to keep it from happening again.

The following day it happened again. On our first trips we had no trouble because we flew for other shippers, but on our last trip the overload artists showed up again. I told them that I would take their word for the weights, but anything over 3200 kilos belonged to me. They agreed.

At Phnom Penh the shippers began trying every trick to avoid weighing the cargo. I kept them from backing their truck up to the aircraft and sent for the Air Cambodge scales. The shippers whined that their fish would spoil and their live pigs would die. They promised to weigh the cargo at their offices in town, which, of course, was nonsense.

The Air Cambodge representative informed us that the scales were not available because an Air France flight was due in. I strongly suspected that the shipper had paid off the Air Cambodge staff, so I told the group around the aircraft that I was taking the cargo back to Kompong Chhnang. I called my copilot and we climbed aboard, shut the doors, and went to the cockpit. Within two minutes, the scales were there.

As each item was put on the scales, the shippers insisted that the weight should be read at the lower scale marking. If an item weighed 88.9 kg, they would scream out the weight as 88 kg and argue bitterly should 89 be written down. Taking advantage of the distraction, the obnoxious teenager sneaked a few parcels off, so I insisted that he leave. The Air Cambodge employees were of little help, so much of the time I was alone among the shippers and their employees. I had to watch them all to keep them from sneaking more cargo off. As the total weight of 3200 kilos was reached, we still had several pigs and bags of beans aboard. I closed the aircraft cargo doors and informed all parties that the rest was mine.

More vehement arguing ensued, but I remained adamant. I was determined to dissuade these shippers from making more difficulties by hitting them where it hurt most, in the pocketbook. I was relieved to see our maintenance jeep arrive with the copilot and our Thai mechanics. The shippers started to look dejected.

Beside me in the doorway was a pig, tied up with its rear end sticking out of the doorway. The thin, sneaky-looking shipper was standing outside the door, still arguing bitterly, when the pig's bowels let loose and sprayed watery excrement right in his face and down the front of his shirt. The

Live pigs from Kompong Chhnang aboard N83AC (photo courtesy of Bill Ernst).

argument ended to the raucous laughter of the Khmer laborers. Bill Ernst laughed every time he thought about the incident for several weeks.

I agreed to let the shippers take the live pigs in exchange for an equal weight of peanuts and roots. I suggested that the Air Cambodge staff could sell them and give a small party for the employees, but under no circumstances should they be returned to the shippers. The mechanics took the cargo to the hotel.

The next day we returned to Kompong Chhnang and the same shipper loaded the aircraft again. The load appeared to be too heavy, so I insisted that he take off a sack of peanuts. He refused, so I threw off two sacks. The shipper then sent his workmen on board to unload everything and we returned to Phnom Penh empty.

The chief pilot had been telling Air Cambodge's station manager that we should cancel our trips to Kompong Chhnang, but the station manager kept pleading for us to continue. From the shippers' point of view, I was acting unreasonably because other companies allowed the pilots to take money for carrying overloads, and they claimed that some Chinese pilots would carry 4400 kilos in their DC-3s. My refusal to do the same was attributed to a lack of skill.

Cedric was annoyed that I was having trouble with one group of shippers. He would not tell me to carry more than the legal limit, but he gave the distinct impression that he would not mind if I did. I had flown with much more than 3200 kilos many times before, but in DC-3s registered in Laos where the maximum gross weight conforms with the limit set by the United States Air Force for the C-47 rather than the lower limit set for the DC-3 by the American civilian controlling authority, the FAA.

In this situation, I could have carried overweights and kept quiet about it. The FAA had no way of finding out, and the SEAAT management did not want to know. If a tire blew or an engine quit at a critical time, the aircraft would be scrapped, and the company would collect several times its value from the insurance company. Should the circumstances be investigated, I alone would be blamed for violating published company policies.

I was not willing to break the rules on my own to please the company management in this way. As retired American military officers, the SEAAT managers were certainly familiar with the practice of suggesting indirectly that subordinates surreptitiously break laws or regulations. As long as everything goes fine, everyone is happy, but if something goes wrong, all the blame is placed on the subordinate, who "obviously acted without the knowledge of his superiors."

The other pilots were very pleased that I had seized the shippers' cargo. Several pilots who had been flying for other companies since the beginning of the airlift congratulated me. They knew of several serious accidents caused by aircraft being overloaded without the pilot's knowledge. Most of these had involved engine failure and the inability of greatly overloaded machines to make it to an airport on one engine.

That same week, one of the DC-3s belonging to Stan Booker was seriously damaged at Kompong Chhnang. A short field take-off had been attempted with a huge overload. The plane stalled near the ground, and its wingtip and outboard end of its aileron were badly damaged. The stories told by the captain and the copilot vastly differed. The Chinese captain was from Taiwan, and the copilot was an American who had come from California to work for SEAAT but quit immediately after arrival to work for Stan Booker. The copilot claimed that the captain had pulled the aircraft off the ground at low speed, stalled, and allowed the left wing tip to hit the ground. The captain said that he was demonstrating a short field take-off to the new copilot and had asked for quarter flaps. The copilot did not know how to operate the flaps correctly and had extended full flaps, causing the aircraft to "balloon" into the air. He then retracted the flaps again to correct his mistake, causing the aircraft to stall.

The end result of whatever really happened was a damaged airplane. A few days later, some mechanics arrived with sledge hammers and straightened out the aileron hinges and wing tip until they looked to be at the correct angles. The empty aircraft was then flown back to Phnom Penh for repairs.

At a company meeting, Cedric lectured us on dealing with our customers. He had spoken with the Air Cambodge vice president for operations and claimed to have the absolute last word in dealing with all Khmers. He admitted that they were quite different from all other people in Southeast Asia and stressed the importance of keeping one's composure. The worst thing a person could do was lose his temper. Anyone who did would be ostracized, no matter how slow, crooked, or stupid another person behaved. He was convinced that my problem stemmed from a lack of patience or politeness, and he said that we should not keep the cargo we had confiscated.

My answer made it clear that I thought his opinions were nonsense, and I was greatly disappointed with SEAAT for failing to become involved in overcoming this operational impasse. All of the shippers and their assistants were Chinese, not Khmer. Many of them could hardly speak the Khmer language and needed translators at the airport. While most of the shippers had abided by the rules, one group wanted to increase the profit margin by shipping several hundred kilos of cargo free of charge each time we flew from Kompong Chhnang. If I took the overloads and kicked them in the teeth each time, they would have been happy. If I refused, I would be a villain no matter how polite I was.

Americans like stereotypes, and even though Cedric would accept the fact that some Americans will degrade themselves in any imaginable way for a buck, he would not believe that people of other nationalities would fall out of their stereotyped role and do the same thing. The Chinese shippers we were dealing with were just like any other group of people in the world. Some did business honestly, others dishonestly. They could not be classified collectively. One group of crooks was causing us problems, and if we returned their confiscated cargo, we would either have to accept overloads or forfeit at least one trip per day due to time lost arguing.

From the time of my arrival in Phnom Penh, I studied the Khmer language as much as I could. I learned the language quite rapidly by asking the SEAAT employees how to pronounce various phrases. I then began to study the written language, which is more complicated.

If someone works in a foreign country and does not read and write the language, he is actually a functional illiterate. If he cannot speak the language, he is much less able to function in the local society than a deaf mute. I often wondered how the American Embassy staff could even go through the motions of functioning in the country as conditions became more and more chaotic, being totally isolated from what was going on around them by their formidable language barrier.

When one of the Thai or Chinese copilots was flying with me, I was often the only American at the small airports far from the capital. I do not believe that I could have done my job properly without being able to communicate with the shippers, passengers, and local civilian and military policemen. Some of the American pilots who spoke no Khmer seemed to manage, but they encountered difficulties with the local authorities and certainly missed most of what was going on around them.

Talking to the Khmers convinced me of the difficulty of their situation. They were definitely less sophisticated and less aware of events abroad than most other people in Southeast Asia. Their ideas about sanitation and public health were primitive, and they were guileless in their business dealings. They had therefore been at the mercy of the Chinese and Vietnamese businessmen, but to expel these people would have reduced the economy of the country to chaos. It was nevertheless clear why the Khmers expressed such antipathy against the Vietnamese in their conversation. The millennium-long process of being displaced by smarter and more energetic people was nearing its end. The American advisors and diplomats, who might have played a role of conciliators, convincing the people of Southeast Asia to forget traditional hatreds and work together, stayed in the embassy and waited for their tours of duty to end, anticipating transfer to somewhere else they would rather be. When they finally departed, events resumed their old course.

Chapter 5

On November 1 I made my first trip to Kompong Thom, which we were to visit very often during the following year. There was a large airport north of the town, but it was too far from the settlement for the Khmer Army to defend. The runway we used was a well-travelled highway just to the north of the main part of town. Soldiers were stationed at both ends to stop traffic while the aircraft took off and landed. The highway, which ran along a low embankment with rice fields on both sides, was straight but rather narrow. When a DC-3 landed in the middle, both main wheels were on the unpaved shoulders. Straying too far from the centerline would spell disaster.

The city had been the scene of very heavy fighting. The communists had suffered severe losses in direct attacks on its stubbornly defended perimeter. The finest group of soldiers that I observed in the Khmer Republic were those at Kompong Thom, although other outposts without airports were reportedly defended by soldiers of similar quality. The city was nevertheless increasingly cut off from the surrounding countryside, and as the communist control spread, the flow of refugees into the city increased. They were very poor, having left their possessions behind when they fled to escape being recruited as forced labor for the communists. The families were settled in provisional camps, where they had to live on small rice rations provided by charitable organizations.

The defense perimeter was located just five kilometers from the airport. Due to the ground fire hazard, we crossed the field at an altitude of 3000 feet, then circled down. The rainy season had just ended, so the rice fields were filled to overflowing, and the ground was rather soft. A crosswind was blowing, but it was not too strong. The runway was long enough, about 3500 feet, but on my first landing, I was impressed by its narrowness. Captain Sangob had had a surprise during his first landing at Kompong Thom. He called for the flaps up immediately after touching down, which is a common practice among DC-3 pilots. His aircraft, N83AC, was so out of rig from years of rough field operations and hard landings that it had developed a strong tendency to turn to the left when the flaps were retracted.

As the flaps came up, Sangob felt his aircraft swerve and head for the rice paddies. He managed to recover without a mishap, but he stopped calling for the flaps up immediately after landing.

After my landing, I taxied to the end, where I was a little concerned about how to turn the aircraft around. Turning required us to go quite far off the paved surface, and the ground was wet and looked very soft. I was relieved when the wheels did not sink in.

Our cargo was rice for the refugees. On our first trips, we returned empty. The unloading time was very short, and it was a pleasure to be ready to go again so quickly after the long loading times I was used to at Kompong Chhnang. As time went on, the number of trips to Kompong Thom increased. We were happy because we spent more time in the air and less on the ground, and SEAAT was happy because the company received money from Air Cambodge for each trip we made. The people at Air Cambodge were not happy at all. Each of them was a civil servant working for the government-owned airline. The opportunities for graft were so good that any of them would have gladly worked without the small government salary. Many of them bragged to employees of other companies at the airport about how much they could make, and most of them drove luxury cars. The offices downtown and at the airport were overstaffed with high level managers bearing impressive titles. Each one had supplemental private sources of income from various outside business enterprises, usually facilitated by his official connections. If such enterprises entailed legitimate business rather than graft, a front man was necessary. It was illegal for a Khmer government official to be involved in a private business, and it was also considered somewhat degrading by Khmer civil servants to be involved in commerce.

The rice we carried for the government to Kompong Thom was packed in preweighed sacks. If passengers were sent, a number of sacks had to be unloaded to match their weight. The government refugee authorities and the army insisted that the rice cargo not be reduced below 53 sacks weighing 100 lbs. each. That limited the number of passengers and private cargo that we could carry, and also the amount of graft and kick-backs from shippers. There was little profit to be made by Air Cambodge employees from the rice runs to Kompong Thom.

One of the best sources of private income was seat reservation. Before almost every trip from Phnom Penh, we were approached by one or another Air Cambodge employee with the request that we take a sister, aunt, uncle, father, or grandmother as an extra passenger. The legal price of tickets for air travel was kept very low, but passenger flights to almost all destinations were fully booked for weeks in advance. The payment of a reasonable sum, usually several times the official price of a ticket, allowed a person to be temporarily adopted as an honorary relative of an Air

Cambodge employee and be permitted immediate travel to a desired destination. As the families of the airline employees grew, so did the number of brand new automobiles parked in front of the Air Cambodge office each day.

The problem of overloads at Kompong Chhnang rapidly reached a crisis. On November 7, 1973, I threatened to throw some overweight cargo off, and the shipper responded by removing all his cargo and refusing to send it with us. The shipper asked Air Cambodge to send another pilot, and the next day I made my last trip there for more than a month. The shipper, wishing to avoid trouble before the new pilot started making the run, showed up with a load weighed correctly to the last kilo. The aircraft tires were compressed properly, and the trail wheel strut sat at the correct angle for a fully loaded DC-3.

Our chief pilot had told me that I was the only pilot that the shipper had complained about by name. He was new to Southeast Asia and had never had the experience of directly dealing with our customers, so he suspected that I had been rude to them in some way or had inadvertently insulted them. I responded that the "insult" had been to their bank accounts, and that this was the only insult that they could not bear. The chief pilot, like Cedric, was under the false impression that the people of Southeast Asia are "noble savages," proud and honest but rather stupid. In fact, our Chinese shippers' ancestors had been doing business at a very sophisticated level while the ancestors of the Americans were still living in caves somewhere in Europe. In cunning and trickery, these shippers were several classes ahead of the SEAAT managers, and profit was more interesting to them than amenities, and certainly much more important than flight safety. Only one of the four groups of shippers I dealt with was creating problems; all difficulties with the others had been quickly and amicably resolved.

Captain Sangob, the only other SEAAT DC-3 captain, was no more ready to put up with the shippers' overloads than I had been. Within two days after I switched airplanes and routes with him, new problems arose. He was expecting the tricks I had told him about, but the shippers had already thought up some new ones. Twice, the shippers had opened the cargo door after I had started the engines to sneak on two or three extra passengers. Both times I sent the copilot back to throw them off again. With Sangob, they carried the trick a little further. He had started the engines, taxied out onto the runway and was preparing for take-off, when his door warning light suddenly illuminated. The copilot went back to close the door and noticed that they had gained three passengers.

On November 10, I inaugurated a new route to an airport about 7 km north of Kampot, a seaport south southeast of Phnom Penh, not too far from the Vietnamese border. The runway was the shortest one for DC-3 operations in the country at the time, and it deserved its bad reputation very well. Its 2300 feet should have been sufficient for a DC-3 if the runway had not been built on the crown of a hill. The last half of the landing roll was always steeply downhill.

The landing approach from the northeast was considered hazardous by the local military authorities because it crossed over a hilly, forest-covered region where the North Vietnamese had bases and the Khmer soldiers were afraid to go. Ground fire was not uncommon, and some airplanes had been hit in the past. The worst feature, however, was the wind. It was generally a gusty crosswind, rather strong because the field was near the sea and turbulent because the mountains to the west interrupted its flow. The tall palm trees on the runway approaches were an added hazard. The tops of several had already been removed by DC-3s in 1971.

An American pilot had clipped the tops off two of the palm trees. The first, he removed with his wheels on take-off, causing minor damage to the gear. The second, a week or two later, was also hit on take-off. This time, the damage was more substantial, so he flew directly to Saigon for repairs. He left the Khmer Republic for good shortly after.

During the ill-fated attempt by Continental Air Services to operate in the Khmer Republic, one of their DC-3s crashed near Kampot under mysterious circumstances. The captain was one of the most experienced DC-3 pilots in the world with over 12,000 flying hours in the type. The wreckage came down several miles from Kampot. The trouble occurred while the aircraft was rather high, and it is difficult to think of an emergency that a pilot with so much experience could not have handled.

The ramp at Kampot was decorated with the hulks of two other DC-3s. One belonged to the Khmer Air Force, and the other was a Cambodia Air Commercial wreck. Before the country fell, two more would be added to the scenery around the little airstrip. The first mishap occurred shortly after I arrived. A Khmer Airlines flight, tremendously overloaded with passengers, had had engine failure on take-off. It crashed on runway heading and scraped along the ground on its belly through a coconut palm plantation. It stopped just short of a tree. Very few passengers were killed or injured, apparently because they were packed in so tightly that they had no chance to be thrown against anything harder than other passengers. The first action the company took was to paint over the name on the side of the wreck. The aircraft made an interesting picture sitting in the middle of the plantation surrounded by palm trees.

The next aircraft demolition at Kampot was performed by the American who had been the copilot on Stan Booker's DC-3 during its mishap at Kompong Chhnang. Pilots seeking employment were avoiding Cambodia at the time because many companies were not meeting their payrolls. In order to keep the DC-3s flying, Stan quickly promoted the American to captain. One of the Chinese pilots commented, "I'll give him a week."

The town of Kampot on the Gulf of Thailand (photo courtesy of Bill Ernst).

One week later he touched down a little short at Kampot, rolling over some sharp rocks on the runway approach. The tracks left on the ground made the course of events absolutely plain. The right tire had blown, causing the plane to veer to the right. The wheel dropped into a deep hole and was ripped off. The aircraft scraped to a halt and caught fire. It burned so completely that not a single usable spare part remained. Before the wreck, the aircraft had been in excellent condition, far better than the average for the fleet. No one aboard had been seriously hurt.

The day I made my first landing at Kampot, a typhoon was approaching and some unseasonal rainstorms were moving across the country. I had not been there before, so I flew in and out of the clouds to the seacoast, then turned west to descend below the rain clouds over the sea. We were clear of the bad weather at about 1000 feet, but there was a heavy rainstorm just inland from the coast. The seacoast is very scenic; high, forested mountains drop off into the water, leaving secluded coves with sandy beaches between them. The ruins of an old French Army post and a few plantation houses stood right at the point where the mountain range meets the sea.

We turned into a large cove. Beside it we spotted the city of Kampot. A river flows past the city, and a short distance farther upstream, we spotted the airport. The front edge of the rainstorm had already lowered a dark grey curtain across the northern end of the town. We headed right for the field to see if we could beat the rain. High wind gusts bounced us around as we approached the field, which was still clearly visible. As we crossed its southern boundary to check the wind sock, huge rain drops snapped across the windshield. A strong wind blew from the north. As we turned downwind, the full force of the storm hit the field. Everything disappeared, and we were flying on instruments for about 15 seconds. We raised the landing gear that we had just lowered. Suddenly, we were in the clear again. As we turned west and looked toward the airport, only the palm trees at the end were still visible. Even if navigation radios had been available, a landing at such a short field would have been impossible.

Tropical rainstorms are characteristically very heavy but of short duration. I could have returned to Phnom Penh with the cargo, but I decided that the best thing to do was wait. I turned back toward the sea, checked the fuel, then retarded the power to hold 90 knots with the gear and flaps retracted. In that way, we would have the lowest possible fuel consumption. We cruised slowly up and down the coast, looking again at the old French ruins. The road that had once wound around the point of land toward nearby Vietnam was now blocked with dense vegetation. Another road led up the hill to one of the plantation houses. They were remnants of an age, already long past, when the European powers had spread empires and planted colonies around the world. These relics now seemed out of place in Southeast Asia, and the jungle was reclaiming its territory.

Another small rainstorm followed immediately behind the first, and about 35 minutes passed before the field finally cleared. By waiting, we were able to deliver a load of cargo and take another back to Phnom Penh instead of wasting fuel for an incomplete mission. At our low power setting, we had burned relatively little fuel. As we landed, the last drops of rain were still falling, but the sun shone brightly from the southern edge of the clouds. The wind had shifted, so we landed to the south.

The first part of the runway was very steeply uphill, and the wheels slipped and slithered in the sticky mud. Small rivulets were deepening the ruts in the runway. As we crested the hill and started down, we were already slowed to a fast taxi speed. We slid to a stop on the soggy ground and turned back toward the parking ramp.

We were unloaded, then reloaded with a cargo of fresh fruit. We were often to carry many kinds of cargo brought by boat from Vietnam. Fresh fish and nu'o'c mam (Vietnamese fish source) were the most common exports to Phnom Penh. I explained to the shipper that we had to strictly adhere to the contract weights. Because the field was too short for overloads, our chief pilot had limited us to 3000 kilos instead of the usual 3200. The military airport commander showed us a map with the approach pattern and possible enemy antiaircraft positions. This route seemed a pleasant alternative to Kompong Chhnang.

We made a second trip to Kampot that day without any further problems from the weather.

SEAAT was not the only company leasing aircraft and crews to Air Cambodge. China Airlines had been operating two DC-4s for them before SEAAT arrived on the scene. One day China Airlines added a DC-3 to its fleet and relieved us of our biggest problem. Captain Sangob had been complaining bitterly about the shippers since inheriting the Kompong Chhnang route from me, and now he too was scheduled elsewhere.

China Airline's DC-3 had been in passenger service, and its interior was beautiful. Everyone remarked what a pity it was to turn it over to the pigs and fishes. Several pilots suggested that each pig could be strapped in a seat and served coffee during the flight.

Without the loading delays at Kompong Chhnang, we completed three or four round trips daily for the next two weeks. We were both soon tired because of difficulties caused by a typhoon. There were 60 to 80 knot winds at altitude, and thick layers of clouds coverd the entire country. With no radio navigation aids anywhere but Phnom Penh and Battambang, no information about wind direction and velocity, and little chance to see the ground, navigation was sometimes tricky. I knew the landmarks fairly well already, however, so I was always able to find my destination without any delay. Take-offs and landings were hard work because of the rain storms. The wet, slippery runways at Kampot and Kompong Thom were no pleasure to land on with some of the highest crosswind velocities that I was ever to experience while flying in the country.

Unfortunately, on November 17, our two-plane, two-pilot operation ended. The first trip of the morning took me to Kompong Thom. After taking off to the north on the return trip, circling the town, and heading south, I noticed that the oil temperature gauge was showing a steady rise, indicating a problem with the right engine. I increased the airspeed to improve cooling, but the temperature climbed from the green range into the orange. At about 3000 feet, the gauge reached 100°C, the maximum allowable temperature, so I punched the feather button and shut down the engine. We were empty, so I left the other engine at climb power and continued to 3500 feet.

After the oil temperature cooled, I motored the right engine with the starter preparatory to a restart, should it be necessary. We would be crossing enemy territory, and it would have been comforting to be a little higher. An erratic RPM indicated that something was seriously wrong with the engine. We would have to make it back to Phnom Penh on one. I leveled off and reduced the power to cruise. Because we were light, the left engine was able to give us 100 knots without any difficulty.

At Phnom Penh the mechanics removed the oil screen. Along with the oil, shiny flakes of metal flowed out. They sparkled in the tropical sunshine like diamonds imbedded in the thick ooze of black oil. The mechanics then began pulling out metal filings by the handful. The prop was very hard to turn, and it was obvious that the main bearings had disintegrated. The engine was finished with only about 1100 hours recorded on its log books.

The immediate result of the loss was that Sangob and I would be on a day-on, day-off schedule. I had flown every single day from October 26 through November 17, and now I was suddenly faced with more days off than I wanted.

More problems arose as the mechanics started to examine the log books. One engine on N83AC had logged 1400 hours; the other, 1800. The mechanics decided to take the 1400 hour engine off N83AC and use it to replace the one on N82AC that had failed. The manufacturer, Pratt & Whitney, recommends a major overhaul after 1500 hours. As the work progressed, however, someone noticed that the serial numbers and log books did not match. An engine, supposedly with over 1500 hours logged, had been crated up for shipment to an overhaul shop. It actually had only 53 hours of flight time, while the one we had been using had logged about 2200 hours, a time-in-service that probably approaches some kind of a record for the Pratt & Whitney 1830 engine. It was disturbing to learn that it was that very engine that had brought us back from Kompong Thom after the other one had failed.

Just how the confusion occurred was never clear to me. The log books in the aircraft had had the correct numbers in them; only the times had been incorrectly transcribed. My opinion of the SEAAT management had been steadily eroding, and I was not really sure that they were not trying to manipulate the records to make a high-time engine look like a low-time one. I made it a habit to watch the engine performance especially closely.

On November 26 Air Cambodge inaugurated two new routes. My first two trips were normal cargo flights to Kampot. The third and fourth were made to carry government rice and soldiers, first to Svay Rieng, a town located in the so-called "parrot's beak" along Highway 1, the route to Saigon, and then to Kompong Cham.

The runway at Svay Rieng was a section of Highway 1 west of the town, which was surrounded by communist forces. A small winding river passed the town as it cut its way through an immense flat expanse of rice fields and marshes. The Vietnam border snaked around the district and could be reached by a short trip to the north, south, or east. The only prominent landmark in the vast, green ocean of rice fields was Nui Ba Dinh, the great conical mountain that stands beside the city of Tay Ninh, Vietnam.

For pilots, Svay Rieng was worse than the other improvised airports in

The road below served as the runway for Svay Rieng. A DC-3 (left center) has just taken off (photo courtesy of Bill Ernst).

several ways. There were more enemy soldiers with better weapons in the district than at our other destinations. The limit of government control extended just a few miles down the highway from the landing strip. The other disadvantages concerned the runway itself.

At Kompong Thom, the road segment that served as the runway was relatively flat, and the crosswinds were usually light. Svay Rieng, on the other hand, usually had rather strong crosswinds that invariably blew across Highway 1 at a 70° to 110° angle. The high crown in the road served to maneuver an aircraft toward the rice paddies if it got the slightest bit off the center line. These water-filled fields were much closer to the road than those at Kompong Thom, and it is doubtful if an aircraft with a flat tire could have escaped complete destruction.

Events a few days later demonstrated the structural inadequacies of the hastily fabricated airport. A DC-3 belonging to Cambodia Air Commercial (CACO) taxied across the seemingly firm ground at the entrance to the parking ramp. One wheel sank into the earth. Another DC-3, this one belonging to Tri-9, taxied on the highway shoulder opposite the CACO machine to get around it. Its wheel also broke through the surface causing the propeller to hit the ground. The pilot judged the tips of each prop blade to be bent around at the same angle, so he flew the aircraft back to Phnom Penh. He claimed to have experienced very little vibration because the prop was balanced.

Another disagreeable feature of the airport was the very heavy traffic on the highway. On final approach, it was not unusual to see one or two bicycles still rolling slowly down the road. Water buffaloes often climbed out of the rice paddies and crossed the runway while aircraft took off and landed, and the guards did not seem too concerned about chasing them off.

Our landing approach was steep, and our turns were tight to keep close to the runway. Wide traffic patterns were not recommended because the enemy sometimes fired heat-seeking missiles. CACO lost one DC-3 to such a missile, and several military aircraft had also been lost in the same manner not too far away. The last part of the approach also had to be very steep to avoid very tall palm trees that lined the highway just beyond the touch-down point. On the ground, the problems were still not over. The tiny parking ramp was not adequate for the volume of air traffic, and taxiing was tricky. We really earned our pay at Svay Rieng.

After returning from the "parrot's beak," we took off for Kompong Cham. The town, that was formerly an important Mekong River port in the rubber plantation region, was already a ruin. Ours was among the first flights into the airport after the battle that had destroyed the community. Anti-aircraft fire was still reported from among the burned-out buildings, and many communist troops were still in the vicinity. As we circled down over the town, we spotted the hospital complex near the airport and noted that it was one of the centers of destruction. The communist soldiers had gone through the buildings throwing hand grenades into each room to kill the patients. The stories of the atrocities never reached the American press. It was not in fashion to print derogatory things about the communist side. America was trying to pull out of Southeast Asia gracefully, and the people were not to be reminded of what our government was leaving behind. The reporters stayed in the bars of the Phnom and Monorom hotels and never went to Kompong Cham.

As we taxied to the parking ramp, we noticed a large number of holes dug in the concrete runway surface by the enemy artillery fire. The Khmer soldiers had pitched their camp in the airport terminal building. Tents were put up because the large hole in the roof exposed the interior to the elements. The ground was littered with ammunition of various caliber. We asked the soldiers about the enormous hole in the roof. We were surprised to learn that it had been made not by enemy fire but rather by a very poorly executed ammunition drop from a Khmer Air Force C-123. A pallet of howitzer shells that was supposed to come down on the runway plummeted instead into the terminal 50 meters away among the sleeping troops.

The soldiers guarding the field were in a wretched state. They looked very scared and crowded around the aircraft hoping to get on and be taken somewhere else. Several asked for rides to Phnom Penh. When I told them that I could take only the authorized cargo, one threatened to shoot at the aircraft after we took off. Those not engaged in trying to escape from their situation were busily probing the engines with pointed sticks and bayonets. They behaved in a way stone age tribesmen would be expected to in the presence of technology beyond their comprehension. I had never seen such behavior in Southeast Asia before. Most of the people there seemed cleverer than the Americans who were supposed to be advising them, but these Khmer soldiers were cut from another cloth. They fought with great bravery at times, and often with great savagery, but they were obviously not mentally equipped to combat the North Vietnamese who were leading the array of their enemies.

I called to the military policeman and told him to keep the soldiers away from the aircraft. The policemen were afraid to rile the mob of dirty, mutinous soldiers, so I had to tell them to keep away myself. The chance of a mutiny would have been very good if there had been any officers there for the soldiers to mutiny against. The commanders were safe in Phnom Penh, however, collecting their soldiers' pay from the United States aid mission and spending it for their own amusement. The soldiers had to stay together and fight at Kompong Cham because they had no way out. It was simply a battle for survival, but they had beaten the Khmer Rouge and driven them from the ruins of the city.

We taxied out to take off, leaving the misery behind us. The mob that had been around the aircraft drifted back in the direction of the terminal. The runway was very wide, although not particularly long, so we were able to choose a take-off path that avoided most of the shell holes in the surface.

Air France had inadvertently proven the adequacy of the runway one day by landing a loaded Boeing 707 on it. The pilot had mistaken the field for Phnom Penh. After touching down, he was barely able to stop his machine before going off the end and over the cliff that begins a few meters beyond. The airport is on a plateau, and anyone overshooting would have a long downhill ride. The plane had to be completely unloaded before it could take off again. The passengers had been carried to Phnom Penh in DC-3s.

Chapter 6

The personnel of the American Military Mission were rarely seen around the country, but when they were, they really stood out. One morning at Kompong Thom, as I stood beside the aircraft with Max Vernon who usually flew as the Convair copilot, we heard the whine of a turboprop approaching for a landing. It was a Helio Courier, a single-engine aircraft designed especially for very short fields. This model had been used by Air America for many years, but the one approaching for landing had "United States of America" painted on its side in large white letters. It belonged to the embassy.

The Helio Courier is known to be tricky to control in crosswinds, but that morning there was only a very light breeze from the left. As the plane passed our DC-3, about 50 feet in the air, we could see that it was brand new, spotlessly clean, and obviously well maintained. The pilot made several swoops and dives as he searched for the ground. He touched down hard nearly halfway down the runway. The little aircraft bounced back into the air and cocked about 30° into the wind. A large rice paddy was located about 30 yards from the runway. The fuselages of two Otters, old single-engine machines that had once belonged to the United States Army, rested in the water in the middle of the paddy. They were inhabited by soldiers during the dry season. As the Helio crashed down on the runway again, it scooted straight for the Otters. At the last moment, the pilot performed a ground loop. Only the tail plopped into the water. A great whirr and cloud of spray arose as the pilot applied full power to try to pull his aircraft out. Because it was already pointed more than 45° from the horizontal position, there was no chance that it would budge without a rocket assist. The pilot finally realized his predicament and shut down his engine.

A black Army major, a white Navy commander, and a Khmer Air Force captain emerged, looking somewhat sheepish. A large group of Khmer soldiers gathered around the stricken aircraft. They quickly determined what had to be done, waded into the water, and lifted the aircraft out. From a distance it looked like ants carrying a large beetle. They carried the Helio to the runway and set it down.

We walked over to look at the damage. The tailwheel had been twisted around the fuselage until it was almost on top. We noted that the major had been the pilot. The commander asked us for a ride back to Phnom Penh. The major first decided to stay with his aircraft, but the thought of being left alone seemed to disturb him, so he also rode with us, boarding at the last minute. As we taxied out to take off, the commander said, "Well, I hope you have more luck than we did."

Some words jumped to my tongue, but I choked them back because I felt a little sorry for the pilot. What I almost said was, "Luck doesn't have anything to do with it, pal."

I found out later that the pilot had no difficulties because of his mishap. He simply reported that he had gotten stuck in the mud, and the Khmer soldiers who pulled his aircraft out had dropped it, causing all of the damage. The United States Army, unlike the Air Force, never makes much trouble for pilots because of accidents. The story looked good on paper, and that was what the United States government cared about.

While looking at the Helio, we thought we were about to see a DC-3 crash. A Khmer Airlines flight approached the end of the runway on a base leg, 90° to the runway heading. At the last second, the pilot made a steep turn to line up with the runway. The left wing came so close to the ground that I thought it had hit. The tire touched down before the turn was fully completed. Both Max and I were convinced that the pilot wouldn't make it, but he did. We would soon hear more about acrobatic landings.

Later that day, I had some problems of my own. The regular DC-3 copilots, Bill Ernst and David Chester, had started their careers in the DC-3 with SEAAT. Captain Sangob and I had painstakingly trained them until they possessed a high degree of competence as copilots. I thought that it was important for copilots to be able to land the aircraft, should the pilot become disabled. I gave them practice and was convinced that they could.

The SEAAT managers had other goals. We were paid a base salary assuming that we would fly 70 hours per month. Overtime was paid for additional hours. Our licenses to fly as captain made Sangob and me indispensable, but the copilots were not. As they reached 70 hours, they were grounded, and the low-time Convair and DC-4 copilots were sent in their place. To save a few dollars, SEAAT made us give additional training to copilots who would rarely, if ever, fly with us again.

Because the DC-3 was designed before automatic landing gear sequencing had been developed, raising and lowering the gear is a rather complicated process, and a mistake in the sequence can badly damage the locking mechanism. It is also easy to confuse the landing gear and flap handles. If the copilot was not sure of what he was doing, I would raise or lower the wheels myself.

As Max lowered the gear in the traffic pattern at Phnom Penh, he inadvertently made an error in the sequence causing a spring lock to hold the gear lever in the down position. Because the handle could not be returned to neutral, a red warning light was illuminated and a warning horn sounded. I could see that the gear was down, but I had no time on the final approach to deactivate the safety lock and return the handle to neutral. The mechanics came aboard after we parked, and I found out that none of them knew what to do about the problem, or for that matter, what the problem actually was. I slipped the safety lock back and moved the handle to neutral myself and left with my confidence in our mechanics badly shaken.

On November 27 a new flight was inaugurated that promised to add significantly to our flying time. A friend of our chief pilot had recently come to work for SEAAT. The two had flown together in Africa, so the new man was made assistant chief pilot. He took over the DC-3 for the first flight on the new route. It was the last time he ever flew a DC-3 for SEAAT.

The flight was successful, so the next day, it was assigned to me. We took off before 5:30 P.M., so that the staff could leave the airport before curfew, and flew north by northwest for almost two hours as the sun set and the day faded quickly into night, as it does in the tropics. Beneath us was a sea of blackness concealing the jungles and mountains of southern Laos. Finally, the faint lights of Pakse appeared in front of us. We maintained our 8000 feet until we could see the airport and city clearly. We had to be sure to avoid the mountain to the southeast of the city. This peak reaches almost 6000 feet and is shrouded completely by the darkness and often by clouds.

We descended over the city and landed on the darkened runway, guided only by faint runway lights. We parked the aircraft, then proceeded to the terminal to deliver the flight plan and customs forms. The atmosphere in Pakse was relaxed and friendly, in sharp contrast to Phnom Penh. The officials were surprised that I was able to carry on all necessary conversations in Lao. I had flown for a company in Vientiane for about two years and could converse in Lao far better than in Khmer.

The shipper took us to eat at the Lao Officer's Club. It was operated as a private restaurant and managed by one of our cargo shippers. In colonial times, it had belonged to the French Army. One of the little pleasures of the trip to Laos was being able to eat a meal in a restaurant without running a high risk of becoming violently ill.

Other pleasures of the trip were many. We had a real airport with lights as well as functional radios for communication and navigation. The runway had a smooth concrete surface, and there were ample concrete parking ramps. Fuel was sold on request and no permits or ration cards were required. The tower personnel spoke distinctly on the radio and concerned themselves with directing air traffic rather than looking for ways to solicit bribes. It was also comforting to know that the fuel would not be drained from the aircraft by thieving security personnel during the night. The air-craft was also safe from enemy rockets. It was a very good trip for us, and we had the chance to make up for some of the flying time we were losing because of the grounding of N83AC.

The shipper put us up overnight in a small hotel. The weather is very cool at night in November, and we felt very chilly in our short-sleeved uniforms. My copilot went to bed shortly after supper, but I walked to the shopping district to buy some newspapers. It was a real luxury to be able to buy a *Bangkok Post* with the news of the day. The Khmer government had banned all foreign-made articles, including newspapers and magazines, supposedly to conserve the currency. Occasionally, a Phnom Penh street vendor would peddle a copy of *Time* or the *Far Eastern Economic Review* obtained through some sort of black market, but these were never less than two weeks old. One could read what was already history, but current news was unobtainable.

Besides buying papers for myself, I purchased a *Thai Rath* and *Daily News*, Thai language newspapers, to give to our mechanics. I then returned to the hotel, noting that the people on the street with their winter coats were looking at me as if I was crazy for walking around in short sleeves.

We did not have much time to sleep. During the night, the DC-3 was loaded with freshly slaughtered pigs, and at about 3:00 A.M., our crew car picked us up. We took off at about 4:30 and arrived at Phnom Penh a little after 6:00 A.M., just as the airport opened. For the rest of the day, we flew local flights. In the late afternoon, Sangob's crew arrived and took over for the next Pakse flight. We alternated this way each day for a while, but in December we decided that we would each take a week's vacation.

Sangob took his leave first. He left for Bangkok to visit his wife, and I had a solid week of getting up at 3:30 in the morning at Pakse and flying for the rest of the day out of Phnom Penh. With one aircraft, we only needed one captain. Every morning, my copilot was changed before the first local trip. It was an interesting week. It was also the week the rockets started falling.

On one of the trips to Kampot, I flew with a newly hired copilot, Ed Bower. He was a retired Army pilot who lived with his Thai wife in Udorn Thani. His other occupation was reporting covertly to the defense attaché's office on the airlift. He had flown in Vietnam and was smart enough to in-terpret the events he had witnessed very accurately. I'm sure he would have been successful as a civilian engineer, but he completed his education dur-ing the 1950s when there was practically no demand for a black man in pro-fessional or management positions, so he made a career in the Army.

We were standing by the aircraft just as the loading was finished, when two mortar rounds dropped on the road leading to the airport cargo ramp. Our passengers took off in all directions. We jumped behind a mound of dirt. Many trenches had been dug at the edge of the parking ramp, and the passengers huddled terror-stricken in these mortar shelters. The exploding rounds did no damage, but we did hear some fragments hit the ramp. I shouted to the shipper and told him to get everyone going to Phnom Penh on the aircraft right away. The passengers scurried back and jumped aboard, and we pulled up the ladder and shut the door. One man got scared and jumped off again. As we shut the door, he had second thoughts and decided to scramble on again without the ladder. The shipper got off, and as Ed latched the door, I started the engines. I expected the communists to lob some more mortar rounds at us as we taxied, so I used plenty of speed. At the end of the runway, I made a fast turn and took off without hesitation. No more mortar fire was noticed, but later in the day, three more rounds landed on the other side of the runway. At Phnom Penh I checked the aircraft for shrapnel holes. Although the projectiles impacted only 20 to 30 yards from the DC-3, we were partially shielded by a thick stand of banana trees, so we sustained no damage.

Kampot was not the only target of the communists. Rockets began to fall on Phnom Penh's Pochentong Airport as well. Accompanying the rocket explosions was heavy machine gun and artillery fire just four or five kilometers away. From the air, we could see the countryside to the west of the field being chewed up.

Two days after the incident at Kampot, I was preparing to start engines on the ramp under the Phnom Penh tower. Two rockets landed on the grass between us and the runway. The passengers opened the door and ran for the little pavilion beside the terminal. My copilot David Chester followed them. I jumped out of the airplane and called them back. David led most of them back while I started the engines. I wanted to take off before shrapnel damaged the aircraft. I taxied out while David called the tower. Our radios were still not warmed up, so I checked that the approaches were clear and took off. Another rocket landed in a rice paddy to the east of the field, but that was the last one for the day.

I was surprised when the tower called and asked why we had not called them for take-off permission. I told them that we would not wait on formality while the airport was under attack. They seemed rather upset about the matter, and I was temporarily filled with admiration for their devotion to duty. I had expected them to leave the tower at the first sign of trouble.

For the next few days, rockets landed on the airport at regular intervals, killing several people. The worst attack involved seven rockets, one of which apparently went through the tower, smashing one big window going in and another going out. It landed on the grass near the runway, where it finally exploded. During most of these attacks, I was at other airports or en route. The mechanics who had to stay behind were noticeably jittery.

The fighting finally got very close to the airport, and on one occasion a Helio Stallion of the Khmer Air Force was circling right above the tower firing to the west. We noted that the pilot was flying too high to be very effective, but he avoided the ground fire, keeping himself and the enemy relatively safe. I noted that the commercial pilots were less cautious than the military ones, and a few were hit by small arms fire. More damage was done to the aircraft on the ground than in the air. One Cambodia Air Commercial DC-3 was perforated with holes, and N82AC had its skin punctured in one place by shrapnel during the night after one of our Pakse trips had been cancelled.

During the early phase of the battle, the communists occupied two small hills along the outer perimeter road about seven kilometers from the airport. The SEAAT DC-4 was returning from a flight and descending over these hills when it came under intense AK-47 fire. As the aircraft descended through 2000 feet, seven bullets ripped into it. One round passed through the aircraft's nose, several layers of sheet metal, and finally hit the copilot, Max Vernon, in the arm. The lead had been knocked out of the bullet by the metal it had passed through, and the copper jacket was just able to break the skin on Max's forearm before it deflected off and landed on his stomach. It was still red hot and Max received a small burn.

Judging from the usual inaccuracy of AK-47 fire at moving aircraft, the number of rounds fired must have been astronomical. The other hits were scattered all over the aircraft, including one in a fuel tank. The pilot, Edgar Wesley, had many years of experience in Southeast Asia with Continental Air Services. He was not used to such intense fire so close to the home base, so he generally had descended en route rather than circling down over the field. After that incident, the chief pilot made it a fast rule that all aircraft circle down from 3500 feet directly over the airport.

The treatment at the local hospital turned out to be more dangerous than the bullet would. Max was given about six injections of unknown substances. These made him very sick, but fortunately, he recovered. He kept the bullet jacket as a souvenir.

The fighting near the airport lasted several days, during which the battlefield moved closer and closer. After some intense ground combat, the communists finally pulled back. They had taken a terrible beating, and the positions they had held were abandoned to the government forces. I was convinced that the bulk of the enemy forces were Khmers because they seemed incompetent in their attacks. A minimum amount of damage had been done, probably less in monetary terms than the ammunition expended by the enemy was worth. The attacks did succeed in spreading terror, however, and the civilians at the airport were noticeably nervous.

After the thrust from the west of Pochentong had been repulsed, rocket teams east of the city began a systematic campaign of terror against the people in the city itself. Every day rockets landed in the populated downtown area. They were generally fired two or three at a time, and those fired in each salvo usually impacted only one or two blocks apart. They were apparently fired without any particular target in mind. Only a few did any damage, but there were occasional fatalities. The second and third weeks of December saw the implementation of a campaign to psychologically demoralize the population of the city.

For three nights in a row, two or three rockets landed between 7:00 and 9:00 P.M. All of these hit in the downtown section, far from any military installations. One hit the courtyard of the Catholic cathedral, two slammed into the road behind the main market, another impacted near Le Phnom Hotel, and others struck various locations at random. The attacks then switched to the early morning hours to drop explosive warheads in among the rush hour traffic of people bicycling to work. Day by day the attacks intensified.

Some of our mechanics began talking about quitting. Two or three actually did. The pay was not nearly as much as they had been receiving before they had been laid off by Air America or Continental Air Services, and it certainly was not enough to compensate for the risks they were taking and the discomfort that they were suffering. Rockets were landing near them during the day while they worked and at night near their quarters. The American chief mechanic took a trip to Bangkok for two weeks to look for spare parts at the height of the attacks.

Some of the mechanics asked me what I thought about the situation. I told them that I didn't think there was much chance of being hit by a rocket. The odds were about like the chance of winning a lottery. The weapon was used only for terror purposes.

After Captain Sangob returned from his leave, he talked to them, too. We managed to calm most of them down. I personally thought that the low pay they were receiving should have been a much greater incentive to quit than the efforts of the enemy.

During my week off, I planned to visit my fiancée in Taipei, so I made several trips to the downtown office of Air Cambodge to obtain my discount air tickets. One morning I found that the glass front of the main ticket office was no longer there. A rocket had landed in the street right in front of the office, blowing away the entire front face of the building. The sidewalk was littered with bricks and broken glass.

My busy flight schedule kept me away from Phnom Penh for much of the time, so I did not get to witness much of what went on. I had been able to get a particularly close look at the fighting around the city from the air, however. What had once been beautiful countryside was in the process of being chewed to bits by huge quantities of ammunition.

The Khmer Army and Air Force had learned the lessons taught by their

American mentors all too well. They did not risk close combat with the enemy or seek to protect the civilian population. Instead, they pounded away at long range with artillery and air strikes. Every few minutes, a United States Air Force C-130 landed with a full load of ordnance, which was consumed almost immediately. At more than arm's length, complete destruction of the enemy units was not possible, and pressure could be put on the government positions somewhere around the perimeter without interruption.

The theory propagated by American military planners during the Vietnam War was that the use of huge amounts of fire power would save the lives of allied soldiers. In the long run, this proved false. By telegraphing all moves through frequent "reconnaissance by fire," the allies gave the enemy the chance to avoid all battles not on his own terms. Naturally, the casualties from day to day could be minimized, but the war could be protracted forever, if the enemy wished, and far more allied soldiers died over the long term than would have been killed in short periods of close combat with the enemy forces. A general lack of fire discipline developed, and even in zones where United States units were in close contact with the enemy, more Americans were killed or wounded by their own fire than by that of the communists. The civilians also suffered unspeakably from this kind of warfare. The cost of the ammunition and bombs that the allies sprayed wildly into the bushes and the lack of tangible success finally became too much for America to bear, and the war was lost.

Where Americans sometimes exercised care to minimize the number of civilian casualties and amount of property damage, the Khmer Army deliberately practiced a scorched earth policy to deny the communists shelter and support. Massive numbers of homeless refugees streamed steadily into the capital. Even if the Khmer officials had wanted to, they could not have taken proper care of so many people.

The United States Congress finally decided it would be better to let our allies die than to pay the bills for the massive amounts of ammunition that the form of warfare we had taught them required. While it is true that the Khmers were somewhat more frugal with their supplies than their American counterparts had been, the Congress did not have the option of cutting off funds while American boys were still involved in combat.

The communist forces accomplished their objectives with cold and deliberate efficiency. They made their fire power count. By lobbing their rockets into the refugee-filled capital, they could accomplish the maximum possible damage with their very inaccurate missiles. Their small units infiltrated villages loyal to the government knowing that the government forces would destroy these villages to drive them out again. The communists sacrificed the lives of their own soldiers in the manner that the Americans squandered their ammunition. To be sentimental about human life is considered a contemptible characteristic of a reactionary. The communists always kept their political goals in mind and uncompromisingly destroyed anything and anybody not under their control.

The effectiveness of the communists was enhanced by their ability to operate as very small units. They could have been effectively combatted by small units if the Khmer government had had the ability to organize, motivate, and discipline an army capable of performing efficiently. The Khmer enlisted men fought surprisingly well on their own, but there were almost no officers in the field. If broken up into small units, these would have undoubtedly degenerated into small bandit gangs.

Officers' commissions were granted almost exclusively to members of rich and influential families, who usually bought them with bribes. Mobs of these officers and high civilian officials crowded the restaurants and night clubs of Phnom Penh. To properly enjoy the *dolce vita* required money, and this was obtained through every imaginable kind of official corruption, including extortion from local merchants at gunpoint. Winning the offensive back from the communists and saving their country were considerations that never entered their minds.

Against the rapid degeneration of the armed forces, effective countermeasures should have been applied by the United States. But what had they learned from the American advisors?

A close look at the organization that should have had the responsibility of correcting the faults of the allied forces reveals the underlying reason for all of the problems. The Congressional investigations of the early 1970s revealed a little of what was going on. Top officers and NCOs involved in the PX scandals were the very people charged with correcting the abuses of the Asian allies. Could they be expected to effectively stop bribery and theft when they were deeply involved in these activities themselves? What the Khmers were learning from their American advisors was not what the average American imagines. The bills for the little pleasures enjoyed by the brass were paid in blood by the low ranking enlisted men, American and Asian, who fought without the benefit of guidance and support from their commanders.

A sidelight of the corruption problem was the traffic in weapons. While returning to Vientiane by bus to renew my Lao pilot license, a Lao from Vientiane struck up a conversation with me. He told me he was looking for a .45 automatic and wondered if I had one to sell. I told him that I didn't, but he gave me his address anyway in case I should find one for him. My friends in Vientiane told me that Americans were looked upon as the most reliable sources of weapons. GIs, in particular, were known to do a booming firearms business. Guns were easily certified as "captured from the enemy" and kept as personal property. The sale of a few war souvenirs, however, was just a symptom of a greater evil.

Khmer Army trucks loaded with artillery ammunition were occasionally sighted headed into territory supposedly controlled by the enemy. Rumors circulated in Phnom Penh that these trucks contained supplies sold to the enemy. It was known that the communists had captured several 105 howitzers from the government forces, and they needed ammunition for them. No one expressed any doubt or surprise at these rumors.

The extent of the corruption within the allied forces will never be fully brought to light. Neither will American participation in the rackets. Problems were routinely covered up by shrouds of bureaucratic jargon and meaningless reports. The "secret" or "top secret" stamps effectively keep reports of official misconduct from the public eye. Even those caught red-handed during the Congressional investigations were never brought to trial. What is known is certainly only the tip of the iceberg. The harsh punishment meted out by the communists to those who betrayed their comrades-in-arms for personal gain was certainly one of the keys to their success.

Chapter 7

On December 29 I returned from Taipei. That afternoon the Pakse flight had been cancelled. I learned that trouble with the shipper was brewing.

In Pakse we had always spent the night in an old army quarters, called the bungalow, or in a very dirty hotel. I was not too fussy because both were better than our rat-trap in Phnom Penh. Sangob, however, objected strongly to the conditions and made his feelings known to our chief pilot. He said that we were treated no better than the "driver of a ten-wheel truck."

The chief pilot backed Sangob to some extent, suggesting to the SEAAT management that they put up part of the cost for our overnight stay. On the night of my last prevacation flight, I had arranged for us to stay in the Air America Hostel. There was always room, thanks to the cut-back in the Air America flights, and the cost was only $5 per night. The food there was excellent, and we were located just across the street from our aircraft parking ramp. Everyone seemed to agree to our staying there, including the shipper.

After I left for my vacation, these quarters were never used again. The cargo owner reportedly objected to spending so much money for lodging. The result was a steady conflict with Sangob. For this reason, or perhaps for other reasons unknown to us, the Pakse trip was cancelled for a few days, then turned over to China Airlines.

The morning of its first pig run, the China Airlines DC-3 did not show up. The meat inspector and customs officials waited all morning in vain. Finally, late in the afternoon, it arrived loaded with 3000 kilos of pork spoiled after a full day in the hot sun, plus perhaps 100 kilos of flies. The crew claimed to have missed Phnom Penh somehow. Then they reached the sea and landed at the nearest airport, Kompong Som, nearly out of fuel. They had to wait all day until the Khmer Air Force got around to flying in some gasoline.

Some of the pilots made wisecracks about the "real cargo" that was being smuggled out through Kompong Som, but I was sure it was just a case of a lost pilot. The shipper had lost the price of all that pork just to save the $2 difference between the hostel and the dirty hotel. This was the last trip anybody made to Pakse.

December 30 was a good day for me. I flew 7¼ hours. That night, Sangob, two Thai mechanics, and I were discussing the future of SEAAT when a rocket landed right across the street from us. It demolished the penthouse on top of the six-story building that housed the Golden Pagoda Restaurant. Amazingly, no one was hurt, but the fire engines had to be called to extinguish the fire. A Khmer girlfriend of one of the mechanics became hysterical with fear. We all stood on the street to watch the firemen do their work. The communists were showing the urban community that Lon Nol could not protect them.

The next day I flew for another 7 hours and 15 minutes to bring my total for the month to more than 120 hours. That brought me over 50 hours of overtime pay, and I had enjoyed a short vacation. I also felt pleased to have brought so much food into the city in spite of active opposition from both the communists and the crooked officials at the airport.

January started off as a busy month. My attitude toward the company management, nevertheless, was turning sour. Keeping the aircraft in condition to fly was their job, but they found it convenient to remain out of town during the rocket attacks. If we wanted to fly, we had to maintain our own aircraft. The mechanics were working very hard, but there was a limit to what they could do without spare parts. No one was making any effort to buy the parts we needed, while rumors circulated about the funds set aside to pay for their being diverted into other business ventures. These rumors proved to be true. We knew that N83AC could also have been flying and earning revenue for the company if one good DC-3 engine had been purchased. On the ground, it served as the only reliable source of spare parts for N82AC. Once an aircraft starts to be stripped, it usually is not too far from the scrap heap.

Our supply chief, an Australian named Pete, had no previous experience in the aviation business. He had been an entertainer in Vietnam for a short while, and shortly after meeting the top management of SEAAT during their aircraft buying junket to Australia, he was hired to head the supply section. He himself often wondered why he had been hired for the job, but more about this later.

Even spark plugs were not to be had. Things had deteriorated to the point where we were having problems on almost every flight. We often returned with backfiring engines, and all the mechanics could do was wash the spark plugs. Pilots from other companies made jokes about our spark plug laundry. The gaps were eroded beyond the acceptable tolerances, and on runup, the engines took turns backfiring. To avoid damaging the manifolds, I stopped running the engines up. The runup was unnecessary anyway; we already knew that the RPM drop on single magnetos was too great. After each flight I performed a runup to determine which of our spark plug banks was still functioning passably. The mechanics got right to work on their washing duties while the cargo was being unloaded. Mysteriously, after the cleaning of one improperly functioning set of plugs, both sets would function poorly. After several days of this nonsense, while hearing repeated promises that in the near future we would have all the spare parts we needed, I set out on a trip to Kampot with Ed Bower as copilot. I purposely ran the throttles up roughly as we started to taxi to see if we had any major problems. We did. The right engine started backfiring and the RPM dropped rapidly. I informed the tower that we would hold position to perform spark plug defouling procedures. After that, the engine ran smoother, so we taxied to the runway. As we held for take-off, I again roughly pushed the throttles forward. The only response was two or three loud backfires and rapid loss of RPM. That was enough for me. I told the tower we were taxiing back to maintenance. I told the washing crew not to waste their time any more; we had to have new spark plugs.

I told Ed that I could overlook a slightly excessive mag drop if I was sure of its cause, but the further use of our worn out spark plugs would be ridiculous. He said that he didn't usually raise any objections to captains' decisions, but he would have had some words with anyone who wanted to fly N82AC in the condition it was in.

Not wanting to lose flying time for myself, the company, and the shippers because the management was not doing its job, I set out to see if I could find some DC-3 spark plugs. I had to go no further than the terminal restaurant. The Tri-9 corporation had one DC-3 operating under contract to Khemera Air Transport. It was reputed to have a better organized operation than the other companies doing business in Phnom Penh. I went over to their pilot and chief mechanic, who were sitting in the restaurant, and asked them where they bought their spark plugs. They told me that most of the companies were supplied by the Khmer Air Force, which received free supplies through United States military assistance programs and resold them for personal profit. Their prices were very reasonable. The Tri-9 mechanic, Joe Weaver, said that he had a good supply he had purchased for $1 each. He said that he would very generously sell us a set for $2 each. Since the lowest stateside price was at least $5 each, he was actually doing us a great favor.

Pete was at the airport that day — an unusual event indeed. Tom, our hardworking Australian mechanic, often complained bitterly about Pete's perpetual absence from work. It was only some personal business that brought him to the airport that day.

I introduced Pete to the Tri-9 staff and told him of their offer, privately reminding him of the revenue we were losing. When Joe Weaver asked $2 each for the plugs, Pete commented, "That sounds like a seller's price to me."

His remark so irritated Joe Weaver that he retracted his offer and told Pete that if he wanted the plugs, he would have to pay the catalog price. Pete maintained that since Tri-9 had obtained them for $1 each, they should sell them for $1 each. He then informed me that he could make no decision anyway because there were no SEAAT executives around to give him permission.

After Pete left, I soothed Joe Weaver's feelings and told him that I would like to buy the spark plugs out of my own pocket to keep N82AC flying. I paid about $60 for one whole set of 28 plugs. Our mechanics quickly installed them, and our engines ran like new. One of our electricians found that the magneto switch was wired backwards. Thus, when we had reported that the engine was running roughly on the right magneto, the problem actually involved the left magneto system. The spark plug crew had therefore been washing the wrong set of plugs each time, thus making the good side of the system function poorly, as well as demonstrating that washing makes plugs worse and not better.

Vic Ibay, our Filipino electrician, corrected the wiring while the plugs were being changed, and we completed our last trip of the day after all.

Now I had the problem of trying to collect the $60 from the company that I had advanced them for the spark plugs. Many of the pilots had asked the executives for pay advances to meet some of their families' moving expenses and were told that the company was simply out of cash. Air Cambodge was blamed for not paying their bills promptly, but we suspected other problems as well. That evening the chief pilot paid me the $60 out of his pocket, saving me the trouble of listening to the financial woes of Lyman Brinkwell, the administrative vice-president. I am rather sure that the chief pilot never got his money back.

The handwriting on the wall was now clear to all but the greatest optimists. Prior to my trip to Taipei, I had advanced some money from SEAAT. All Lyman could come up with were two $100 bills and $200 in travelers' checks already cashed by a Khmer bank. The New Nana Hotel in Bangkok was the "company hotel" of SEAAT, which received all of our business. Lyman had assured me that the checks were as good as cash because of the bank stamp on the back, but the cashier at the "company hotel" only laughed at the idea of taking them. They turned out to be fully non-negotiable.

Pay day for December was late, but only by a couple of days. In the flying business, pilots are seldom sure if and when they will get paid for their work. Many "fly-by-night" companies flourish briefly, then fold, leaving piles of outstanding debts and unpaid salaries. The Khmer Republic was certainly not the only place that this happened.

SEAAT's chronic lack of cash grounded not only the DC-3s but also the rest of the fleet. When I arrived in the country, SEAAT had a normal DC-4 and a Carvair, a DC-4 with an enormously bloated fuselage, originally designed for transporting automobiles. Unfortunately, they had only seven engines for both and had to decide which to fly and which to use for spare parts. The Carvair flew and the DC-4 was cannibalized. As more engines began to fail, the Carvair service became more and more irregular.

SEAAT also had Convairs that were perpetually on the disabled list and rarely flew. Several times, they had taken off fully loaded with passengers but turned back before reaching the destination. The annoyance of the passengers and airport staff mounted with each new "baggage drill," and soon Air Cambodge was reluctant to schedule the Convairs for any flights, even when they weren't broken.

The pilots not flying remained theoretically on the payroll and by January most of them were spending the day in the Khemera Hotel restaurant with nothing to do. Our DC-3 was the only aircraft steadily making money, and we were supporting the company. Nevertheless, the SEAAT executives were still actively recruiting pilots.

A newly purchased DC-4 arrived from the States with several new pilots who told harrowing tales about the ferry flight. The aircraft had been purchased in Fort Lauderdale, where it had been parked and abandoned in the beautiful Florida sunshine and salt air since 1968. After its purchase, the SEAAT crew simply started it up. It was incredible that the engines ran, in spite of the rust and probable hydraulic lock in the cylinders. Hydraulic lock is caused by oil seeping into the lower cylinders. Because fluids are not compressible, forcing the engine to turn results in cracked pistons or connecting rods or ruptured cylinder heads. The damage is not always immediately apparent.

During the ferry flight, the DC-4 had broken down at every intermediate stop. The crew received no money for repairs, and they paid the bills out of their own pockets. After a long delay at one stop, the mechanics assigned to maintain it en route almost destroyed one engine. They kept trying to turn the prop with the starter even though it appeared to be jammed. The flight crew finally stopped them. As the spark plugs were removed from the lower cylinders, at least one liter of oil flowed out of the holes.

The arrival of that aircraft had to be considered a miracle, but the cumulative damage had been considerable. The aircraft made two revenue flights in the Khmer Republic, then proceeded to the scrap heap. The engines were scavenged to keep the other DC-4s flying, but none of these engines, so grossly abused, lasted very long.

The SEAAT executives had recruited the newly hired pilots in California by painting a rosy picture of the future in Southeast Asia. When they arrived in Phnom Penh, they were confronted by the harsh realities of life. One quit immediately and returned to the States; another quit to work for another company in Phnom Penh. Two others stuck it out for a while before returning to the States.

SEAAT had paid an enormous sum of money to transport a pile of scrap from a junkyard in Florida to one in the Khmer Republic and to bring over more pilots who would have nothing to fly.

My chief reason for not being happy with SEAAT was the lack of ability shown by the management in attempting to run a fast-paced operation. The future promised no improvement. The operation was steadily deteriorating, and I saw myself winding up idle like the DC-4 and Convair pilots sooner or later. All of the executives had left the country on urgent business during the rocket attacks, but none of them had brought back any replacement engines.

Travel discounts are one great advantage of working with the airlines, and SEAAT had assured us that we would receive the benefits of many interline agreements. When I requested some discount tickets to use during my time off, Lyman informed me that the management had more important things to do in Bangkok than requesting tickets for the pilots. Of course, they were frequently in the airline ticket offices to get tickets for their own nonstop excursions, but they could not spare a few minutes to request tickets for employees bringing a steady flow of income into the company.

The man hired by SEAAT to do the leg work was Aby, a Filipino who had formerly worked as a nightclub entertainer. He never seemed to have time to perform his essential duties, and I found out that it was useless to ask him to get us discount tickets. When his name was mentioned to any of the other SEAAT pilots, they would invariably snarl. Thus, I personally learned how to buy discount tickets during my short periods of time off. I learned that letters from SEAAT were not accepted by most airlines. The interline agreements were mainly with Air Cambodge. First, I had to get a letter from SEAAT requesting a letter from Air Cambodge. The government employees of the national airline were not used to doing things without a payoff, so it normally took several days to get the letter. After that, I had to search for the proper ticket agent, who usually had to send a Telex to Bangkok to get permission to sell the ticket. It turned out to be easier to take the letter from Air Cambodge to Bangkok and buy the ticket there.

Lack of consideration by the management, low pay, and poor working conditions alone would not have been sufficient cause for me to quit, but I had hoped to be able to work for a company with potential for future growth, and that company was obviously not SEAAT. In late December several people in charge of other companies had spoken to me about going to work for them. I had told them that I was not presently interested. By January, however, my dissatisfaction with the company operation had increased to the point that I would be ready to quit if one more thing went wrong.

The "last straw" came on pay day in January. During his long trip out of the country, Cedric Warren had decided that the pilots were cheating the company on their flying times. Air Cambodge had supposedly complained to him that they were being charged for more flying time per trip than the other companies were logging. This, of course, was true. Our chief pilot had directed us to circle over the field to 3000 feet before departure and to circle down from the same altitude on arrival. Most of the pilots for other companies simply departed straight out and came straight in for landing. Our times were naturally five or six minutes more than theirs. After Max was hit in the arm and the DC-4 shot full of holes, the chief pilot had stressed that his procedure was mandatory.

To control the "cheating," a set of fixed "block times" had been instituted in late December. Instead of being paid for the actual time between leaving the parking place at one airport and parking at another, we recorded a time for pay purposes that was arbitrarily determined by the management for each destination. I had no objection to this, in principle, even though we would no longer be paid for delays en route. A fixed time of 42 minutes had been allowed to the run to Kampot, however, and this was so unrealistically low, that we would be losing pay for over a quarter of an hour of actual working time on each trip. Cedric had arrived at this figure only because one of Stan Booker's pilots had bragged to him about being able to make the run in 42 minutes: 38 minutes in the air and 4 minutes taxiing. Cedric failed to add that this pilot's company paid him for a fixed block time of 47 minutes. Some SEAAT pilots referred to this pilot's flights as "low level gun runs" because he climbed straight out and descended straight in without regard for the enemy firing positions. I had seen him tell the police chief of Kampot to mind his own business when this conscientious official tried to show him the maps depicting the enemy positions. I did not want to decry the actions of this pilot, whose company regulations were quite different from mine, but I greatly resented having the vice-president of SEAAT use him as a model for our flying performance.

It was not too long thereafter that the fast-flying pilot picked up a reported ten bullet holes — I only counted seven — during a low-level, straight-in approach to Kompong Cham.

When we received our pay for December in the middle of January, we found that the fixed times had been applied to calculate our flying time. All of these company times agreed very closely to those we had logged, except that for the Kampot trip. Since we flew to Kampot so often, however, I had a total loss of $35 out of my paycheck of $1840. This was particularly annoying because Sangob and I were the only pilots consistently flying more than our minimum of 70 hours. The DC-4 and Convair pilots were paid for

The Air Cambodge DC-3 N83AC, northwest of Phnom Penh with the Mekong River in the background (photo courtesy of Bill Ernst).

their basic time of 70 hours even though they were actually flying only 30 or 40. The hourly wage of these pilots was also higher, so one of them who had flown 20 hours in a month received the same pay as I did for flying 100. I decided that if the management did not want to pay me for complying with their own circling procedures, they could put the money toward the plane ticket of my replacement.

As I was handed my pay, the new SEAAT office manager told me that it was $40 short because he had only $100 bills. I strongly suggested that he should pay me an extra $60 and have it counted as an advance toward the following month. He accepted my idea.

Because of my complaint about the time allowed for Kampot, Cedric scheduled a meeting with Sangob and me for the evening. I ran into him in the office during the afternoon, and we discussed the matter informally. His only grounds for this particular block time was the boast of Stan Booker's pilot. He had allowed 51 minutes for the flight to Kompong Thom, 71 nautical miles away, and only 42 for the 70 nautical mile leg to Kampot. He said that my average time for this flight was higher than Sangob's, but he included the long holding time because of the rainstorms during my first flight. Disregarding this trip, both of our averages were only a few tenths of a minute apart, falling between 53 and 54 minutes. Usually, I had logged 52 minutes, but he pointed out that I had once logged exactly one hour. I told him that on that day, we had had 50 to 60 knot headwinds at cruising altitude because of a passing typhoon, and showed him that only 45 minutes were logged for the return flight, when tailwinds prevailed.

He finally took out his pocket computer to figure out a theoretical flight time. Because he regularly flew only the DC-4 and Convair, he had no idea how fast we could climb to 3000 feet and cruise. He used a cruising speed of 160 knots, when, in fact, we would have been lucky to get 120 knots out of the overloaded machines with the numerous skin dents from years of abuse. After he added only 5 minutes as the total taxi time for the trip, his computer told him the block time should be 53 minutes, one minute more than we usually logged.

With all of his arguments exhausted, I could not imagine what remained to be discussed. That evening, however, he arrived with the chief pilot and a vast array of statistics. His display gave one of the best examples of misusing mathematics to support a fraudulent case that I have ever seen. As a retired military man, he certainly had had plenty of opportunity to learn how to make figures lie. Of course, enough trips had not yet been flown to provide a meaningful average, and my average had apparently been increased by 1½ minutes due to the holding time on my first flight. When I looked at the data, however, I immediately saw that his whole case was phoney. He had included a large number of flights supposedly logged in October, before the aircraft had even been authorized to fly. He nevertheless insisted that all his data were correct. I asked to see the records, so he sent his secretary to get them. After a while, she returned to say that there were no records for October in the files. Cedric claimed again that his data were correct to the last detail and that the records would be found later. I thought that he might have confused October and November, but when I checked my log book, the dates did not match his. I then told Cedric that his records obviously did not exist, and that the statistics he had presented were nonsense. It was galling to be given such an idiotic treatment, suitable only for a Department of Defense briefing or a Liars' Club meeting.

The following morning I had a letter of resignation on the desk of the chief pilot. I gave SEAAT a period of notice so that they could find a replacement, but the chief of administration said that this was unnecessary. SEAAT had only one plane still flying, so they neeeded only one pilot. He also said that the company was planning to hire a DC-3 pilot who was being laid off by Continental Air Services in Laos.

Because the SEAAT treasurer claimed to have no cash, I had to wait two days for my pay. The time actually logged for January was worth about $30 more than the time the company paid me for, due to the unrealistic block time used for the Kampot trips. When I received my pay, the $60 advance was forgotten, so although I had been shortchanged for December and January, this $60 almost made it good again. I therefore left SEAAT without being cheated out of any pay at all, a record very few were to achieve.

Lyman handed me my pay, telling me how generous he was for giving it to me. Someone had told him that I was planning to go to work for Tri-9, so he told me that the head of that company was a drunk who would give me nothing if I quit. I considered the source of this information and took it *cum grano salis*. The SEAAT managers had all previously worked for Tri-9 themselves and stolen the Air Cambodge contract behind the back of their employer. I had been given a letter by the SEAAT management to get a 75 percent discount ticket on an Air Cambodge flight to Vientiane, Laos. The sales manager, an enormous fat man, told me that 75 percent discounts were given only to the SEAAT executives. He offered me a 50 percent rebate. I turned him down and left Phnom Penh for Battambang on January 18 on one of Stan Booker's aircraft and took a taxi from there to Poipet. The ride cost a dollar and lasted five hours, during which I had the experience of traveling one of the worst roads in the world. At Poipet I walked across the Thai border, then proceeded by bus to Vientiane.

Chapter 8

Before leaving Phnom Penh, I had spoken with several people about employment. John Yim, the vice-president of Tri-9, had already hired Cary Seavers from SEAAT after first having offered me the job in December. He had two DC-3 captains and one DC-3, but he planned to buy another DC-3 and promised to hire me when he did. Stan Booker also asked me to contact him when I returned from Vientiane because he also needed another DC-3 captain.

I spent two weeks in Vientiane helping my fiancée get her visas to study in the United States. I also flew some Cessnas there, carrying passengers to Ban Houey Sai and instructing some private pilots in instrument flying.

Before my planned return to Phnom Penh at the end of January, I received a telegram from John Yim requesting my immediate return. Tri-9's new DC-3 would be purchased in Vientiane and maintained with a Lao registration. Although I possessed a Lao *Pilote de Ligne* license, I first had to obtain the necessary Khmer papers to ferry the aircraft to Phnom Penh. The Khmer bureaucracy had become worse as the war situation became more and more critical.

On February 1, the day after my arrival in Phnom Penh, I flew with the Tri-9 chief pilot, Bill Davis, to get my company check-out. The DC-3, registered in the United States with the number N64422, was in much better condition than SEAAT's aircraft. It was the fastest DC-3 I have ever flown. At normal cruise power, it held an airspeed 15 to 20 knots faster than SEAAT's Skytrains. I found that it was difficult to make a good landing approach the first couple of times because it refused to descend as steeply as the aircraft I had been flying. It had considerably less drag than the average decrepit "gooney bird," and it became famous with the other pilots who tried to race it to the traffic pattern. On descent, with somewhat less than cruise power, it would acccelerate to 160 knots in a few seconds and speed past other "gooney birds" holding cruise power during descent. When I told the pilots of these aircraft that I was holding only 21 inches of manifold pressure, they would look at me incredulously and ask whether my jets had been turned on.

My first trips with 422 included the usual disputes with dishonest shippers. John Yim was planning to hire stewards to relieve the pilots of the loading problems. The first ones were soon in training and flying with us. We had hopes of being able to forget about the loading, allowing the Khmer stewards to handle all the work on the ground.

Our second flight on February 1 took us to Kompong Cham. Here our problems were aggravated by the mobs of unsupervised soldiers who hung around the aircraft. They tried to steal fuel out of the sump drains, poked bayonets into the engines, and insisted that we take them as unauthorized passengers to Phnom Penh. Officers were rare and seemed terrified of their own men.

Our cargo was soldiers, heavy mortars and other weapons. One unit was replacing another one there, and we were participating in the airlift. Our third flight of the day was a repeat of the second. I made the take-off and turned the aircraft sharply to the right at the northeast boundary of the field. I made a tight 180° turn and headed straight toward the city. A few seconds after levelling the wings and while only about 300 feet above the ground, we heard a noise like a heavy mortar falling over. Bill Davis decided to investigate. Behind the copilot's seat, in the compartment once occupied by a radio operator, there was a hole in the aircraft skin.

In Phnom Penh we discovered what had happened. One blade of the right propeller had a deep hole punched about halfway through. We found the steel core of an armor-piercing small arms round under the floor near the hole in the fuselage. We deduced that the round had hit the propeller blade dead center, gone about halfway through, and then been slung off through the fuselage skin. The inside layer of sheet metal had stopped it and deflected it under the floor. Bill kept it as a souvenir. It was interesting to speculate on the source of the bullet. The city was occupied by government soldiers, and the shot had certainly come from the direction of the city.

This episode ended 422's flying for a couple of days. The prop had to be changed. Undetected structural damage to the steel could have caused the blade to disintegrate in the air. It was also nearly time for the 100 hour inspection, so all the work was to be done at the same time. Unlike SEAAT, Tri-9 actually carried out inspections every 100 hours rather than just stamping the log books.

Whenever possible, John Yim tried to send the aircraft away from Phnom Penh for the night. Our usual overnight stop was Battambang. It was a pleasant change from Phnom Penh, although the hotels were usually without electricity and often without water. Battambang was far from the war and well stocked with food grown locally or imported by road from Thailand. The shops were better supplied than those in Phnom Penh, and the restaurants had more to offer. We logged almost an hour and five minutes en route, a relatively long trip.

On February 5, I made my first overnight stop with 422. Jim Devore, a retired American soldier who made his home in Bangkok, flew as my co-pilot. He had learned to fly in military aeroclubs. We flew a straight line course over the mountains to the northwest of Phnom Penh, flying parallel to the south shore of the Great Lake for its whole length. We then crossed marshland that would be dry until the onset of the southwest monsoon in April.

Toward the end of the dry season, the windless atmosphere becomes very hazy, and the smoke from numerous fires hangs in the air for weeks at a time. The setting sun ahead of us made visibility almost nil. As we passed the western end of the Great Lake, we saw the set of curious animal-shaped ponds that gave the region the nickname "barnyard." As we approached Battambang, I called the tower to tell them that we estimated our arrival in ten minutes. Jim was not familiar with the area, so he tuned our radio compass (ADF) to the Battambang station. We received a strong aural identifier, and the needle pointed straight ahead. Our set of charts lacked the one showing Battambang itself, although we had one that reached to about a mile east of the city limits. When I estimated that we were about abeam of the airport, I turned southwest. In that direction, we would have to cross the highway and railroad that run through the city. Through the thick haze, we could see some of the trees that lined a river. Then the road and railroad tracks emerged from the murkiness. The ADF needle pointed northwest along the road, so I turned in that direction and followed the twin transportation arteries toward Thailand.

After following the parallel road and railroad tracks for five minutes, I saw two low hills resembling rock piles. They looked familiar. I recognized them as the hills I had passed in the taxi on my journeys from Battambang to the Thai border. I immediately made a 180° turn and headed back. The ADF now pointed behind us, still persisting in telling us that Battambang lay to the northwest. In seven minutes, we were in the airport traffic pattern. The visibility in the direction away from the sun was not too bad, and I was able to see that the trees we had first spotted were located at the western edge of the city. I felt pretty stupid for having passed the field. The flight took about 15 minutes longer than it should have. Tri-9 paid according to fixed block times, so it did not matter for pay purposes.

On the return trip the next morning, the Phnom Penh area was blanketed by clouds. There were unseasonal rainstorms and low clouds around the field. I could not descend under visual flight rules (VFR), so I made an ADF approach. Needless to say, I was not very confident in Khmer ADF stations after the experience the night before, but we broke out of the clouds exactly where we should have been. The Phnom Penh ADF seemed to work very well. Even if it had misled us, the fact that there are no hills or other obstructions near the city precluded any possible danger.

Radio aids in the Khmer Republic could never be counted upon. False stations had been reportedly set up by the communists, and a good many aircraft had been lost in Southeast Asia as a direct result of the pilot relying on some approach aid instead of maintaining visual contact with the field. Knowing the terrain and using reliable charts were indispensable for survival. Only a few major airports had fully reliable and correctly maintained radio navigation and approach aids. These included Saigon and Bangkok. Elsewhere, even radar was not always trustworthy. For example, incorrectly calibrated ground control approach (GCA) radar at Danang Air Base had resulted in several aircraft being directed into mountainsides.

On February 7 we returned to Kampot. The field had been closed for a while because of frequent shelling by the enemy. The fighting around the town had been heavy, but the communists had been driven off. Our cargo was wounded soldiers. We met some of our shippers there, who told of paying 1000 to 2000 United States dollars to the crews of the Khmer medical evacuation helicopters to temporarily leave the town during the fighting. Wounded soldiers had been left to die so that the Khmer Air Force crews could accommodate their paying passengers. These stories were credible to me because of many events that I personally witnessed.

On February 10 I again travelled overland to Vientiane, Laos, after hitching a ride on Stan Booker's DC-4 to Battambang. John Yim arrived the day after I did, and we flew the acceptance flight of the aircraft that Tri-9 was to buy. It was registered in Laos as XW-TFB, and I had previously flown it for a year and a half out of Vientiane. I knew that it was in good condition, since Roger, the chief pilot of Xieng Khouang Air Transport, had made sure that all regular maintenance had been performed.

Because the unnecessary sheet metal in the navigator's and radio operator's compartments had been removed, TFB had a much lower empty weight than most other DC-3s. This would allow us to accept much greater cargo weights than our competitors and to receive better charter rates.

We prepared to leave for Phnom Penh on February 19. The paperwork required to get permission for the flight was enormous, and only by visiting the Director of Civil Aviation (DCA) office and the airport officials personally was I able to collect everything I needed to depart on time. Here again, I found knowledge of the language indispensable. The clerks whom I had to ask for the typing of various forms spoke little or no English, and if I had been unable to speak Lao, our departure would have been delayed one or two days. The Lao officials at the airport had expedited our departure. They were pleasant to deal with, sharply contrasting with the Khmers in this respect. Permission to overfly Thailand was required, and the official documents take several days to obtain. I knew a way to circumvent that problem, however. I knew the radio frequencies to contact the radar sites that monitor flights in Thai airspace, so after taking off, we were able to get immediate permission by radio to cross Northeastern Thailand under radar supervision.

Jim Devore was my copilot, and three pilots from other Phnom Penh companies were on board as passengers. We had a very pleasant 3 hour and 15 minute flight that took us across Udorn and Ubon in Thailand, then along the Tonle Sap. Jim wanted to use the ADF, but I made sure that it was not turned on. No radio aids are better than false ones. Haze and smoke made the visibility poor, but there were no clouds. The radar station at Udorn, Brigham, monitored us for a short distance, then lost us from the scopes. We were told to contact Lion at Ubon, but they were not answering their radios that day. We navigated solely by dead reckoning and pilotage, giving our position to Ubon tower for relay.

The long stretch from Udorn to Ubon is relatively free from prominent landmarks. The charts of the route had been prepared many years earlier. Since then, lakes and ponds had dried up, and new ones had formed. Trails and villages had long been abandoned, and new ones had replaced them. This long leg had to be flown by dead reckoning alone. At the time we estimated reaching Ubon, we were only about 10 miles north of Ubon Air Base.

South of Ubon, we could see the remarkable topography that marked the border between Thailand and the Khmer Republic. It is a straight cliff running through the middle of a vast plain for a great many miles. On the Khmer side of the border, the land gradually slopes upward to the north, then it drops off abruptly into Thailand. A network of trails connects numerous villages on the Thai side of the border, but south of the cliff, signs of human life vanish. A vast stretch of unpopulated open woodland and forest welcomed us into the Khmer Republic.

Human life had not always been absent from the region. As we proceeded southward, we tried to spot the numerous ruins marked on the charts. Evidently, an extensive civilization had flourished here many centuries ago. Only scattered stone monuments attest to its existence. West of our route lay Siemriep, with the ruins of Angkor nearby. Even these impressive ruins of the old Khmer capital and its enormous temples had lain hidden beneath the jungle for centuries.

Soon the Great Lake of the Tonle Sap loomed into view. We flew parallel to its northern coast for a while until we could see the winding Mekong as it crossed the plain to the east. At the confluence of the Mekong and Tonle Sap stands Phnom Penh.

After the experience with the cooperative Lao officials and our pleasant journey, we were suddenly confronted again by the rude unpleasantries of everyday life in Phnom Penh. After presenting TFB's papers to the authorities, we were naturally refused permission to remove any of the spare parts or tools we had brought with us. One low-ranking Khmer

The Air Cambodge DC-4 operated by Southeast Asia Air Transport taxies from the parking ramp at Pochentong Airport, Phnom Penh (photo by Bill Ernst, courtesy of Charley Pennington).

customs guard stood watch, greedily eyeing the contents of the aircraft. He wanted to see our cargo manifest. Since we had no cargo, we had not made one out. That delayed us about one hour. One of the officials finally reluctantly agreed to let us make one out. It consisted of the date, the aircraft registration number, the number of crew members, the weight of the spare parts, then the words "passengers — none" after a blank half page and "cargo — none" after another blank half page. After I signed this important document, which was worth an hour's work to the customs officials, we were free to proceed to the immigration office. Of course, a little grease could have speeded up the procedures, but when it became apparent that I was not good for any bribes, they tired of the game.

After we located the immigration official, who was quite drunk, he stamped my re-entry visa. The pilots who had come with us as extra crew members did not have re-entry visas. The normal fee to enter at the airport was United States $5, and some haggling ensued about whether they should pay more or come back the next day when the chief of immigration would be there. I did not ask how the matter was settled, but the pilots got their entry visas.

As we left the airport that day, I well realized that a long delay would ensue before TFB would have all the necessary papers to start flying commercially. The capital was surviving on the food brought in by the airlift, but the corrupt officials in each department were only interested in what they could get for putting their signatures on some meaningless documents required before an aircraft was allowed to fly.

Many new companies were being organized to begin operations in May under a campaign by the government to increase the volume of the airlift. The minister of transportation was behind the move to step up our operations to save the starving capital. He used his power to suppress the crooks in his own ministry and promised to expedite the issuance of permits for any new company that would operate aircraft in the country. For those who snapped at the bait and brought in new aircraft, the unseen hook lay in the ministry of commerce. The minister of transportation kept his promise about the permits, but aircraft need fuel to operate, and the minister of commerce issued the authorizations to buy avgas.

In mid–May, the new companies got together and offered to pay the minister of commerce 1,200,000 riels to release the fuel. Each of the six companies was to contribute 200,000 riels. This proved to be insufficient, and the aircraft remained grounded. A tanker with fuel rode at anchor in the Tonle Sap but could not unload because all of the tanks on shore were full. Meanwhile, the parking ramp of the airport was congested with idle aircraft. Food supplies in the city dwindled. Prices rose. The riel continued its precipitous depreciation.

Finally, pressure on the minister of commerce forced him to release the fuel, but he did so only on a month to month basis so that the shake-down process could be repeated at regular intervals.

The central executive power of the country rested in the wheelchair of the brain-crippled Lon Nol, while the actual organization of the supply effort took place in the United States Embassy. Incredibly, the American officials sided with the minister of commerce on the issue of the permits. An enormous amount of fuel was being stolen, but the bulk of the thefts were taking place in the harbor. For the embassy bureaucrats, however, the new paperwork would exonerate them from charges of carelessness in their stewardship over American aid, while the Khmer officials made the situation as lucrative as possible for themselves.

Both TFB and 422 were to fly under contract with the new companies. Between the time of its arrival in Phnom Penh and May 1, however, TFB flew under contract with Khemera Air Transport, one of the old companies with a long-term fuel authorization. Thus, we could count on working during March and April.

Chapter 9

Flying resumed for me the day following my return from Vientiane. I took over as captain of 422 until TFB could get its papers and be repainted. Every day was a mad scramble to finish our scheduled flights in time to fly to Battambang for the night. The tower at Battambang was scheduled to close each day at 5:00 P.M., although it would stay open later if aircraft were due in. The tower at Phnom Penh, however, forbad flights to take off for Battambang if they could not be sure of landing before five o'clock. We were sometimes allowed to depart as late as 4:30, if our airport representative "talked" to the tower personnel first.

The cargo for Battambang always consisted of fuel in 55 gallon drums. Gasoline and diesel oil were shipped to Phnom Penh through the courtesy of the American taxpayers, then sold at cost plus to oil companies for profit. The fuel in Thailand, where the free market operates, was about twice as expensive. Hence, the fuel that made the risky run up the Mekong past the enemy gun positions was flown to Battambang, or sometimes Krakor, to be smuggled into Thailand and sold for a great profit. The United States Embassy made no effort to stop this but instead satisfied itself with strangling the airlift by making it very hard for the companies to get fuel for bona fide operations. Whether or not the Khmer and American officials kept their paperwork honestly is another question.

At about this time, a check was made of the fuel storage facility in the port of Phnom Penh, and a loss of about 8 million liters (over 2 million gallons) was discovered. For us, a set of stricter controls meant that we had to fly without enough reserve fuel to make it to an alternate field if our destination was closed because of a rocket attack or bad weather. Joey Johns, a Convair pilot, was particularly bitter about the situation. He claimed to be sure that an American official at the embassy had been behind the fuel thefts.

Joey claimed to be looking for some proof that this American was involved, but the chances of finding such proof are almost nil. Of course, it boggles the imagination to think that even an American civil servant could be so stupid as to allow 8 million liters of fuel to disappear under his nose.

The fact that the system called for fuel to be placed under Khmer control, however, permitted the responsible Americans to pass the buck. Even in the few cases where American officials were caught red-handed in the theft of enormous quantities of government property, they were not prosecuted. This would create a bad precedent for other thieves who might be caught later. Apparently, too many people were involved in these activities, at least if we can believe the testimony at Congressional hearings. Trials of public officials are also discouraged because it might make the public "lose faith in the government."

During a visit to the United States, I drove down the Parkway to Washington, D.C. I had to chuckle when I read the sign claiming that the 55 m.p.h. speed limit was saving a million gallons of fuel per year. Twice that amount had disappeared in a couple of months in the Khmer Republic.

For corruption to flourish in the way that it did all through the Vietnam War, three fundamental principles had to be followed:

1. Public officials who oversee American aid programs must be allowed to work under the assumption, "It's not our country, we cannot be held responsible for what the local officials do with our aid after they receive it."

2. To account for all aid to the client country, only a list of the funds or goods turned over is required. No accounting is required to show the use to which the aid is put.

3. The proper use of the aid is mutually agreed upon by the American advisors and their counterparts in the client country without a responsibility for the effective use of the funds and goods being assigned to either.

If these three ground rules are followed, anything goes and the Swiss banks will be sure to prosper. Under this sytem, a dishonest American official is in the position to commit perfect crimes. No one has jurisdiction over what he does. Besides being protected by diplomatic immunity, he is invariably involved with the families and friends of the richest and most powerful men in the client country, men who stand above the law. They will certainly protect their American benefactor who looks the other way while they channel the aid funds into their own pockets. Since the funds and goods are misappropriated after they are turned over to the foreign government, that American cannot be held responsible by his agency, either. The American can deposit his kickbacks in a confidential Swiss bank account and keep it out of the reach of the Internal Revenue Service.

There were only two possible explanations for what I was witnessing in the Khmer Republic: either the Americans working in the Embassy were so incredibly stupid that they really did not know what was going on, or they were committing "perfect crimes" in the manner just discussed. Were the representatives of the United States really incapable of being dishonest and sharing in what they were permitting the Khmer officials to do with the aid?

The Khmer Army consisted of hundreds of thousands of soldiers who existed only on paper. Because of their "official" existence, they were provided with pay and equipment by the United States. Moreover, those real soldiers I met at the outposts far from the capital were often at the point of mutiny because they had not been paid in months, lacked food, and were usually short of ammunition. Where was all of the aid money going? Everyone in Phnom Penh knew that "phantom soldiers" were being supported, and many people knew to which units the phantoms were assigned. Why did the responsible officials at the Embassy just look the other way?

The rate of exchange between United States dollars and Khmer riels fluctuated wildly, but the overall trend for the riel remained downward. The price paid in the banks and exchange shops was the rate used by the United States Embassy. Its dollars were changed at what was called the "official rate," which was often less than half the actual rate. American officials had to pay Khmer employees and buy riels for other purposes. What did they do with the difference between the real and "official" rates? If an American diplomat needed 300,000 riels for a payroll, he could take $1000 to the government bank and change it at a rate of 300 to 1. Instead, he might also decide to pay a Khmer confederate at the bank $100 and receive an official paper stating that $1000 had been changed. Now he could take the remaining $900 to the market, where 600 riels were paid for each dollar. He could then return to the Embassy with the 300,000 riels plus $400, which would officially be unaccounted for.

Although the $400 profit in the example is insignificant, similar profits on the hundreds of millions handled by the Embassy are certainly not. It is noteworthy that "official rates" of exchange have been maintained in many developing countries, including all three of the Indochinese states involved in the Vietnam War. These were instituted ostensibly to "help support the local currency," but all that it actually did was to make millionaires out of many black marketeers and speculators, and also out of several Americans who later testified about it before Congress.

That the Khmer government was totally corrupt remains undisputed, but how it could remain that way and keep its close ties with the American diplomatic mission, which was providing all its support, leaves much room for speculation. The staff at the United States Embassy was burdened with many old career civil servants and retired military people. If they had wanted to be dishonest and share in the graft, they had had plenty of time to learn how. Were they really involved, or did their consciences and sense of honor keep them from profiting personally?

Considering the many shortcomings of the system we were working under or questioning our shipper about the source of his petroleum products were not part of my job. My problem was seeing to it that the drums of flammable fuel were properly tied down and that the drums with leaking bungs were not loaded on the aircraft. Whenever I told one of the Khmer loading crew to tie a heavy drum down securely, he would laugh and explain that the item was heavy. They considered me a little crazy for wanting such heavy things tied down. I grew tired of explaining how heavy things can fly around in the aircraft during turbulence.

Particularly annoying was the shipper's habit of using the drums for passenger seats. Normally, he would find his passengers seats on those drums that showed signs of leaking. Each time I witnessed this, I began a heated explanation in broken Khmer about how the reduced pressure at altitude would cause the flammable fumes to spew out of the drums, then possibly explode. During my tirade, the shipper's passengers would leap from their "seats" as if they had suddenly become hot.

This scene repeated itself almost every time we flew to Battambang. Each cargo seemed to contain at least two or three leaky drums, and the shipper never learned to pick these out himself before his men loaded them.

Tri-9 was in the process of expanding. I had always thought that the DC-3 was the only reliable aircraft for making money in the Khmer Republic, but the majority of the company managers did not share my opinion. The maintenance of the larger, newer aircraft was simply too complicated, and the revenue they generated did not cover their repair bills. Still, new dinosaurs kept arriving.

Our company purchased two Convair 240s from Garuda Airlines in Indonesia. The management also acted as agents to purchase a C-46 and an AT-11, an ancient forerunner of the Twin-Beech, for two local companies. Our chief pilot wanted to fly the Convairs himself, so he paid some money under the table and bought a Lao license for the make and model. Cary Seavers, a pilot who had worked for Tri-9 several times before, had been standing by to fly the Convairs, but John Yim released him because he allegedly would not fly if the weather conditions were not perfect and continually complained about the maintenance. Although Cary had quit SEAAT with hard feelings before going to Tri-9, this company was glad to get him back. Such was the shortage of qualified captains that one need not be long unemployed.

Since our chief pilot planned to get out of the DC-3 business for a while, we would be short one captain. I recommended that John Yim hire two Thai pilots with whom I was acquainted. One of them, Soonthorn Pradith, nicknamed Tony, had been working for Stan Booker's outfit, which had gone out of business about a week earlier. He was hired as a copilot. The other, Sawai, had flown many years with the Thai Air Force and had much experience with the DC-3. John Yim hired him as our new DC-3 captain.

Sawai had a very bad opinion of the local operation and with good reason. He had initially been hired as a copilot by Cambodia Air Commercial (CACO), a low budget company, about two weeks earlier. He noted with dismay that the captain he was assigned to fly with had little idea of what he was doing, and on one of his first flights, he had to sit in the right seat and watch as his aircraft commander landed long at Svay Rieng, ran off the end of the runway, demolished a house, killed several of its inhabitants, and badly damaged the landing gear. Enough of the landing gear was later welded back on for a flight back to Phnom Penh, where the aircraft remained on the ramp for a long time awaiting major repairs.

Sawai started out flying as my copilot until Bill Davis switched to the Convairs. The company started off on the wrong foot with him by promoting him to captain on a "probationary employment status." In this way, he could be excluded for two or three months from a new pay raise to $17 per hour for DC-3 captains. He made no secret of the fact that he considered this a deceptive excuse to cheat him out of $2 per hour.

Until May both of our DC-3s bore the colors of Khemera Air Transport. Mr. Muku, the owner, was a very rich man and one of the few truthful and upright businessmen that I met in the Khmer Republic. His company and Khmer Airlines were the two best run aviation enterprises in the country. The operations of Khmer Airlines were handled by China Airlines. Their maintenance was good, and their DC-3s were in excellent shape. They were periodically sent to Saigon for overhaul and major maintenance. Khmer Airlines handled almost all the regularly scheduled domestic passenger flights.

Air Cambodge, the government airline, contrasted strongly with these companies. Overstaffed with corrupt employees who were incapable of managing effectively, the national airline remained a drain on the treasury, and hence, a drain on the American taxpayers. Most other companies operating in the country failed to follow good maintenance practices and ignored many sensible safety requirements.

Our company had two airport representatives, Mr. Nien and Mr. Ping, who were very efficient at soothing the aching palms of the airport officials with "grease." They kept our operations running very smoothly as much of the time as we had a right to expect. However, problems did arise.

Only Khmer Airlines and Air Cambodge had authorizations to carry passengers on their aircraft. The other companies preferred cargo flights because the profit was greater. The government had set the price of passenger tickets so low that there was no profit in carrying them on unsubsidized flights. In fact, many small merchants began supporting themselves by buying round trip air tickets from Phnom Penh to some city outside of the blockade, such as Krakor or Kampot, to buy as much sugar as they could carry. This was brought back into the capital as hand baggage and sold for enough to pay for the trip plus a handsome profit.

Since there were very few passenger flights and many travelers, most aircraft leaving Phnom Penh were full of passengers. "Black market" tickets on unauthorized aircraft cost much more than the official price, but there were plenty of buyers. Passage was booked by the airport police or Air Force personnel, who asked each company representative to put on a number of their clients as a courtesy. Our airport representatives feared that refusal of their requests would prompt the policeman or airman to find some reason for not approving some document that we required for the flight. The passengers were usually introduced to the pilot as relatives of the policeman. Several times, I questioned these "relatives" on how much they had paid for passage. Two persons actually were relatives engaged in transporting sugar for profit, but all others I spoke to had paid about twice the official price of a ticket to join the policeman's family.

To take their cut of the profits, the tower employees began regulating this black market passenger business. I first learned about this one day late in February. On our last flight of the day to Kompong Chhnang, we were carrying 7 persons plus the crew. Two of these were cargo conveyors, who were permitted on cargo flights, and the rest were soldiers.

When we called for taxi instructions, the tower asked how many passengers we had on board. The copilot quickly responded, "Five plus two conveyors."

The tower controller then told us that the passengers would have to disembark because we had no authorization to carry them. We complied, to the great dismay of the soldiers, then started our engines again. The controller, whose whining nasal tone I quickly recognized as belonging to one of the least efficient directors of airport traffic, called again to tell us, "You still have passengers aboard. I see a woman through the window."

Our steward informed me that the woman was the cargo owner, who was going along to carry the money and invoices. I told the controller that the woman was a conveyor. The controller whined back that a woman was not allowed to be a cargo conveyor. I told him that it was none of his business, and I told the woman to tell him on the radio that the cargo was hers. The controller responded that no woman was permitted to talk on a radio in the Khmer Republic and that I had broken their radio regulations. I forget my exact words, but I let him know that I thought he was an idiot. I shut down the engines and explained the problem to our mechanics. The soldiers who had been kicked off the flight were still standing beside the aircraft, so I made my explanations in Khmer to make sure that they all understood why they could not fly with us. As the tower operator looked down at us through his field glasses, he could see only hostile faces.

At the time, an American, Reb Simpleton, who knew nothing about aircraft, was working for Tri-9 as an electrician's helper. He took it upon himself to try to ask someone in the tower what was wrong. He ran inside and headed up the stairs. The tower personnel saw him coming and fled into the tower control room, bolting the door behind them. In panic, they began calling the airport security police to save them, claiming that the tower was under attack. When Reb returned, he told us that a policeman had told him to leave the tower and never come back. Soon, the Khemera Air Transport staff arrived, and the matter was quickly settled for an undisclosed amount. We took off with a delay of about 45 minutes.

The next day the tower commander sent word that he wanted to see me. He spoke no English, so his assistant was there to translate. I decided to speak English so that I would not express myself inaccurately. I explained what had happened. After I was through, the tower commander told me that he had been away on business the previous day and that sometimes the tower employees tried to engage in private business. The enforcement of the passenger authorization was up to the director of civil aviation and not the duty of the tower controllers. He advised me in the future not to tell them whether I had passengers on board or not.

He went on to explain that the tower's function was only to give instructions for take-off, landing, taxi, and traffic pattern entry. He said that he was concerned because the personnel on duty that day had reported that Reb had been sent to the tower to attack them, and he had entered the restricted area. I explained that Reb had only wanted to talk to them, but they had panicked and fled at his approach. He had not seen the sign marking the entrance to the restricted area.

Later, our company representatives explained the situation to me. The tower commander was a good man, but his subordinates were racketeers. It had been arranged with him privately that Khemera Air Transport would be allowed to carry passengers in exchange for certain favors, such as carrying people for him free of charge when we had space. When the tower commander was not in his office, however, some of the underlings often tried to get in on the graft by soliciting bribes in exchange for allowing passengers to fly in cargo aircraft.

Supposedly, there were behind the scenes activities to get rid of the worst individual on the tower staff, and I began to hope that I could aid in speeding his departure. This was not an easy matter. Like all Khmer civil servants, the tower employees owed their lucrative sinecures to influential persons high in the government. Most had paid for their jobs, which could only be taken away after conviction for some serious crime.

After my interview with the tower commander, I went to the flight plan room to file for my first flight. The functionary, a weasely looking Khmer with thick glasses who could have modeled for a picture of the typical bureaucrat, began thumbing through a book listing DC-3 captains. He announced that my authorization to fly was valid only for United States registered aircraft, and my flight in the Lao-registered TFB could not be approved. I had a Lao authorization in the DCA's office, but I did not waste time with explanations. I grabbed the book and came around the counter. The weasel fled in panic. I noted that a tall Khmer, who always seemed to be around when skullduggery was afoot, watched us intently. After ordering the weasel to go right upstairs to the commander's office, I took the book there and asked the commander if his personnel were trying to exact retribution because I had talked to him. After listening to the problem, he dismissed the seedy looking bureaucrat, explaining to me that this individual was not very smart and was incapable of doing anything like this on his own. Someone had obviously put him up to it. The flight plan was sent back to the sheepish official, who quickly approved it, and I began my day's flying.

Reb was not the only American who had terrorized the crooks in the tower. Frank Hines, one of the copilots for SEAAT, had quietly taken the harassment for several months. He had always been particularly easygoing and polite while submitting his flight plans, a chore which SEAAT assigned to its copilots. His conscientious efforts at friendship and cooperation were constantly rebuffed by various idiotic objections to small details on his flight plans and unreasonable delays. After making as much trouble as possible for him each day, they would then ask him to buy some 5-kilo sacks of sugar for them at one of his destination airports. He frequently did them this favor.

By late January SEAAT's flight schedule had reached its nadir due to the lack of spare parts, and Frank's patience was wearing thin. One day he submitted flight plans for his two scheduled flights of the day to a flight plan clerk. In the past he had always received simultaneous approval, but that day, the clerk approved only one and told him to come back and resubmit the other before his second flight. Frank insisted that his flight plans were always approved without delay, but the clerk simply shrugged his argument off. Frank now had reached the breaking point. He tore up the flight plan and threw it in the clerk's face. He then started to leave, but suddenly changed his mind, turned around, and demanded his flight plan back. Frank is over six feet tall and heavily built. He came around the desk and the Khmer officials all fled in panic. Frank pursued. The terrified bureaucrats ran up the stairs and barricaded themselves in the office. Frank thought the situation over and decided he needed a rest. He left on the next available flight to take a month's vacation in the States, where he took his test for his airline transport pilot rating in the DC-3. When he returned, he flew skillfully as a DC-3 captain for SEAAT, and I saw him save his aircraft at Kompong Thom after he landed with a flat tire which could easily have caused him to skid off the narrow runway into the deep ditch if he had not used extraordinary skill to control the aircraft.

In my subsequent dealings with the Khmer airport personnel, I found that I possessed an enormous advantage over my fellow pilots because of my limited fluency in the language. I began treating the bureaucrats with an attitude of studied disdain and sometimes open contempt. I insulted them in Khmer using a casual tone but loudly enough to be heard by the laborers and coolies standing around. I would candidly ask how much of a bribe they wanted from a representative of another company or shipper and made plays on words in Khmer, turning the word for "airman" into "air thief," *jao agat*. My insults, which were not made jokingly, were often accompanied by the guffaws of the coolies, who may have been earning less than $1 per day but were not too ignorant to know where the officials were getting the money to pay for their new Mercedes. Soon I was one of the only pilots whose flight plans and authorizations were approved quickly and efficiently. The clerks were afraid that if they created delays for our company representative who submitted the flight plan, I might show up in the office, and that was something they wished to avoid.

Acting in this way went against the grain because I well knew that the arrogant and overbearing attitude of many American government officials and businessmen in Vietnam or Thailand had ruined their chances of accomplishing anything and subjected them to much frustration. Some people do not let themselves be pushed around, regardless of their social status. In the Khmer Republic, I found that I had to forget everything I had learned for getting along elsewhere in Southeast Asia. A totally opposite set of values prevailed, and it was difficult to find the logic behind the behavior of the officials, if indeed logic was involved at all.

Those pilots who were most courteous and obliging to the demands of these low grade civil servants were rewarded by endless problems. The Chinese pilots, with a few very notable exceptions, were the most cooperative, acting in a manner that they knew would guarantee them success almost anywhere else in Southeast Asia. They returned from almost every trip loaded down with fresh fruit or sugar for their friends in the flight plan office. They then confessed bewilderment at the problems their beneficiaries created for them. They were often required to make repeated pilgrimages to the tower before their flight plans were approved. Sometimes they were simply refused clearance to taxi or, after they had taxied out for take-off, they were told to return to the ramp. If the pilot brought them a bag of sugar, they ordered him to bring five the next time.

I formulated a hypothesis to explain this behavior. Apparently, when someone did a favor for one of these jungle bureaucrats, he placed himself in the position of an inferior. From that time on, he would be expected to do favors whenever asked, and he could be subjected to humiliation so that the bureaucrat could demonstrate his personal importance before his peers. By adopting a contemptuous attitude, I secured myself excellent cooperation from the airport officials. No one ever seriously attempted retribution for my insults, no matter how blatant. I think, perhaps, these people really felt guilt for the advantages they were taking over their less fortunate countrymen.

An interesting sidelight of this story is the fate of Reb Simpleton, an individual of subnormal intelligence who had been left behind by the American Forces in Vietnam. He had reputedly spent some time in a Saigon prison for a drug violation, and he arrived destitute in Phnom Penh. Apparently, he had been recruited by SEAAT, but even its management could see that he would be of no use. To help him survive, John Yim had given him a job as assistant electrician although he knew nothing about the work.

During his short tenure with Tri-9, his only ambition seemed to be amusing himself by taking airplane rides. He would announce that he needed to fly with us to observe the operation of the radios. I took him along once, then refused his requests. He reacted like a small boy whose parents had just refused him an ice cream cone. Our gross weight was already too great on most of our trips, and he obviously could do nothing with the radios anyway. He would remove tubes to test them because that was all he knew how to do. The ADFs worked fine, but the needles in the indicator were about 3° out of adjustment. He never succeeded in correcting the problem, although for a real technician, the job would have been simple.

One day Reb noticed that one of the thermocouple leads to the cylinder head temperature gauge was too long. The extra wire was rolled up and taped to the side of the engine compartment. He cut the extra wire off. Every aircraft electrician's helper knows that a precise amount of resistance in the system is required for the calibration of a cylinder head temperature gauge. By cutting off part of the lead, Reb had reduced the resistance and made one of our gauges inoperative. This cost him his job.

Reb began borrowing money from various people in order to buy food — and drink. Soon he ran out of benefactors and faced the real danger of starvation. Because the American consulate is supposed to provide emergency loans to repatriate Americans, Reb decided to speak with the vice-consul. Unfortunately for Reb, the vice-consul was rather typical of the United States Foreign Service. He was quite young, and his hair, carefully curled, hung down well below his shoulders. When I once described him as "hippie," I was corrected by my former SEAAT copilot, Bill Ernst, who explained: "He's not hippie, he's 'mod,' Charlie!"

This was apparently true, because his flower-covered clothing was clean and probably very expensive. His belongings were carried in a small purse with a draw string tied at the waist. I never saw him outside of the fortress-like consulate building. What would the Khmers have said if they had seen him on the street?

The vice-counsul made it clear to Reb that no help whatsoever would be forthcoming from the representatives of his country. Reb explained humbly that he had no money to eat, and the vice-consul replied, "Then I guess you'll have to tighten your belt."

Tiring of the interview, the vice-consul called the Marine guard to throw Reb out of the building. As Reb departed, the vice-consul added that he had to refuse the loan because Reb could still find a job in Phnom Penh, perhaps teaching English.

The suggestion that Reb could find a job was ridiculous. He had already been fired by two airline companies, and it was unthinkable that any of the others would hire him. He could not speak grammatical English and was at best marginally literate, so his value as an English teacher was almost nil. Why the vice-consul wanted to keep an ex-convict of marginal intelligence in a combat zone is difficult to understand. There are those who believe that such people as deserters, fugitives, ex-convicts, and narcotics addicts are always in demand by agencies of our government overseas. Such people are desperate and will often do anything for a ticket home. If a need to do an unpleasant or disreputable job arises, a supply of such renegades could be very useful. Was there a purpose in keeping Reb in the Khmer Republic? Perhaps the vice-consul realized that such a person was not literate enough to file an official complaint. So why help him?

Reb eventually wandered to Kompong Som, where a Frenchman gave him a small loan and a place to stay. Shortly thereafter, the communists attacked Khmer outposts along the highway between the port and Kompong Som Airport, isolating the two enclaves. The house in which Reb had taken shelter was in the communist controlled area, and Reb was reported missing. First reports in the American press stated that an American lieutenant (Reb) had been captured by the Khmer Rouge. After a lengthy search of American records at the embassy, the reports were denied. Later on Reb turned up again. He had no idea that he had achieved such notoriety and apparently did not know that his house had ostensibly been under Khmer Rouge control. What happened to Reb after that I do not know.

The staff of the consulate was not very popular with the pilots or with any other Americans in Phnom Penh. Cary Seavers once had some business with the vice-consul, and he was given an appointment at 9:00 A.M. He arrived 20 minutes early and watched through a glass partition as the vice-consul, who had seen him come in, read a magazine with his feet up on the desk until the appointed time. The discussion lasted less than 10 minutes.

On one occasion I brought my passport to the consulate for extra pages. The vice-consul was not in, but the secretary was able to paste the pages in. She then told me that I would have to come back in the afternoon because the vice-consul was required to apply the official stamp himself. Since I worked all day, often for seven days per week, I did not appreciate having to make two trips to the consulate because the personnel wanted to take vacations during their duty hours.

Chapter 10

The day after my interview with the tower commander, we were scheduled for another trip to Kompong Chhnang. The copilot called for taxi instructions, and the controller inquired, "How many passengers do you have on board?" The copilot started to answer, but I waved him away from the microphone.

"That's none of your business," I replied into my hand mike.

There was a pause, then the tower repeated, "I say again, how many passengers do you have on board your aircraft?"

Again I said, "That's none of your business!"

The controller responded, "Cleared to taxi."

At Kompong Chhnang, after the usual long arguments with the shippers about weights and numbers of passengers, I noticed a soldier with sunglasses putting a large canvas bag aboard the aircraft. It was labeled, "tower." I inquired about it and was told that it contained sugar. Every aircraft departing Kompong Chhnang carried one large bag of sugar for the Phnom Penh tower staff, without the crew's permission and usually without their knowledge. Each kilo of sugar sold for 500 riels at Kompong Chhnang, which was less than $1 at the time. In Phnom Penh, sugar sold for between 1500 and 2500 riels per kilo, depending on the daily market fluctuation. The tower staff's bag held two or three kilos, and sometimes two of these bags were placed on board. A tower representative met the planes at Phnom Penh to pick up the sugar. With a $9 or $10 profit per bag and 40 or 50 bags delivered per day, the tower officials could count on a net gain of up to $500 per day, just from Kompong Chhnang sugar. There were similar profits being made on oranges and a wide variety of other basic food items, which were in critically short supply in the capital.

Before take-off I booted the bag of sugar off like a football and gave strict instructions to the steward never to allow it on the aircraft again.

A few days later, because of a heated argument between our steward and the cargo shipper over the cargo weight, the tower representative managed to sneak his bag of sugar on board. The climb performance of the aircraft told me that the steward had been outfoxed by the shippers, so I ordered that the cargo be sent to the company scales at Phnom Penh and weighed before release to the shipper. As the tower messenger grabbed the sugar and started to leave, I snatched it out of his hand, threw it on the truck, and said in Khmer, "To the scales."

The bag was carried off in the truck with the cargo. I never learned who got the sugar, but I know it wasn't the tower staff.

The next day a sinister-looking Khmer with sunglasses approached the aircraft as we were loading. He identified himself as the "tower sugar conveyor," and informed me that I had to take him to Kompong Chhnang. I told him in no uncertain terms to get lost fast. He turned and beat a hasty retreat to the tower building.

During the next few days, I reaped the rewards of my open hostility toward the tower staff. There were absolutely no bureaucratic delays. Time and again, I heard pilots from other companies being queried about their passengers, then told to taxi back to the parking ramp. Some pilots had long waits in the airport terminal restaurant while their companies negotiated for the approval of their flight plans. I saw many a harried Chinese pilot carrying watermelons, bags of oranges, crabs from Kampot, and other goodies to the flight plan room—all to no avail. My crew had standing orders to avoid doing the slightest favor for any of the tower personnel.

Ben Crawford, an old friend from Laos, arrived in Phnom Penh to seek employment. He had an FAA airline transport pilot rating in the DC-3 and hoped to get some operational experience. He was hired as a copilot by Tri-9. Before one of his first flights, a young woman who worked at the flight plan desk asked him to buy her two watermelons at Krakor. He complied in spite of my disapproval of the practice.

While we were waiting in the restaurant for the shipper to finish loading the aircraft for the next trip, Ben was called away on company business and replaced by another copilot. The watermelons were still in the aircraft. After the last flight, I spotted a workman hurrying away with them. I retrieved them and carried them to town in the maintenance jeep. Ben told me that they were for the girl in the flight plan room. I warned him of the consequences of doing favors, but he did not believe me. He asked incredulously, "How can buying a couple of watermelons for someone hurt anything?"

Since he was the one who had to submit the flight plans, I decided that he better find out for himself. Ben delivered the melons to the girl the next day, apologizing for the delay. The girl then asked him if he was going to Krakor again. Ben said he was. She then told him to buy her four watermelons, while a colleague ordered him to bring back a bag of oranges. Before the other staff members could put in their orders, Ben told them that his aircraft commander did not want him to make a habit of taking private cargo on the aircraft. The girl replied that his flight plan could not be approved right away, and he would have to come back. For the next few days, Ben continued being harassed by the menials employed in the tower offices. He had marked himself as an inferior by doing a favor and was treated accordingly. His attitude toward the bureaucracy quickly soured, and as he became more sullen, he gradually began to win their respect.

We did do favors for people on occasion. When returning empty from our rice flights to various outposts, we carried soldiers and their families, as well as refugees, but I objected if the local police were making them pay for the permission to fly with us. We knew that the common soldiers were unable to pay, but refugees were frequently taken advantage of by the local authorities. We also let our stewards carry sugar and oranges for themselves as long as they kept our weights correct. By carrying one kilo of sugar per flight, they could earn several times their monthly salaries.

In February the national ban against carrying passengers on cargo flights was countermanded by the province governors. Since the aircraft returning to Phnom Penh were almost always fully loaded with cargo, more and more stranded passengers were waiting in vain for the few available passenger flights. To cope with this problem, the governor of Kompong Chhnang Province ordered that at least 10 passengers be carried on every flight departing from airports in his province. The governor of Pursat followed suit by setting a minimum number of 5 passengers for all flights departing Krakor. The military police at the airports were ordered to prevent any departures of aircraft not complying with these regulations. Thus, we violated one law if we carried passengers and another if we did not.

The country was obviously lawless anyway, so the situation did not bother me at all. My concerns were that the passengers had seats with seat belts and that we kept the gross weight within safe limits. The rest of the rules were only nonsense designed to keep the graft flowing to the government employees. When a large load of perishable fresh fish at Kompong Chhnang was waiting to go, the shippers paid off the Air Force security police, and we carried no passengers.

The military police handled the waiting lists, so those wanting to travel paid not only the official price of a ticket but also a considerably larger sum for a "reservation." When many people were waiting to go, the airport police could auction off the places on the aircraft. The passenger fares should have gone to the shippers who had chartered the aircraft, but the policemen normally kept two or three of the fares in addition to the "reservation" fees. A bewildering array of petty officials had descended on the airports to share in the shippers' profits by finding ways of creating difficulties that required bribes to solve. This not only drained the merchants' pockets, it also wasted enormous amounts of time. Occasionally, one of the shippers

The crowd on the parking ramp at Kompong Chhnang airport (photo courtesy of Bill Ernst).

lost his temper with a policeman, but most resigned themselves to paying whatever was asked and trying to make up for the loss by sneaking on some extra freight.

The policemen often tried to increase their incomes by asking the aircrews to take one or two extra passengers who were said to have some urgent reason for immediately going to Phnom Penh. My standard answer to these requests was, "Ask the shipper."

Our shippers were accustomed to shifting the blame for refusing passengers to the captain. In real or pretended emergencies, the shipper would ask the captain if the person could go. The captain would usually tell the shipper to reduce his cargo weight and take the passenger. The shipper would refuse to reduce his profits, but would plead that an exception be made to the weight limitation because the person really needed to go to Phnom Penh. The captain, who had heard the same story dozens of times before, would generally refuse. The shipper would then turn to the crowd and tell them in their own language that he had tried his best, but the captain just would not agree to taking the emergency case. The Chinese and American pilots who spoke no Khmer became the unwitting targets of scorn from every disappointed passenger. Some would wonder why they were receiving so many nasty glances from the crowd. At the same time, the shippers, who were usually Tae Chou Chinese, were able to ingratiate themselves with the local population by appearing to champion their cause.

Most aircraft that were hit by ground fire accumulated their bullet holes very close to "friendly" positions. I often wondered how many shots were fired by disappointed passengers who blamed the aircrews for not taking them. This is not unlikely because a large number of these prospective travelers were armed soldiers without the necessary funds to pay for a place on the waiting list.

On the few occasions that the shippers tried to make me the villain, I turned the tables on them. Speaking Khmer in a voice loud enough to be heard by all, I would tell the shipper that he had misunderstood me. I would gladly take the extra passengers. All the shipper had to do was take off some bags of peas to keep the aircraft from being too heavy to fly. Now the shipper could either agree or make himself the villain. In a few cases, the shipper was forced to remove cargo because the crowd was large and the case really needy. Usually, however, he would just tell the passenger to get lost. The shippers showed great consternation and annoyance when the tables were turned on them like this.

Some shippers resorted to sneaking passengers aboard. If we were supposed to have 10, a count often revealed 12 or 13. An argument would then ensue about who had to get off. The shippers would try to protract the argument until the pilot would lose patience and agree to take everyone. The result was an overload of 140 to 210 kg in addition to the extra cargo that was sneaked on as a matter of course.

To give in was unthinkable. At the beginning of my career, I found that every time I let everyone go, the situation repeated itself on the next trip with even more extra passengers involved. I finally came up with the ideal solution. If the argument exceeded five minutes, I would order the doors closed, start the engines, and taxi to the end of the runway. Parking the aircraft at the runway's edge, I left the copilot holding the brakes, went to the rear, and personally jettisoned cargo weighing at least as much as the extra passengers. This procedure allowed the engines to warm up properly, gave me a little exercise, and kept our gross weight within the allowable limits for take-off.

The shippers never figured out a way to circumvent this sytem, so they went to John Yim regularly to complain bitterly about it. Some threatened to cancel their contracts with Tri-9, and several actually did, but they invariably came back pleading to charter our aircraft again. There was no shortage of customers, and most of the companies could pick and choose. We never had to sit on the ground for lack of customers.

Chapter 11

In early March I left for a short trip to the United States. I had run into the usual problem getting a discount ticket to leave the country, but Air Cambodge agreed to let another pilot sign his ticket to Vientiane, Laos, over to me, saving me another overland trip. Because Tri-9 had interline agreements with more than a dozen first rate international airlines, getting tickets to New York in Vientiane or Bangkok was no problem.

I was only in the United States for five days, but I found out how much we were appreciated for the risks we were taking in support of American foreign policy by the American business community, which had benefited immensely from the prosperity generated by the Vietnam War. First, we were given discounts by almost all foreign but not one single American airline company. To accompany my fiancée from New York to her college in southern Utah, I had to pay full fare in spite of my profession. In Las Vegas, both major car rental companies refused to rent me a car because I had no credit card. Another pilot in Phnom Penh later told me that he was also refused a car rental by a leading company. Fortunately a local company was willing to accept a cash deposit, and we were able to drive to Utah for much less than we would have paid the big-name companies.

Bill Davis and Sawai had taken over the DC-3s in my absence, so I rushed to return to Phnom Penh before Bill's Convair was ready to fly. When I arrived, I learned that a severe fuel shortage had grounded almost the whole fleet, except for Air Cambodge. We did not fly again until March 29.

I must now digress and explain what had been happening at SEAAT. When I quit in January, I was the last SEAAT pilot to receive full pay before April. On payday, February 1, the pilots were told that the company had no more money, and they would have to wait until some unspecified time in the future to get paid. They could stay in the Sokhalay Hotel free because SEAAT had rented the whole building, but they could only draw small amounts of money in local currency for their expenses.

Before long, several of the pilots quit and returned home. Those few whose aircraft were in condition to fly at all were not logging many flying hours, and their prospect of getting their pay looked very poor. On March 1 there was still no money. The mechanics, who were even worse off, were being billed for their rooms at the Sokhalay, which they had formerly occupied free of charge. The SEAAT management contended that only aircrews had been promised free quarters.

The whereabouts of the company president were unknown, and the vice-president for operations was almost always out of town. He made one quick trip to Phnom Penh during this period to fire Lyman, the administrative vice-president, on whom the whole mess was blamed.

Actually Lyman was the only one who had not left town and was therefore the one who had been listening to all the gripes of the employees. With him out of the way, a new man was needed to shield the big executives, who had found themselves private offices in which to hide from the pilots and other underlings during their short stays in the country. This man was Harry Jones, who had come to work for SEAAT after being released by Air America.

It was remarked that the vice-president for operations was starting to suffer from paranoid delusions because he saw the need to hire Donny Slugger, whom he found in a Saigon bar, as chief of security to protect him from the pilots. Although energetic in manner, Cedric was small in stature, and he reportedly stationed his new M-16 toting bodyguard between himself and the pilots whenever they met.

According to his own boasts, Slugger had taken part in every he-man operation ever conducted in Vietnam. He let it be known that he was tough (Green Beret service, etc.). Cedric felt secure enough in his presence to actually call a few pilot meetings. He told his employees that the future looked rosy, and their pay would be available in a month or two. They just had to stick it out.

After the communists were repulsed from the approaches to the city and the rocket attacks abated, the SEAAT managers again began to see a chance for profit. They had to get their aircraft flying again, and two more DC-3s were actually imported from Taiwan.

Part of the infusion of money to keep SEAAT in operation came from a payment to Cedric from the United States Embassy. After some behind-the-scenes dealing, SEAAT had been awarded a contract to ferry T-28 aircraft back from overhaul in Thailand. This involved finding some Thai pilots to fly the aircraft. Sangob's contacts with many former Thai Air Force pilots got him the job of hiring them for the ferry flights. Sangob's reward was getting paid in full for his own flying time, while the other pilots waited. He was naturally told to tell no one about the arrangement. The SEAAT management could not afford to have him quit, and they knew he had been thinking about it.

The United States Embassy could have hired Sangob directly, thereby saving the taxpayers a considerable amount of money. The American civil servants never succeeded in finding reliable people to deal with, however, and as a result, Southeast Asia was full of "sharp operators" with embassy and USAID contracts. As retired military men, the SEAAT managers knew just what to say and how to say it, and it did not bother the "powers that were" in the embassy that their contractors didn't even pay the wages to their employees, and this was not the only case that I knew about. Maybe the embassy staff could excuse their actions by arguing that SEAAT should get money from someone to stay in business, but from past experience, they should have known that their money would be used for purposes other than the air operation. I speculated that SEAAT must have been getting covert backing, but I had no way of finding out.

While Sangob was efficiently organizing the return of the newly over-hauled T-28s, Cedric was spending long periods of time in Saigon, reportedly looking for spare parts. While there, he found another non-flying employee. "Biggy" Smathers was another former military man who had found a new home in the vice warrens of Saigon. When Cedric discovered his talents, Biggy was working as a bouncer in a house of prostitution, although his work probably carried another official job title. He had never been involved in aviation, so he was hired in some administrative capacity. One of his first duties for the company was to return to Saigon with a suitcase containing $10,000 in cash to pay for a shipment of spare parts. After he returned, the management circulated the story that the suitcase had been stolen from him at the airport. Of course, everyone knew how dishonest the Vietnamese are, so no more questions were asked. The pilots' payment was postponed for another month.

Biggy was what is called a "good old boy" in his home state of Alabama. Unfortunately, he got into the "firewater" one night and didn't stay good very long. While drunk in the lobby of the Sokhalay Hotel, he dropped some of his money. One of SEAAT's Thai mechanics picked the money up and handed it back to him. Having done his good deed, the young man turned around and walked away. Biggy followed him to the front desk and for no apparent reason grabbed him from behind in a strangle hold. The Thai was very small, under 100 pounds, while Biggy weighed well over 200. After choking him unconscious, Biggy let his victim drop face down on the floor. When the mechanic fell, several of his teeth were broken, and he had to spend some time in a local hospital.

Biggy's next stop was the Khemera Hotel Restaurant, which was the favorite hang-out for many of the pilots, particularly the American and European ones. Inside, Biggy began harassing some of the customers and some of the street girls, who often entered looking for boyfriends. Finally, he blocked the door and announced that nobody was allowed to leave. After a while, a Khmer girl tried to go past him, and he threw her to the ground. At this point, Ed, the former Army pilot who worked for SEAAT, told Biggy that he had better go home and sleep it off. Since Biggy was bigger than Ed, he decided to enforce his orders. He slugged Ed in the face. Ed quickly demolished his big but stupid opponent, leaving him unconscious in the street. No one was particularly looking for trouble with Biggy because the news of what he had done in the hotel lobby had not yet reached anyone.

Biggy came to and dragged himself back to the Sokhalay Hotel to get his knife. When he returned, it was after the 9 P.M. curfew, and the Khemera Restaurant was closed. He began to menace the passersby with his knife and threatened a military policeman who tried to interfere.

Before Biggy could get into real trouble for what he had done, the embassy intervened. He was picked up in an embassy car and rushed to the airport, where he was hiddden among United States Army CONEX containers. By this time, the Khmer police were looking for him, but they were not allowed in the American military section of the parking ramp.

Every day a procession of United States Air Force C-130s carried ammunition to Phnom Penh and returned empty to Thailand. The first of these the morning after Biggy's rampage carried him to Thailand. From there, he returned immediately to the States, courtesy of the government at the expense of the taxpayers. The only concern of the embassy staff was that the mechanic's friends might seek revenge.

Whenever I have been tempted to say that I never knew anybody overseas that American diplomats helped in time of difficulty, I have to stop myself. Biggy was the one American I know of who actually received the full support of his government in his hour of need.

During my five-hour overland journeys to the Thai border, I would think about all of those empty C-130s flying from where I had been to where I was going. The United States Air Force never breaks its rules about civilians flying on their aircraft, except for certain people.

While we were grounded in March because of the alleged fuel shortage, I had to seek new quarters. After I left SEAAT, I had to give up my room at the Sokhalay Hotel, but Sangob let me use his while he was in Thailand. First, he had taken a vacation to attend a ceremony in which King Bhumiphol bestowed a master's degree on his wife. Then he was busy recruiting T-28 pilots. While I was in the United States, he returned to Phnom Penh, and he had taken the room key with him. I wanted to leave a small bag in the hotel, and I found that the door to the next room was open. It was Frank's room, and he had already been in the States for over a month on extended leave, so I left my bag inside and closed the door. A little later, I met Sangob, who assured me that it would be all right there for the day. I was not on good terms with the room boy on the floor, however. He was a seedy, sneaky dwarf who liked to steal small items. He was seen on many occasions searching through the personal effects of residents whose rooms he was supposed to be cleaning. On two occasions, I noticed that small items were missing from my room, and I had told him menacingly that I expected to have the items back. When I returned several hours later, they were on my desk.

Apparently, he had seen me put the bag in Frank's room and reported to SEAAT's security chief that a person no longer working for SEAAT was staying in one of the rooms. Slugger decided that this was a chance for him to show that he was not someone to be trifled with. He saw my name on the small bag and found out that I was working for Tri-9. With the help of the room boy, he then packed up all of Frank's personal effects that were in the closets and took them all to the Tri-9 office.

As I arrived there after some shopping, Slugger was just leaving. He saw me and said that he had left my things at Tri-9, adding cynically that my new company would be happy to find me a place to stay. I gazed at the enormous pile of clothing and personal belongings but said nothing as Slugger drove away. John Yim was in the office. He asked me what I was going to do with all the things. I told him that I had to take them back to SEAAT. He asked incredulously, "Do you mean they're not yours?"

I replied, "No, they all belong to Frank Hines, except this one small bag."

"Why did he bring them here?" asked John, puzzled.

"I don't know. Maybe he thought they were mine," I said.

It took John Yim a few minutes to stop laughing, then he told me that I had better take them back soon because he didn't want to be responsible for them.

The next day when the crew car wasn't busy, I took the various bags and boxes to the villa that served as the SEAAT office. Slugger was there talking to Harry Jones in the office. I placed the things on the reception desk in front of Vanny, the Khmer secretary. I announced in a loud voice that I was returning some of Frank Hines's personal belongings that had been taken to the Tri-9 office. I asked her to provide for their safe-keeping until Frank returned. Slugger peered out of the office and asked, "Don't those things belong to you?"

"No, they belong to Frank," I said matter-of-factly.

"Didn't one bag have your name on it?" he asked sheepishly.

"Just one bag," I said, "Sangob had kept it for me in his room, and since it was in the way, I put it in Frank's room for the day. I didn't think it would bother anybody. The room boy doesn't keep the door locked, and Frank is in the States."

Slugger retreated into Harry's office with a rather disturbed look on his face. I overheard him ask Harry, "Frank doesn't work for us anymore. He quit, didn't he?"

"I'm afraid he does still work for us," replied Harry.

There was a long pause, followed by Slugger's voice asking, "Are you sure he still works for us? I thought he quit."

They were still discussing the matter when I left.

When Frank returned, he reported that a radio was missing. I assume that the room boy had rewarded himself for his good deed.

For the rest of my stay in Phnom Penh, I shared a large apartment with Ben on Okhna In Street near the main market. It was far from the usual hang-outs of the pilots, which was an advantage in many ways. On occasions when I had any spare time, I used it to try to improve my knowledge of the Khmer language. It is the easiest of the national languages in Southeast Asia, with the exception of Malay. It is not a tonal language. The meaning of the words depends only on the vowel and consonant combinations, as in European languages, and not by voice inflections, as in Chinese, Vietnamese, Thai, and Lao. The Khmer vocabulary is poor, and many scientific and technical terms cannot be expressed in the language. The few educated Khmers who know about such things discuss them in French, the language in which many advanced courses in the schools are conducted. The Khmer language had simply not progressed into the machine age. The Buddhist and Hindu scriptures, on the other hand, are quite complex and have a vocabulary of their own. The words used for common speech are few, and the grammar is simple.

There were special problems learning Khmer, however. People capable of teaching the language were few, and text books and dictionaries that came close to being correct were even harder to locate. Khmers generally had a very poor knowledge of their own language, and the rate of illiteracy was higher than in any other land in Southeast Asia, with the possible exception of Burma, where I had never been. Prince Sihanouk obviously had bizarre ideas on the meaning of education and knew the advantages of keeping his subjects ignorant.

The most beautiful university buildings in Southeast Asia were located along the highway between Phnom Penh and Pochentong Airport. It had been given to Sihanouk by the Russians for services rendered. In spite of its impressive physical facilities, the university had not educated the Khmer students well enough to hold their own in competition with other Asian students.

Bookstores in Phnom Penh were filled with books for learning English. The English sentences in these texts ranged from pidgin to nonsense. I bought a Khmer-English and an English-Khmer pocket dictionary, only to find that many of the English words it contained came from the imagination of the author. Of the "10,000 most-used words in the English language" mentioned on the cover, 20 to 30 percent were such nonsense words as "disbehaviour," "misjudgingly" and "misobey." Many common words were missing, and the Khmer words given as translations of the English were often either incorrect or represented the most obscure meaning of the English word.

I met the American owner of a large English language school, who mentioned that the manuscript for the dictionary had been presented to him for editing. He had to make so many corrections on the first page that he recommended that the author revise the entire work. The Khmer lexicographer simply took his manuscript back and sent it unchanged to the printer. It was just not worth the trouble to him to do the job correctly.

Ben decided to learn Khmer properly, so he hired the head of a local private school to instruct him. The man needed the money because the government had closed all of the schools as a response to a student protest. His 600 young pupils just had to stay home.

Ben progressed well, but he found that the headmaster was no more reliable than most of his countrymen. Ben often rushed home from supper for his lesson only to wait in vain for his teacher to show up. At first, there was a 50-50 chance of his arrival, but as time went on, the attendance record became poorer. He finally stopped showing up at all. I had had a similar experience with Buon, a former driver for SEAAT who later took a job as a steward for Tri-9. He had agreed to exchange English for Khmer lessons, but he failed to show up for every single appointment.

The disputes between the students and the army had become quite serious. The university had already been closed for about a year, so the high schools became the scenes of the unrest. Under Sihanouk's system, education was reserved strictly for the children of the richest and most influential families. It was therefore easy to understand the impatience of the soldiers, who came from the poor and hungry masses of the common people, when dealing with protests by those far more fortunate. One group of students arranged several serious confrontations with the government officials, and finally the minister of education was taken hostage. During the ensuing negotiations, one of the students shot and killed the high ranking hostage. The soldiers, who had been standing by, could no longer restrain themselves. Several students were killed, and many others were arrested.

A great source of irritation to the young people that helped to stir the unrest was the draft system, which was fundamentally conscription by capture. Anyone looking fit for duty was picked up on the streets by press gangs and shipped off to basic training. Children from wealthy families had no desire to go to war, the conditions of combat being what they were. The parents had to purchase their children's freedom with generous bribes, but as the inflation rate soared, the price of immunity from conscription became more and more of a burden. The progressive conquest of the rural regions by the communists had taken this great source of manpower out of the government's hands, so the pressure on the urban population steadily increased. Our company employees were often picked up by press gangs, and John Yim had to go to the induction center to verify that the captured individuals were performing services vital to the survival of the country.

Some slogans painted on the walls near the government buildings along 9 Tola (9th of October, the date of the coup deposing Sihanouk) Boulevard gave evidence not only of the discontent but also of the literary level attained by the Khmer students. For the benefit of visiting diplomats and reporters, the protests were written in French and English and included such slogans as "Having no ability, go away!" and "I don't want to die for a single!"

After the elimination of the few fanatics who had killed the minister of education, the rather minor protests of the other students were crushed with brutal force. The actions of the Khmer Army succeeded in restoring order, but they also intimidated anyone who might have wanted to fight for necessary reforms. While the government wallowed in stagnation, vast amounts of vital American aid were channelled into private pockets, and the communists were able to consolidate their control over the countryside.

Draft reform was sorely needed. In the communist controlled areas the draft was universal, and everyone who could not fight was put to work carrying munitions or digging deep ditches across the highways. The government, on the other hand, permitted the privileged few to avoid combat and make plenty of money, while everyone else had to fight. It was even less equitable than the American draft system of the '60s that had done so much to fill the ranks of the anti-war protestors.

Conspicuous in the capital were the hordes of officers in the entertainment centers, which had been officially closed by the government but found ways of staying open, and the many deserters in uniform, who terrorized local businessmen, stole cars and motorcycles, and occasionally got drunk and threw their grenades in crowded places. The movie theaters were always full, and one soldier who could not get in threw a hand grenade into the crowd. Another grenade was later thrown into the theater because a soldier's girlfriend went to the movies with someone else.

Not only common soldiers stole money from merchants at gunpoint, high ranking officers did, as well. Lon Nol's brother, also named Lon Nol, reputedly practiced this kind of extortion whenever he needed money. Several merchants who balked at raising the sums demanded were shot.

In spite of the shortcomings of their government, many soldiers in the field were fighting with astounding valor. The government could have won back the initiative if it had been able to deal with the corruption. The United States held the power of the pursestrings over the Khmer government, but the American Embassy gave no impetus toward reform. Instead, the staff would report to the Congress that they needed more money to replace the supplies that were being stolen.

Responsible for overseeing the aid programs was the American ambassador, who had changed his name to John Gunther Dean from the name he had been given at his birth in Berlin. Prior to his appointment, he had been chargé d'affaires of the United States Embassy in Laos. In this capacity, he had personally negotiated the agreement to form a coalition government including communists and noncommunists. Great concessions were made to the communists to get them to agree, while pressure was used to force the undesirable terms on Souvannapouma's "neutralist" government.

Every knowledgeable person on the scene agreed that the implementation of the coalition would turn the whole country into a time bomb. Hordes of machine gun toting Pathet Lao troops distributed themselves at checkpoints set up on each street corner.

No such coalition government had ever survived any longer than it took the communists to kill or intimidate the other members into resigning. Predictably, the Lao attempt failed quickly. It had surprised me that the anticommunists offered such little resistance. The murder of only one government minister was all it took to induce the others to flee the country. The victim was Boun Oum, the minister of culture. He was killed by a hand grenade, gangster style. The flight of the neutralists and rightists meant less bloodshed during the initial phases of the takeover. After that, the western reporters were kicked out or restricted to the immediate vicinity of their hotels. The campaign of genocide against many of the ethnic minorities in Laos therefore went unreported. The Meos were particular targets of the communists' revenge, and the new government in Vientiane made it a national policy to eliminate these mountain people "as an ethnic and cultural group." That meant killing all of those who failed to escape to Thailand.

The communists correctly judged the American reaction. With no reporters, there were no reports, and what the people in the States did not know did not bother them.

As a reward for successfully ramming the coalition agreement through the weak resistance put up by the Lao leadership, Dean was made ambassador to the Khmer Republic. The American press began hinting that a new coalition agreement was in the works for the Khmers. To Americans in Asia and to the Khmers themselves, this boded nothing but ill.

While the embassy staff was engaged in formulating grandiose utopian peace plans to "bring the communists into the government," nothing realistic was done to combat the real problems of inefficiency and corruption. The Khmers proved less agreeable than the Laos when pressed to discuss the formation of a coalition. They realized that they were being asked to place guns against their own heads. The Khmers had to face reality, while Dean did not. If the plan failed and the Khmer Rouge started shooting when they entered Phnom Penh, Dean would just jump into an airplane and head for Washington, while the Khmer leaders would suffer gruesome deaths. It may well be that the impetus to the massive corruption was the desire by some of the high officials to accumulate enough money to escape the country and support themselves in exile in case of the worst. At least some of their family members could be saved by sending them abroad to school.

The internal problems of the Khmers were aggravated by the lack of a united leadership. When I arrived in the country, the chief-of-state was already practically a vegetable with much of his brain destroyed by strokes. It was only logical to conclude that the uniting force for the Khmer leadership would come from the supplier of financial support, the Embassy of the United States of America.

Unfortunately, logic had little to do with America's political philosophy in Southeast Asia. Although agencies of the United States government had been dropping hundreds of tons of bombs daily on Vietnam, Laos, and the Khmer Republic for many years, the embassy officials would indignantly declare their unwillingness to "interfere in the internal affairs" of those lands. The fine distinction between removing a corrupt minor official and covertly arranging for a coup and the assassination of the chief-of-state can only really be understood by one steeped in the lore of American foreign affairs. Insistence on the removal of a corrupt civil servant would be an "official act" of interference, while the coup is "unofficial," whatever that means.

The official American representatives in Southeast Asia were caught in a complex web of conflicting regulations, fine legalistic distinctions and rationalizations, and poorly thought-out theoretical extensions and limitations of their powers. In practical application, this meant that the ambassador could do pretty much what he pleased, as long as he did not assume responsibility for doing it. It was convenient to have a local leader on whom to heap the blame in case of failure. In the Khmer Republic, that man was strapped to a wheelchair in the Presidential Palace.

The men who held the power in the Khmer Republic included Long Boret, Sirik Matak and In Tam. Sosthenes Fernandez, the Armed Forces Commander, was a broken and useless man after his great defeat in Operation Chenla IV. It would be an injustice to brand these men as crooks; they had a genuine interest in their country. Agreement among them about the best way to preserve the Khmer Republic, however, was seldom achieved. Each tried to place as many of his supporters as possible into powerful positions. Even if these underlings were proven to be crooks, they were nevertheless almost impossible to remove from office or bring to trial because this would be an affront to their powerful patron. If one of the leaders attempted to clean up the government, he would have to limit himself to his own supporters. To fire or arrest a member of another leader's party might bring him into open conflict with one of his powerful rivals. The result of this situation was rampant corruption and a general stagnation in the war effort at a time that only dynamic action might have saved the country.

Had Lon Nol been well and active, it is hard to say what might have happened. Perhaps the corruption would have assumed immense proportions anyway. In any case, events in neighboring Vietnam played a greater role in sealing the fate of Cambodia than did internal events. It is well to remember, however, that the main thrust of the North Vietnamese was against Saigon through Tay Ninh Province, and to keep up the pressure on this front, they had to have uncontested control of their supply lines in eastern Cambodia. When the final attack came down the coast from the North, the South Vietnamese Army was still largely deployed to defend against an attack from Cambodia and could not reorganize in time to avert complete disaster. The inability or unwillingness of the United States Embassy in Phnom Penh to deal with the corruption and internal disintegration of this allied government therefore had a catastrophic effect on the entire region.

One of our Khmer employees summed up the decline of his country while we were waiting for the issuance of my exit visa. He said, "When Sihanouk was here, the policeman would take the bribe money, throw it quickly in his drawer, and look around to see if anyone was watching. Now he holds the money up and says in a loud voice, 'What! Only 500 riels!'"

On Sundays after flying, I was in the habit of attending mass at the cathedral near the center of Phnom Penh. If I finished early enough, I went to the Vietnamese mass at 4:45 P.M. When I returned late, I went at 6:00 P.M. to the sparsely attended mass in French and had the experience of seeing the motorcade with sirens blaring drive up to the cathedral to escort Ambassador Dean to mass. After the service police would blow their whistles to clear everyone off the street, the sirens would blare again, and the ambassador's car, flags flying, would rush him back to his bunker.

According to Bernand Fall in *Hell in a Very Small Place*, General Cogny, one of the two French commanders who spent the twenty years following the battle of Dien Bien Phu writing books and letters blaming the other one for the defeat, had been given the nickname *Coco la Sirène* by his soldiers. Whether a predilection for motorcycles with sirens is a trait common to losers of Southeast Asian wars remains for the historians to discover.

Chapter 12

The long delay in getting fuel caused by the embassy's paperwork ended at the end of March, and April was a busy month as we moved the great backlog of cargo to alleviate the severe food shortage that had been created in the capital. I flew every day and was glad to receive a decent pay check for the overtime at the beginning of May.

The first week of April had been particularly hectic as we worked like fanatics against the usual loading delays in order to fly four missions per day. Tri-9 had hired stewards for all of the flights, but we still had to keep a sharp eye on the shippers who knew more tricks than the stewards did. First, we found a set of false weights for the scale. Then, we discovered that another shipper had weights with holes cut for lead plugs. When we checked the scales, the weights were correct. Then the shipper would insert the lead plug, and each bag of cargo would appear to be 10 to 20 kilos lighter than it really was. Another scale had springs placed under the platform. The workmen hired by some of the shippers were trained to keep a foot under the scale platform. We caught two shippers with their notebooks held against the side of the balance arm to stop the needle at the mid-point. After the steward's attention was diverted to the scale, an extra sack or box could be sneaked on behind his back.

Early April is the most uncomfortable time of year in Cambodia. The rainy season does not begin until late in the month, and prior to the first rain storms, there is little wind. The air is hazy, and the sun beats down without interruption from passing clouds. The aircraft heated up on the ground like an oven.

After rushing to complete our local trips on a particularly hot day, we helped the Khemera Air Transport ground crew tie down the cargo properly. Even the station manager pitched in as we all worked fiendishly, bathed in sweat, so that we would be ready in time to take off for an overnight trip to Battambang. We succeeded in getting loaded just before the deadline.

The tower cleared us to taxi, so we rolled to the runway and held short. One aircraft waited ahead of us, and several were circling to land. From high above the airport, a lone T-39 circled down to land. The aircraft ahead of us took off, but we did not have time to follow before the United States Air Force executive jet landed. The pilot used the whole 10,000 feet of runway, rolling slowly to the end, turning around, and taxiing back to take-off at the speed of a fast walk, the way Air Force pilots are instructed to do. At the end of the runway, he turned around again, then held for a while before starting his take-off. He could not seem to understand the tower because he asked to have everything repeated several times. About seven or eight aircraft were circling overhead waiting to land as the T-39 tied up the active runway for 20 minutes. He neither discharged nor picked up anyone or anything.

When the circling aircraft started making their landings, it was already 4:40. The tower controller told us to taxi back because Battambang tower closed at 5:00. This incident was particularly annoying to me because I could surmise what was going on. Only an Air Force veteran can fathom the peculiar mentality and understand the twisted logic behind that organization's practices.

Combat pay was undoubtedly granted for that one landing in a "combat zone," and so was an income tax deduction of $500. No doubt, the flight was a training flight to "check pilots out" for Pochentong Airport, and the T-39 was undoubtedly crammed full of extra crew members to share in the benefits. An Air Force pilot cannot be expected to land on a 10,000 foot runway unless he has been there before with someone who has the certification that he knows how to do it. Civilian Caravelles, Boeing 707s, 727s and DC-10s landed there every day, cleared the runway quickly, and allowed normal operations to resume. They were also fulfilling useful missions. The Air Force was flying for the sake of flying and fringe benefits, logging time, and fulfilling "training requirements" of their own invention. That particular little junket cost the American taxpayers a good deal more than the extra pay and allowances, and perhaps medals, that were awarded to the Air Force pilots for their "combat landing." The taxpayers also paid for the fuel burned in eight cargo aircraft circling the airport for 20 minutes. In my aircraft were 3½ metric tons of cargo that would not be delivered to Battambang. It was unloaded, and the mission cancelled. Another 3½ tons of badly needed food would not be brought back from Battambang. My own loss in flight pay was insignificant. For the round trip, I would have received much less than each of the T-39 pilots received in combat pay for that one landing.

Meanwhile, fighting had been raging about 20 miles west of Phnom Penh. The swath of devastation had been cut from the western edges of the capital itself to the ancient capital of Oudonk, where the communists exacted revenge for their recent losses. Just east of Oudonk was a hill crowned by pagodas which we had always been instructed not to fly over. The city itself had previously been untouched by the war. In a short time it was overrun. During each flight, we were able to follow the progress of the fighting. The main part of the city was totally destroyed. We were able to spot a few bodies from the air. Several weeks after the fighting began, the government forces were again in full possession of the district, including the hill with the pagodas. They found large numbers of skeletons, apparently belonging to the people the communists had taken prisoner. Flies were reported to be extremely thick. Because they had always been so plentiful, the pilots had started referring to the house fly as the "national bird" of the Khmer Republic. For the Khmers to report that the flies were thick must have meant that they had reached plague proportions.

While flying back and forth over the battlefields at 5000 to 7000 feet, we often saw the United States Air Force RF-4 reconnaissance jets from Thailand. They flew high and fast. Now and then one could dive down to get a close look, usually streaking down to 7000 or 8000 feet at a supersonic speed to avoid the clouds that often formed on the leeward side of the 5500 foot mountain to the southeast of Oudonk. They would then go into an afterburner climb back to high altitude. Overcautious is perhaps too mild a word to use to describe the procedure. At least that was the way it impressed me as I flew over the same countryside six to eight times a day, seven days a week, at an altitude of 5000 to 6000 feet and a ground speed of 120 to 140 knots. I often wondered how much combat pay and tax deductions they were receiving, and which medals they were awarded for the few seconds that they spent at an altitude that might be reached by a heavy anti-aircraft gun, if the enemy had had any. I'm sure their union was better than ours.

During the busy month of April, we flew almost exclusively to Krakor and Kompong Chhnang. From Krakor to Phnom Penh, our cargo invariably included cartons of empty wine bottles. We carried more of these than any other kind of cargo. Usually shippers prepared cargoes of pigs, dried fish, sugar or peas for a DC-3 rigged to carry 3200 kilos of cargo. We carried 3500 kilos, so the charterer always had wine bottles at the airport to bring our load up to capacity.

The wine was bottled in Phnom Penh and we carried the refilled bottles to various fields as outbound cargo. Alcoholic drinks as vital war supplies were a concept well established by the United States forces during the Vietnam War. The Khmers gave this kind of cargo a lower priority, however. Fresh fish and live pigs were shipped first. The fish would spoil, and the pigs died, but the wine improved with age.

Weighing the pigs at Krakor and Kompong Chhnang was a terrible chore, and we had to help the stewards, who were badly outmatched by the wily shippers. The pigs were too big for the scales, and they twitched and struggled constantly. The shippers liked to place the pigs on the scales so that the head rested on the wheel beneath the weighing platform. In that way, the pig could be made to appear five to ten kilos lighter. If the pig was particularly large, the hind quarters could be allowed to rest on the floor. If one of the workmen's feet was shoved under the pig, the recorded weight could be reduced even more. These tricks were used to supplement the usual repertoire of deception.

Besides being difficult to weigh, the pigs suffered from various bad breath and body odor problems, and their scent remained in the aircraft long after they departed. Furthermore, pigs can be very noisy. The pig handlers were very rough, and they tied their charges with pieces of vine, which cut into their skin. The pain caused the pigs to squeal loudly. We found that 45 screaming pigs in the cargo compartment could drown out the sound of engines in flight. Even with our cockpit door closed, we had no difficulty hearing the hogs over the engine noise.

We also found out that angry pigs bite. They were loaded in a way that they completely covered the cargo compartment floor. The only way for us to reach the cockpit for departure was to walk over the pigs. By stepping from shoulder to shoulder, the crossing could be made safely. Some of the pilots had made the mistake of stepping on the stomach or head of a pig, enabling the pig to inflict a retaliatory bite. I successfully avoided being bitten, but several pilots were not so lucky. The results were not serious, although somewhat painful. According to general opinion, pig bites are not rated very high on the list of dangers to pilots, but to us, they were an everyday hazard.

If the pig managed to escape its bonds, trouble could ensue. In most cases, however, the pig was too exhausted from its ordeal to accomplish very much.

One of the benefits of our many flights was the education I received in judging hogs. I learned to judge the weight of a live pig better than most residents of Iowa. My estimates were generally within one or two kilos of the weight recorded by the scale. Several times I caught the shippers cheating when I investigated the reason my estimate was rather far from the scale reading. This ability did not enhance my popularity with the shippers. Ed Bower was married to a Thai woman who invested the money he earned in fish and pig farming. He found the experiences he gained judging the weight of pigs to be of great value in dealing with the Chiense hog buyers in Thailand who were used to cheating the farmers shamelessly on the weights.

The cargoes of fish presented other problems. The favorite ploy of the fish shippers at Kompong Chhnang was to arrive with defective scales, assure us on their words of honor that their weights were correct, and tell us to weigh the cargo at Phnom Penh to check their veracity. Each basket of fish contained several kilos of ice, which melted rapidly and ran out, filling the hull of the aircraft with corrosive fish water. By the time we weighed the fish at Phnom Penh, much of the weight had flowed out of the baskets. Even so, we were usually overweight, indicating that we had been greatly overloaded for take-off.

We solved some of the problems by carrying a scale with us. We tied it at the rear of the aircraft and let our steward use it to weigh the cargo. For a few days, our problems with the shippers decreased, although they strongly protested our tactics, telling John Yim that we were getting too strict. Finally, one of the helpers of a particularly troublesome shipper stole one of our scale weights at Kompong Chhnang. That made it more difficult to weigh the cargo, but we managed by combining the remaining weights in various ways. Our weights were hidden to prevent further loss.

The battle never ceased, but I always maintained my tough stand. In case of dispute, the steward was told to always record the lower weight. If I caught a shipper sneaking something on, we fined him by taking 100 kilos less. My goal was to achieve minimum ground times, so I ceased all kinds of arguing. If the shipper did not agree with my decision, I simply taxied to the end of the runway with everything that had been put on and threw all excess items out of the airplane before taking off. The flights were scheduled with so little ground time that the loss of just a few minutes meant that all of the trips could not be completed. Nevertheless, to wheedle a few more kilos on the aircraft, the shipper would gladly cause us to cancel our last mission, which was generally chartered by one of the shipper's competitors. My method worked, and I was able to make one more trip each day than the other DC-3 pilots.

After a while, the shippers began to try an honest and humble approach. They would come to me and admit that they had brought a little bit more cargo than the contract called for, then ask me politely and humbly if they might not carry just a few extra kilos. This gave me the opportunity to institute a system that paid off in short ground times. We had the capability of carrying a little more than the contract weight without exceeding the maximum take-off weight, so I could permit the shipper to take an extra 50 kilos if the loading was completed in minimum time, usually 15 or 20 minutes. Some of the shippers were not sure of the contract weights anyway, so when I told them that they could put on 3550 kilos if we were ready to go in 20 minutes, they thought they were getting an extra 100 kilos or more free of charge.

During the loading operations, the coolies would actually run with heavy bags of cargo. If the shipper was a little slower than his promise, we gave him the benefit of the doubt. If he wasn't trying, we had the option of throwing off 50 kilos, but it never came to that. In the past, loading at Kompong Chhnang had taken about an hour, but with the incentive system we were seldom on the ground more than half of that time.

Some of the pilots from other companies were wondering how we were finishing our trips so quickly. Everyone had problems at Kompong Chhnang, and our quick turnarounds began to attract attention. The SEAAT pilots refused to believe that we could actually weigh the cargo in such a short time, and one accused me of just letting the shippers put on whatever they wanted.

The shippers continued to complain to us that some of the Chinese pilots would carry much more in their DC-3s than we did. They asked why we couldn't carry as much as the competition. We were never able to explain this to their satisfaction. I usually told them about the wrecks caused by overloads that were scattered all over the country. We tried to operate a safe airline, and our chances of an accident were very small compared to those of the DC-3s with the 4500 kilo loads. This was an explanation that they could not accept at all. Sometimes I told them that the Chinese pilots worked for companies that took extra money for the overloads. Why should we do it for nothing? They could fully accept this argument but failed to understand why I turned down their bribe offers on several occasions just because it was against company policy. Policies change, however, and all of the American owned companies were finding out the profits to be made by taking overloads.

After the seedy characters that SEAAT had hired as stewards failed completely in their assignment, the management fired them and decided to encourage their pilots to carry overloads in exchange for extra pay. The overweight charges were to be divided equally between the company and the pilots.

Tri-9 did not adopt this policy right away because our steward system was working well. We had reliable and trustworthy Khmers working with us, and although they were no match for the wily shippers, things could be kept pretty honest when we stood by and watched, too.

In April the companies operating in Phnom Penh were involved in a massive buying spree, and buyers were scouring the world, from Turkey to Australia, as well as Europe and the United States, for old aircraft. There was enough confidence in the Khmer Republic to induce anyone with enough money to buy an airplane. The profits in Phnom Penh were reputed to be fabulous, and everyone wanted to cash in on the opportunities. The aircraft in Southeast Asia that had been rusting away in the corners of airport parking ramps for years were suddenly purchased for fabulous sums and ferried to Phnom Penh. Several DC-3s that could have been had for a few thousand dollars a year earlier were sold for over $50,000. The date for the inauguration of the expanded airlift operation was set for May 1.

Tri-9 was deeply involved in the expansion program. SEAAT had been losing pilots very rapidly, and some of those who quit were coming to Tri-9 to look for work. Their chief pilot had quit and, together with a former

SEAAT DC-4 pilot, was vainly attempting to establish a company of his own. His replacement at SEAAT was seeking employment with Royal Air Lao.

Ford Chapman, one of SEAAT's original captains, quit his job as a Convair captain and came to work at Tri-9. He ferried the AT-11 from Vientiane but then left to work for Byrd-Air in Singapore.

Don Douglas had been a pilot for Tri-9 at the time some of its employees stole the Air Cambodge contract and founded SEAAT. When Stan Booker's operation ceased, he came back to work for Tri-9. He flew with me one or two times, then quit to start his own company in partnership with two other pilots who planned to buy some DC-3s in Turkey.

Continental Air Services and Air America were both reducing their Southeast Asia operations to nothing, gradually but steadily. The pilots who were losing their jobs were, for the most part, returning to the States, but a few wanted to stay in Southeast Asia and were looking for work. Tri-9 hired two former Air America pilots from Vientiane. One was an American, Phil Schneider, who came to work as a Convair captain. The other, Joe Chan, was a Singaporean of Chinese descent with Thai citizenship. Since the Convairs were often grounded because of maintenance problems, Joe flew quite a bit as my copilot. Cal Sherman, a former Continental pilot, was hired to fly the C-46 that John Yim had bought for MASCO, a new Khmer company.

All of the new companies were Khmer owned, at least theoretically. The top managers of most of them were totally unfamiliar with aviation, and their misconceptions were often comical. Several depended on John Yim for technical advice. Many of the new tycoons of the air had plenty of money, and they tended to spend it foolishly. One thing that they did not want to spend it on, however, was pilots' salaries. That led many of them to disaster.

Cal Sherman was so dissatisfied with the delays and complaints by the MASCO management that when it came time for them to pay him he gave them an ultimatum. Either they hand him a $100 bill at the beginning of each day, or he would not fly. Not only was there nobody else available with a C-46 license, there was no one to be had who could fly the machine. MASCO had no choice but to pay. Cal was confident that he could deliver the flying after he received the money, but he had no confidence that his employers would deliver the money after he flew.

John Yim was somewhat upset by Cal's high handed tactics and exclaimed, "Why, do you know that I could hire 1000 coolies for the salary MASCO pays you?"

Cal calmly replied, "Then hire your 1000 coolies and get them to fly your aircraft to Kompong Chhnang for you."

Chapter 13

At the end of April, the Khemera Air Transport contract had expired, and the green and white KAT colors on TFB were painted over with the colors of Golden Eagle Airlines. The MASCO colors appeared on the sides of 422. The paint was long dry before the DC-3s began flying again. In fact, on the inaugural day of the myriad new airline companies, not a single aircraft turned a wheel. The monthly fuel authorizations had not been approved, and more than half a month went by before the minister of commerce accepted an offering and signed over the fuel. It was understood that another and perhaps larger donation would have to be handed over at the beginning of June for the next month's fuel authorization.

While waiting for the negotiations to be completed, I had some time to look around Phnom Penh, which was already one of the dirtiest in Asia but was becoming even dirtier every day. While mountains of trash like those in New York during a sanitation department strike never accumulated, the garbage that did accumulate was of a filthier variety, consisting chiefly of spoiled food and excrement. The city was literally filthy. The sidewalks were black and gummy, and after a day of walking around, the bottoms of my shoes were black and sticky. The stink of human excrement baking in the sun was ever present and especially strong after rainstorms. The northeast wind that prevails for almost six months during the dry season brought the stronger stench from the refugee hovels across the downtown section of the city. These wretched dwellings filled the inactive railroad yards and spread across the fields beyond. To the south of the city, even larger refugee camps had been built.

The stream of refugees pouring into the city had never abated. The people had to leave everything behind to escape the terrors prepared for them by the communists, and many were forced to live in huts made of empty boxes along the streets. The government did as little as possible to help them, since the civil servants were far too busy taking care of their own well-being. Even relatively minor officials were already driving Mercedes, which were still being imported in large numbers in spite of the blockade. The cost of renting one with a driver had dropped to under $100 per month.

A Phnom Penh street scene with the main market building in the background. It is depressing to know that most of the people in the picture met horrible deaths just because they lived in a city and were therefore regarded as "enemies of the people" (photo courtesy of Bill Ernst).

The right of way in the streets was determined strictly by the size of the vehicle. The law dictated that traffic should keep right, but this was generally viewed as a suggestion. The army trucks were the largest vehicles, so they simply took the center of the roads. The drivers seemed to know how to use only the accelerator and horn. They regularly drove through rush-hour crowds at high speed with the horns blaring. It was up to the drivers of private cars and cyclists to get out of the way. Amazingly, only a few people were run over each day. Most had learned the art of self-preservation. The Mercedes followed the army trucks in the order of precedence. If the driver of a high precedence vehicle wanted to drive on the left side for a change, he did. The oncoming vehicles had to clear a path. Many drivers did opt to keep left, and I never saw a policeman stop anyone for doing it. After all, if one has to find a parking place on the left side, one is better off driving there. Unfortunately, there were quite a few head-on collisions.

When the electricity was operating, the traffic signals often worked.

Only small vehicles bothered stopping for red lights, however. Our crew car drivers just kept going past the corner of the Monorom Hotel whether the light was green or red. The smaller vehicles travelling perpendicular had to accommodate. Only at the corner of the two main market streets, Kampuchea Krom and Prachiethipitei, did a military policeman keep some semblance of order. High officials often ignored the policeman and simply drove by as he held out his hand to signal them to stop, but most people followed his instructions.

This is not to say that traffic tickets were not given out. Regular road blocks stopped motorcycles at various parts of the city to check registrations. The penalty for not having one was either the loss of the motorcycle or a small payment to the policeman. These control checks also gave the policeman the chance to check personal identification papers and draft any young man on the spot. That meant that a draft deferment would have to be purchased, unofficially of course. The fact that one or more had already been purchased did not keep the authorities from demanding money again, and many parents with modest incomes had to keep their sons home at all times.

The sons of the local Chinese businessmen never served in the army even though they were native-born Khmer citizens. To avoid constant extortion by minor officials, most of them made modest contributions to a person in authority. They also acted as front men and managers for the business operations of Khmer military officers, who were forbidden by law from doing private business. The Chinese were accorded official protection and received working capital in return for financial counsel, and large profits were reaped by all concerned.

The most amazing thing of all was that the simple Khmer soldiers fought hard and bravely against a tough enemy, and most remained staunchly loyal to their government to the bitter end.

Phnom Penh was a shopper's paradise for objects of art and other hand-made items. The temple rubbings from Angkor Wat and Angkor Thom have been sold for high prices around the world, but in Phnom Penh, they cost only a few cents each. Hand carved stone Buddhas and small statues were produced with great skill and showed very fine detail. They were also comparatively inexpensive. The prices for the various items never seemed to catch up with the inflation, and many families that had been rich were selling everything they owned in order to raise money to flee to Europe. Captain Sangob had always been interested in gemstones, and I often went with him to a dealer who had moved from Thailand to Cambodia about ten years earlier. The gems were mined and cut in the Khmer Republic, mainly at Pailin, and they were sold for comparatively low prices. Sangob was also able to buy some stones from some of the departing Khmers. The price of gems had been even lower in the past but, according to a persistent rumor, the market had been inflated by a group of Japanese buyers who had bought up every ruby and sapphire available at top prices. The rumor further recounted how the group had gone bankrupt in Japan because the stones could not be sold for a profit sufficient to cover the cost of the buying expeditions.

The custom of bargaining in Southeast Asia is vital for any business-man to understand. The American GI had earned a reputation as the "big-gest sucker" among the native Southeast Asians, but tourists from other countries and some of the Japanese businessmen subsequently gave the GI much competition for the championship title in trading gold for glass beads. The custom of doing business is rather simple and not unpleasant. The owner of the item quotes the top price he would like to receive for his goods, and the prospective buyer quotes the price he would like to pay for them. The owner comes down with his offer, while the buyer raises his. The selling price is the meeting point of the bid and ask. Knowing from ex-perience that many foreigners have more money than brains, some busi-nessmen quote an initial price many times higher than he hopes to get for an item. If the foreigner is ignorant of the custom but not of the market price, he might well walk out of the store instead of making a reasonable offer. If he is rather stupid, he buys the item for the price asked. If the seller realizes he has a genuine "sucker" in his shop, he trots out all of his merchan-dise and offers to sell it at astronomical prices. When the victim later finds out he can get the same items for 10 percent of what he paid in any other shop in town, he may feel he was cheated. He was at fault for not knowing the price of the item and for not bargaining with the shopkeeper, according to the local custom. It goes without saying that the local businessmen think that such customers are stupid, not generous.

Bargaining makes it possible to get some great bargains. Some shop-keepers will accept offers just above the price they paid for it. A little profit is better than keeping the goods and making nothing at all. The lack of rigid adherence to some price on a tag gives both the buyer and seller leeway to reach an agreement satisfactory to both. In the Khmer Republic, it was really a buyer's market. The raging inflation outraced the price increases. An item priced at 50,000 riels might cost $100 one month and only $80 the next. Many people were trying to sell belongings to try to catch up with the runaway cost of living. One great bargain was postal service. An aerogram cost only 19 riels. That price had been set when one riel was worth between one and two cents. The dollar had in the meantime become worth 800 riels, decreasing the cost of the aerogram to only 2.4 cents. Telegrams were also extremely cheap in terms of dollars.

All mail was censored. Letters were received with one end neatly clipped open and reclosed with a staple. To indicate that it had passed the censor, the envelope was stamped in red with the words in French and

Khmer, "North Vietnamese and Viet Cong aggressors, leave us alone." I never minded the censorship; it was done openly.

A problem arose for one of the SEAAT pilots. He had escaped from Hungary in 1956 and had resided in the United States ever since. He always complained about not receiving his mail. We finally surmised that his lost letters were being held because none of the Khmer censors could read Hungarian.

Chapter 14

On the evening of May 1 our landlord sent his son to tell me that I had a telephone call. It was Tong Ky, the Tri-9 business manager. He asked me if I would like to fly the Twin-Beech the next day for Indhandu (Rainbow) Airlines. I told him that I wouldn't mind, so he arranged transportation to the airport for me the following afternoon. He was glad that I agreed because nobody else wanted to fly the machine.

Several days earlier Ben Crawford and I had represented Tri-9 at the inaugural celebration for the newly formed Indhandu Airlines. Tri-9, acting as their agent, had purchased and would maintain the Twin-Beech. It was the same AT-11, with the Lao registration number XW-THS, that Ford had flown from Vientiane. As I began using the manual to check myself out, I discovered that this model was a very primitive forerunner of what is usually referred to as a Twin-Beech. Our chief mechanic, Joe Weaver, got in to show me how to start the motors, which actually required at least three hands. The fuel for start was supplied by a wobble pump while the throttle was manipulated and the starter engaged. At the right moment, the prop and mixture controls had to be adjusted. If the hand pumping stopped, the engine died. With five hands, the procedure would have been easy, but with two, it was impossible. Since I would be flying the machine alone, I had to learn to be very fast with the use of my knees, elbows and chin to get the engines turning. To complicate the matter, the motors were not well tuned, and it took about half a minute before they started running, even when all procedures were performed correctly.

By trial and error, I learned that several distinct movements of the mixture control were necessary to complete the start. No mechanical explanation for this sequence was ever offered. Once I had mastered the procedures with these modifications, I was able to start the engines every time I tried. Other pilots who later tried to fly that aircraft were invariably unsuccessful in starting the engines until I showed them all the tricks.

Weaver went with me on my check-out flight. He was interested in seeing if the ancient machine would really run. Having flown only the DC-3 for so long, I found myself overcontrolling the small, light twin. After my first landing, the aircraft swung left about 45°, but swung right back as I overcontrolled in the other direction. The brakes seemed weak compared to those of the DC-3, and the landing roll distance of both aircraft was about the same. My flying rapidly improved, and my second and third landings were quite satisfactory, although I found some flight characteristics very poor. The model was a prototype with the designers' mistakes built in. These defects were eliminated in subsequent models. Three landings were satisfactory to meet the Lao experience requirements, and I was ready to start operations.

The first trip with the Twin-Beech took me to Battambang. I checked the load carefully before take-off, and the fuel consumption turned out to be very close to that reported in the aircraft manual. It was not an unpleasant aircraft to fly, and fully loaded, it cruised somewhat faster than the DC-3, although it climbed slower.

The cargo agent at Battambang was a young Chinese lad, perhaps 18 years old, who had such an energetic manner that one might believe he had some serious glandular imbalance. He apparently mistook the Twin-Beech for a C-46 because he had enough cargo with him for four full loads. As I watched, he attempted to load it all into the aircraft. Eight passengers and two stand-bys expected to go, as well. We were authorized to carry only cargo and had not been told to expect passengers.

The police and airport officials crowded around the aircraft. They had never seen such a small twin. One of the policemen asked to see my flight authorization. After gazing at it for a long time, he informed me that we could not carry passengers. I told him, "Fine, tell them to get off."

The policeman looked surprised. He expected me to hand him some money so that he could forget what the authorization said. I turned to the agent and told him, "The policeman says, 'No passengers!,' so get them off. We have no authorization."

The agent looked slightly annoyed, but he seemed to have complete confidence in his ability to handle the situation.

The policeman looked horrified. "Do you mean that you don't want to take passengers?" he asked.

I took the policeman aside and told him that there was no room in the aircraft for even half the load, and it was unsafe to carry passengers with so much cargo. They could not possibly get out the door in an emergency, and the cargo might fall on them in flight. I said I would appreciate it if the passengers were told that they could not go by the proper authorities, and I asked him to explain the situation to them.

The policeman promptly vanished from the scene. I suspected that some of the passengers were friends or clients of the airport police chief, and they were supposed to go.

Without the proper authorities to back me up, I had to tell the agent the bad news myself. Without blinking an eye, he shoved a handful of money into my fist and continued loading. I handed the money back and told him that I needed a scale. He looked very annoyed and said that there were no scales. My next move was to tell the agent that it was the first trip with the aircraft, and I needed to go a little light and could not take as much as the contract called for. Then, I threw off a good deal of the cargo, but agreed to take two of the passengers, who were manifested as shippers. One of them was an old man, supposedly related to the tower chief, who had to go if we wanted to get take-off clearance from the tower. The other carried the money for the cargo we were taking.

Like everything else in the aircraft, the door latch had a very unusual design, and the passengers had almost managed to break the handle off. I quickly learned that I had to close the door each time personally. It had to be slammed, then not touched again. A passenger would invariably move the latch to what seemed to be the locked position, and the door would open. The slightest movement of the handle in either direction opened the door, on the ground or in flight.

As I taxied to take off, most of the cargo was still on the truck or on the ground where I had thrown it. The ground time had been excessive, about twice as long as a normal DC-3 stop. At Phnom Penh, I weighed the cargo and found that we had actually carried more than the contract weight.

The AT-11 had been scheduled for two trips to Battambang that day, but due to the excessive time on the ground, the second one had to be cancelled. I told the Indhandu representative, a tall and rather stupid individual, that if he could better organize his ground operations and keep the weights correct, we could complete many more trips each day. Private baggage belonging to the shipping agents could not simply be added to the load without weighing it.

The next morning, a trip to Takeo was on the schedule. The field had just opened, and mine would be the first commercial flight to land there. The Khmer Air Force and some short-field aircraft contracted to the United States government were already using the field, but at the time, the runway was not considered long enough for the DC-3 and C-46. Takeo is only 15 minutes flying time from Phnom Penh, but it was completely cut off by the communist blockade. There had been heavy fighting just to the south, and communist troops were still apparently holding the land to the south and west. We were warned not to fly a traffic pattern over the enemy positions, so we descended over the city.

The sand runway was about 1800 feet long. It resembled a stretch of beach with no water around. The last part of the runway was downhill, landing in either direction. The crown of a small hill was about a third of the way from the northeastern end.

Passengers from Takeo to Phnom Penh in the Indhandu Airlines Twin-Beech (photo courtesy of Bill Ernst).

Only passengers were carried on the first trip. The start of the southwest monsoon was late, and the wind had not yet switched from the northeast to the southwest. I landed the fully loaded aircraft into the wind to the northeast, hoping to stop before reaching the crown of the hill. The plane touched down at the recommended speed, and I was relieved to notice that the wheels were digging into the soft sand, stopping the aircraft with little need for brakes. We had slowed to a taxi speed before reaching the top of the hill.

We parked on the little ramp and the passengers quickly departed. As I waited for the cargo, a huge mob of local farmers gathered around the aircraft. They acted as if they had never seen an aircraft on the ground before. Their clothing resembled that of the mountain people in Vietnam. It was amusing to watch the older people explain to the younger ones how they thought an airplane worked. I was not amused by their destructiveness, a trait that I had never witnessed before among inhabitants of Southeast Asia. They felt compelled to poke sharp sticks into every part of the machine, peel the dope off the cloth-covered control surfaces, and try to poke their fingers through the fabric. Their explanations of flight principles could only be made clear to their friends by dissection.

One of the soldiers addressed me in French. I answered in Khmer that I could not speak French. That was a mistake! I was suddenly deluged with all kinds of questions from the onlookers. As I answered them, I was able to explain that the aircraft was breakable and should not be touched. The people complied, and I was pleased for a while, but after a few minutes, some new groups arrived, and the process of dismantling the machine continued.

My final lecture in Khmer was made to impress upon the soldiers and bystanders that the aircraft should not be approached while I started the engines. I told them that this was vital to their well-being because the props are designed perfectly for removing heads. My explanations were satisfactory, and I left the place without killing or injuring anyone.

The next flight took me to Battambang. The radio receiver stopped working en route, and the landing was made on light signals from the tower. The radio worked again briefly during the return trip, then it stopped functioning again. It was repaired in time for me to make one more trip to Takeo that day, but it was again inoperative when I landed at Phnom Penh.

The radio problems kept the aircraft grounded for the next two days. Each day I went to the airport and met the same group of passengers, who were brought to the airport again and again in the false hope that they would fly somewhere. The Indhandu management never seemed to grasp the fact that the tower expected us to have an operational radio.

To help the passengers to get where they wanted to go, I began trying to convince the tower personnel that the flight could be made using light signals. I explained that in the United States, most control towers allowed aircraft without radios to take off and land.

On May 6 I was not scheduled to fly, but as I returned from breakfast at about 10:00 A.M., the Indhandu car drove up with the company president. She was a very pompous, middle-aged woman who was furious that I was not ready to go to the airport. I told her that if she wanted me to fly, she should talk to John Yim about sending me a schedule. She did not appreciate my lack of contrition, but I didn't really care. At the airport, I found that the flight was scheduled for the afternoon, and the fuel had still not arrived.

The DC-3s were grounded because of the fuel shortage, and the Twin-Beech had no allotment either. Its fuel requirements were so small, however, that ordinary black-market gasoline could be purchased for it in town and brought to the airport in the company car. In fact, this fuel had probably been drained from the larger aircraft during the night by the airport security guards.

The radio had been repaired, but it stopped working again while we were checking it. Airport traffic was unusually light because of the fuel shortage, so I gave the tower personnel a long sales talk about the advantages of light signals, and they finally agreed.

We received the light signals to taxi out, but after the run-up, we had a long wait without receiving any more signals. Finally, a United States Army U-3 landed and rolled past the taxiway on which we were holding. I then saw a light in the tower. It was white, the signal to taxi back to the ramp. The glass on the lower part of the tower window was deep green, however, so I rationalized that the light was green enough to mean, "Cleared for take-off."

Under the circumstances, I was not above countering the chicanery of the tower controllers with some of my own. I taxied onto the active runway as the U-3 made a 180° turn and taxied off the runway by the taxiway that I had vacated. No other aircraft were anywhere in sight, so I took off and flew to Takeo. When I returned, I made my no-radio traffic pattern, rocking my wings on my initial approach over the runway. I received a green light from the tower and landed.

When I returned to town, John Yim told me not to fly for Indhandu any more unless I received a schedule from Tri-9. He said that I should refuse to ride with them to the airport and tell them that I was authorized to ride only in the Tri-9 car.

Later, the husband of the Indhandu president spoke with me at my apartment. He asked me to quit Tri-9 and come to work for his company. I declined his offer, telling him that I did not want to fly the Twin-Beech as a permanent occupation but intended to return to the DC-3 after the fuel crisis ended.

The next day another flight to Takeo was on a schedule given me by Tri-9. At the airport I filed a flight plan for an aircraft without radios again. After a delay in the flight plan room, one of the traffic managers arrived with a book explaining the light signals. I told him I knew the signals, but that a white light from the tower looks green. I added that I had a right to expect a green light anyway, because that is the signal that would have been given at the time by any competent air traffic controller. My sales talk was successful, and the flight plan was approved again.

The engines were running, but the tower gave only periodic red light signals for the next 20 minutes. Finally, the Indhandu representative came out to tell me that the flight had been cancelled. The tower personnel had just been playing games. They had stopped me this time before I could taxi because they were afraid that if I got near the runway, I might just take off again. The score was now one for me and one for them, but at least I had had the satisfaction of getting one group of long-suffering passengers to their destination.

It was obvious that we would need a radio before we could fly again. Joe Weaver told me that trouble was brewing between John Yim and the

Indhandu management. There was a radio in the Tri-9 warehouse but Weaver had been ordered not to install it.

A relative of one of the Indhandu owners was a lieutenant in the Khmer Air Force. We asked him to lend us a hand-held walkie-talkie to use for the trip, but he claimed that he did not have one. Some of the mechanics said that he was lying. He carried the radio at the airport on many occasions. He had no inclination to help his relatives but did not want to say so openly.

The next day our scheduled flight was suddenly cancelled. A Khmer Air Force security team had photographed the fueling of the Twin-Beech with the black-market gasoline, and charges were pressed against Indhandu Airlines. The security forces knew that fuel authorizations had not yet been issued, and they were quite knowledgeable about the gasoline black market because they were running it. The pictures were used as leverage for a fat payoff. After Indhandu paid, the charges were dropped, and Indhandu continued to use the black-market fuel. Since the charges would have been serious enough to close the company down, the bribe must have been rather large.

During the short suspension of operations, the mechanics discovered what appeared to be a cracked cylinder. The aircraft was grounded for over a week, but after an examination, the cylinder proved to be sound.

While the aircraft was grounded, I had a chance to talk with Ski, an American pilot and a friend and former tenant of the Indhandu owners. He was convinced that John Yim was trying to cheat them on the contract by sabotaging their operations. His refusal to install the spare radio did indicate a less than helpful attitude.

On the other hand, the Indhandu organization was terrible. The managers were very wealthy and overtly greedy, dealt with shippers who were unusually crooked, even for the Khmer Republic, and showed great annoyance at my attempts to keep the weight and balance within safe limits. They quickly showed that they knew nothing whatever about aviation and refused even to listen to suggestions. I tried explanations but found that only ultimatums were effective, and I bluntly refused to fly overloaded aircraft and demanded that all serious mechanical deficiencies be repaired before each flight. They were, however, glad to have me flying their aircraft because of my willingness to fly anywhere without quibbling about security of the airports or runway conditions.

On May 16th we finally got off the ground again. I made four quick trips to Takeo. After the last flight, I was supposed to check Joe Chan out in the aircraft so that he could take my place when I returned to the DC-3, but the right engine would not run on one of the magnetos.

The following day, I flew four more times to Takeo. Joe went along on the first flight for a check-out in the aircraft. He enjoyed it but didn't ride again because his weight reduced the load and took one seat that Indhandu wanted for a passenger.

On the last flight, a Khmer Air Force C-123 was parked right on the end of the runway. The wind sock indicated that the wind was quite strong and blowing right down the runway toward the C-123. The Khmer Air Force was noted for excessive ground times, and the aircraft was surrounded by an enormous crowd. The Air Force crew was busily selling tickets to prospective passengers and buying cargo to sell in Phnom Penh. The negotiations were carried out behind the aircraft. Since the entire operation was paid for by United States military aid funds, all of the profit was net, and the business was booming because so many commercial companies had been grounded.

Obviously, I would have to land with the C-123 blocking the approach or return to Phnom Penh. I did not want to land with such a strong tailwind, and it was impossible to approach directly over the very high vertical stabilizer of the C-123 and still stop before the end of the runway. I therefore approached the runway at an angle of about 30°, passed beside the large aircraft, then turned sharply 30° just before touching down. There was nothing to it, and I stopped on the first half of the runway. It was like the approach of the commercial jets at Kai Tak Airport in Hong Kong, but on a much smaller scale. The only problem was the stupidity of the people surrounding the C-123. Instead of getting out of the way, they just squatted down and let the aircraft pass right over them. They seemed to think it adventuresome to have the airplane wheels miss their heads by inches. I had to stay a little higher than I would have liked just to be sure of not hitting one of them.

While my aircraft was being loaded, I watched the Air Force crew members with immense wads of riels in their hands selling tickets behind their aircraft. Their mob scene operation was a serious menace to aviation. The runway was dry and sandy, so before take-off, I held the brakes and ran up the engines at take-off power a little longer than necessary to give the crooked crew a good dust bath.

The following day the DC-3s started flying again. I had enjoyed flying the Twin-Beech, both as a light aircraft and as an antique. The DC-3 was even older, but over the years the primitive systems of the Second World War period had been replaced. Boost pumps were installed for the wobble pumps, hydraulic systems for hand cranks, and automatic mixture controls for manual ones.

On the Takeo flights, I was making one landing or take-off for every 15 minutes of flying time. For improving my flying skill, I have always preferred making relatively short flights without an autopilot. Flying time is often falsely equated with experience in flying. A pilot who flies only long intercontinental routes may spend much less time actually controlling his aircraft in 5000 hours of time logged than a pilot flying short legs does in 500. I was glad to get the chance to develop my skill. This was unfortunately not rewarding financially since we were not paid for our long ground times between legs, and the quality of the experience is not taken into consideration for future employment.

My first flight in the DC-3 after the fuel crisis was in 422, newly painted with the MASCO colors. I was accompanied by Ben Crawford, who was beginning his training for captain with Tri-9. The cargo on the first trip was government rice bound for Svay Rieng. After unloading, we flew directly to Kompong Thom for a load of beef and dried fish from the Tonle Sap.

Kompong Thom had become a major source of food for hungry Phnom Penh. The farmers who fled into the province capital to escape the Khmer Rouge took their cattle with them. Because there was little grazing land in the city, the animals had to be slaughtered, and we carried the beef back to Phnom Penh.

The increasing demand that we carry rice was a result of the bizarre economic developments resulting from the American Embassy's failure to come to grips with the corruption. All of the enormous transport capacity supplied to the Khmer Air Force by the American aid mission was used for private commercial operations run by Air Force officers. The rice and ammunition that the C-123s were supposed to be carrying were forced on the commercial airlines, which were paid in riels at the official dollar rate for the trips. The payment did not even cover the cost of the fuel, and it was delayed for months, during which the riel steadily depreciated. In order to finally get the money, the companies would have to meet the demands of some financial official for 20 percent of the payment as his "tip." The government officials had to use every form of leverage to force the companies to take their cargo, while the company representatives tried to avoid these trips by every means. The usual means of forcing compliance was withholding flight plans for revenue flights until a load of rice or ammunition was taken. By flying a triangular route, we could carry some commercial cargo on a flight approved for government rice.

On May 19, 1974, I flew in the Twin-Beech for the last time. It was Sunday, and we had all been invited to John Yim's wedding reception in the evening.

Early in the morning, I went to the airport with the Indhandu crew, where we were told that the scheduled flight had not been authorized. The shipper, a short, fat and very unctuous Chinese merchant with the Khmer name Hour Souk, returned to town with us. At the office, he suddenly suggested that we try to get an authorization for a flight to Krakor. I agreed to fly if he could arrange the details. We drove to the Indhandu office. Hour Souk went inside and returned a few minutes later to say that everything was approved.

We returned to the airport, and after he talked to some of the tower officials, the flight plan was approved. I had a very hard time with Hour Souk during the loading. He wanted to send several leaking jars of fuel together with some passengers. I told him, "No passengers!" and threw off the leaking containers.

I calculated the weight of each container based on the number of liters and the fuel weight per liter. The fuel alone was 100 kilos overweight. After much arguing, we weighed one container. The weight I had calculated was correct, while he had claimed that the containers were 5 kilos lighter than they actually were. He still insisted that all of the containers go, and that the passengers go, too. I turned to leave the airport and return to town when he suddenly accepted my terms. Hour Souk was an individual that one could very quickly come to dislike.

At Krakor the fuel was quickly unloaded, and a huge quantity of dried fish appeared. I knew the approximate weight of the fish from experience, and I knew that it was far beyond the load that a Twin-Beech could safely carry. The shipper's agent, Hour Souk's younger brother, guaranteed in writing that the weight of the cargo was 650 kilos. I asked him if he would agree to let me keep the cargo if it was heavier than he said. He readily agreed, knowing that it would be wheedled away by his brother once it arrived in Phnom Penh. I was curious to know how much heavier than 650 kilos it really was, and I wanted to make a firm case against a particularly annoying overload artist, so I let him load his fish.

The aircraft flew sluggishly at a much lower cruising speed than usual, but its handling characteristics were much better than I had expected. I contemplated throwing the overweight cargo out en route but decided that it would be too much trouble.

At Phnom Penh, Hour Souk and his truck were waiting, but I blocked the door of the aircraft and demanded a scale. The Indhandu representative tried to move me out of the way to open the door, but I shoved him away. He left with the company president's husband, and I was alone with Hour Souk's crew. I stayed in the aircraft until some military policemen arrived, and they agreed to be responsible for the cargo until it could be taken to town and weighed.

It was interesting riding to town in the back of a cargo truck. It was only a few kilometers, but we had to stop at seven check points. Each time the driver had two choices: he could let the workmen unload all of the cargo so the policeman could check the load against the manifest or he could pay the policeman a few hundred riels. The Air Force guards at the exit to the aircraft parking ramp received the first payment, and a motorcycle policeman just inside the Phnom Penh city limits received the last. This last road block was not always there, so I thought that it might just be set up anytime a policeman needed money in a hurry.

We found no scale at the Indhandu office, and one at the market had false weights, so the military policemen decided that we should return to the airport. There the scale was being used for the Air France flight. At that moment Joe Weaver and our crew of mechanics arrived, and we unloaded the cargo from the truck to a wagon we borrowed and attached to the back of our jeep.

At the airport gate, we were stopped by the guards. They informed us that the load manifest listed five baskets of chickens and we had six, so the cargo would have to stay overnight in the airport. We edged closer to the gate, so the guards quickly closed and locked it. A long queue of trucks already waited behind us. I moved into the driver's seat and revved the engine. One of the guards pointed his M-16 at the front tire of the jeep and snapped a round into the chamber. I got out of the jeep and confronted the guard with the M-16. Other guards closed in around us. I was beginning to get angry. Some of the mechanics were looking for the airport comman-dant. We waited as Hour Souk and another shipper left on foot, smiling and confident that they would soon have the cargo back.

An authoritative-looking noncommissioned officer approached the scene. I explained the problem. He examined our cargo authorization very carefully, then shook his head seriously and denied us permission to leave the cargo. I glanced at the paper he was holding and noted that it was up-side down. Although he could not read, he had studied the inverted docu-ment with great care. I should have known that if he could read, he would have been an officer.

Our Khmer steward, who had ridden to town with me in the truck, took me aside and told me that he had overheard Hour Souk offering the guards as much money as they wanted if the cargo were not allowed out of the airport. I had left the jeep in a position that blocked all traffic, so I knew that I would have to get a decision before the airport closed.

The commandant finally arrived. I quickly took him aside to explain that the cargo had already left the airport once but had been returned for weighing because of the overload problem. He had not been offered anything by Hour Souk, so he ordered the gates opened. The guards looked horrified. They hesitated but finally had no other choice. As we drove out the gate, I endeavored to look at them with the greatest amount of con-tempt that my face could express. They looked almost on the verge of tears as they saw their chance for the equivalent of several months' pay evaporate before their eyes.

We took the cargo to the Tri-9 supply house on 9 Tola Avenue. We were not yet inside with the cargo when Hour Souk arrived with an Army major in a jeep. The major limped and carried a cane. I thought to myself that he must have fallen off his motorcycle, because Khmer field grade officers were noted for avoiding combat zones.

The major explained very politely that the cargo was his but that Hour Souk was managing his business for him. It was forbidden for government officials to engage in such business, so he needed Hour Souk as a front man.

I explained politely to the major that his business was of no concern to me and it also did not interest me whether or not Hour Souk cheated on his contracts. I cared only about keeping my aircraft from crashing, and to do that, I planned on keeping my cargo weights within reasonable limits. The cargo would be kept until we could get a scale to weigh it.

The major offered to get a scale, and I agreed to weigh the cargo as soon as he did. In a few minutes, Hour Souk's truck arrived with a scale. The hyperactive agent from Battambang appeared with it and lost no time slipping his foot under the weighing platform. I knew that trick already, so I kicked at the foot as hard as I could. The scoundrel went flying backwards into the street, but the bag on the scale had gotten in the way, saving him from serious injury. I told him that I did not want to see him there anymore, and he disappeared from the scene.

The scale was surrounded by Tri-9 mechanics, so the weighing went unusually smoothly. The cargo weight was over 1100 kilos, almost 500 kilos over the contract weight. The AT-11 did not have full-feathering props, so the loss of an engine would have meant a quick trip down.

Because the cargo contained live pigs and chickens and because the amount of overload was established, I was inclined to let Hour Souk take the cargo. John Yim could settle the matter with the Indhandu management however he wanted. One of our Khmer employees reported that he had overheard Hour Souk telling the major that he should bring a truckload of soldiers to take the cargo back by force, however. I calmly informed Hour Souk that if he was thinking about bringing soldiers, he should realize that before they could get out of the truck, I could douse the cargo with gasoline and burn it up and then take him apart.

It would have been foolish to spend the night guarding the cargo, so I prepared a paper in Khmer and English acknowledging the cargo weight. If Hour Souk would sign it, the major could take the cargo. Hour Souk refused the offer, but the major told him that he better agree. He also apologized unctuously for Hour Souk's threats. Hour Souk agreed to sign but balked again after the cargo was half loaded on his truck. Weaver rushed over and told him that he had better sign it or be beaten to a pulp, and Hour Souk scribbled his name on the paper.

The whole sordid proceedings had taken so long that we missed John Yim's wedding reception. I sent word to the Indhandu people that I would not continue flying their aircraft. John Yim refused to hire another pilot for them, so they had to look for their own.

They first went to their American friend Ski, and he agreed to fly, if necessary, until another pilot could be found. Ski blamed John Yim for the problems, claiming that he was playing an underhanded trick on the Indhandu owners. John Yim attributed the problems to the ignorance of the Indhandu owners and their refusal to accept good advice. He said that they thought nothing of overloading the aircraft because it was insured. When he inquired about the fate of the passengers and crew, the president had replied that they were insured, too.

The husband of Indhandu's president told John Yim that Hour Souk had not spoken to anyone when he went to the office and had then taken the aircraft to Krakor without authorization. He had stolen the aircraft. He went on to say that he thought that I had been his accomplice until he saw me seize the cargo. He offered no explanation for the refusal of the Indhandu crew to weigh the cargo at their office.

The next day I stood by at the airport to fly the Twin-Beech so that the Indhandu management could not claim that Tri-9 had violated the contract. The mechanics had grounded the aircraft, however. By the end of the day, Tri-9 had been released from the Indhandu contract.

On Tuesday I was scheduled for only one flight in the DC-3 to Krakor with Phil Schneider as my copilot. When I saw Hour Souk's brother there, I demanded that he accompany me to Phnom Penh to explain the theft of the Twin-Beech by his brother. The stewards jokingly told him that I intended to throw him out of the aircraft halfway back to Phnom Penh, scaring him so badly that he sought the protection of the police at the airport. I then insisted on settling the matter at the police station six kilometers from the airport in the town of Krakor.

We entered a small wooden station of the Pursat Province Police, built on stilts in the typical Khmer style. I greeted the policeman in my best Khmer and explained what had happened on the previous Sunday.

The police chief wore an undershirt and dirty tan pants. His interest seemed to be in "smoothing the matter over," and he first tried to protect Hour Souk's brother whom he seemed to know.

My goal was to get some financial compensation for Tri-9 and to teach Hour Souk a lesson. Hour Souk's brother had already gotten a scare that he wouldn't forget, and he was willing to agree to anything as long as he didn't have to fly in my airplane.

After a long discussion, the police chief agreed that Hour Souk's brother should pay something for the overload. He mentioned sums from 10,000 to 20,000 riels, at that time worth $12 to $24. I told him that the total cost of taking an aircraft without authorization should be about 240,000 riels.

The police chief and I determined that Hour Souk's brother was carrying a little over 90,000 riels with him. I therefore suggested that the police chief should take 20,000 riels of this money as "bail" to prevent the accused from fleeing to Thailand and give me 70,000 as security that he would not leave Krakor. As the police chief looked at the 20,000 riels I was shoving across the table to him, he began to see that justice was on my side. The proposition was agreed to, the papers drawn up, and I put 70,000 riels in my pocket for Tri-9. The police chief solemnly warned Hour Souk's brother not to leave town and put the 20,000 riels in his drawer. Hour Souk's brother looked very relieved. He believed the price for saving his own skin was cheap.

At the airport, I apologized for making Phil wait almost two hours, but he laughed when I told him how I had picked up about 100 bucks in overload charges for the company.

When I gave the money to John Yim, he was extremely amused. His spies had reported the arrival of Hour Souk's brother on the first flight after mine. "Fine," I told him, "if he skipped bail, keep the money."

The great surprise shown by John Yim at getting the money gave me a great deal of pleasure. His favorite topic of conversation was how an American could never get the better of a Chinese businessman in Southeast Asia. Although Hour Souk had gotten the cargo back, I had gotten much of the money for it. If we had kept the cargo, it would have been taken by the Khmer major's men from the unguarded supply rooms after curfew, anyway.

For Golden Eagle Airlines, to which TFB had been leased, John Yim had what he thought was an ideal solution to all of the overload problems. He made the shippers pay for ten flights in advance. If overloads were detected, the price of an extra flight was to be deducted. In spite of the financial hardship, customers were flocking to John Yim for contracts, and some had to be turned away. I learned where some of the best restaurants in Phnom Penh were located when various groups of shippers began inviting me to dinner to ask me to put in a good word for them to John Yim. Their favorite topic of discussion was the vast profits they claimed they were able to make.

The fate of Indhandu Airlines after they terminated the Tri-9 contract requires only a few lines to tell. The president hired Bill Ernst away from SEAAT. He wanted to fly as captain, and the desire to wear four stripes overcame his reluctance to fly for a company sleazier than the one he was already with. He made several trips to Takeo; then he was sent to Prey Vieng, where no other aircraft had been landing on the nice-looking runway that had been built there. He did not realize that it was in the middle of a battlefield until after he was on the ground. Mortars started falling, and he heard the zip of small arms rounds as he got out of the aircraft. He leaped into the Khmer Army command bunker beside the runway, and was immediately asked for a copy of his landing authorization. Even in the middle of a battle, the paperwork had to be in order.

As he took off again, several more mortar rounds dropped on the field.

After that experience, he told the Indhandu management that he would go to Prey Vieng again only if they paid him $100 per trip. Shortly after, the president found a Chinese pilot, and Bill was fired. Fortunately for Bill, SEAAT was short of pilots, and they were willing to tear up the record of his resignation and take him back.

The Chinese pilot who took Bill's place was a very tall, friendly chap from Taiwan who was desperate for a job. He had been willing to fly for less pay than anyone else in town. His first trip to Prey Vieng ended in the grounding of the Twin-Beech for several weeks. The commandant there had discovered that Indhandu had neglected to get an authorization for the flight. As soon as flying was resumed, disaster struck. The electric motor for lowering the landing gear burned out before landing at Phnom Penh. Cranking the wheels down and locking them by hand are easy for anyone who knows how. The pilot succeeded in getting them down, but he didn't know how to lock them. The gear collapsed when he landed, and that was the end of a fine antique. The mechanics jacked up what was left of the air-craft, cranked the gear down and locked them, and towed the wreckage to the ramp. Indhandu was one of the first of the new companies to go out of business, but not the last.

During the final hours of the Phnom Penh airlift, Ski imported a LodeStar for Indhandu Airlines, but it was too late for them to start a profitable operation.

The same Chinese pilot later went to work as a C-46 copilot and wound up in the Gulf of Siam, but that story will come later.

There was one other Twin-Beech in the country, leased to Hang Meas Airlines, known as "Hang Me" airlines in the local slang. It was owned by an American and flown by an American pilot. They were retired military men who were new in the country and paid dearly for their experience. On the first flight, the shipper overloaded the aircraft without mercy. On take-off, it began to gyrate wildly, porpoising several times as it became air-borne. It continued to gyrate wildly in the air, and the pilot said later that he was sure he would crash. Several times, it almost hit the ground before it began its next upward gyration. The pilot finally succeeded in turning the machine, and he was able to circle the field and land. I heard that his cargo weight was in the neighborhood of 2500 kilos, and the center of gravity was far out of the allowable limits.

Jerry, the pilot, was so shaken by the experience that he refused to fly for a week. He stayed drunk for several days. Finally, he ventured forth again, equipped with a small hand scale to teach himself what the Air Force hadn't taught him about weight and balance.

His next trip was to Takeo. The owner had to go along because he had a Khmer authorization to fly, which his pilot lacked. They took off on a gloomy afternoon as rainstorms moved across the country. I had flown the

Indhandu AT-11 to Takeo that afternoon and found the weather over the field to be satisfactory, but the Hang Meas crew couldn't find the field. After unsuccessfully searching for the sand strip, they returned to Phnom Penh.

The next day I offered to show them where the field was located. We took off at about the same time, but they lagged behind, and we had only radio contact. They succeeded in landing shortly after I did.

Not too long after their first successful trip, one of their engines started to fail. They were inbound to Phnom Penh at the time, but they elected not to shut it down to save it. It completely disintegrated before they landed. Every cylinder sustained internal damage, and several were blown off. The aircraft was out of commission so long that the pilot finally left the country to seek new employment.

After the aircraft had finally been repaired, Joe Bobbs, a pilot formerly with Continental Air Services and SEAAT, was hired to fly it. The rainy season had just started, and Joe was sent to Pailin, a beautiful little town in the mountains very near the Thai border, famous for its gemstones. He circled the field and decided against landing on the short, wet runway.

Another pilot, who had landed at Pailin, decided to show Joe how to do it. Unfortunately, the winds were different during the rainy season, and the two pilots found themselves on a very tricky final approach. The aircraft touched down and immediately nosed over enough to allow both props to contact the muddy runway. The pilots quickly added power and took off again. The plane shook and rattled all the way to Battambang. Several people who looked at the bent prop tips doubted that the aircraft could have flown, but it had. It was never repaired, and no one ever attempted to fly a Twin-Beech in the country again.

Chapter 15

The incident with Hour Souk prompted John Yim and the Tri-9 staff to hold a strategy discussion. We were losing too much time haggling with the shippers, and overloads were taking a steady toll of wrecked aircraft. I still maintained that the shippers could be controlled by being consistent and charging sizeable fines every time the contract weight limits were violated. Appeals to moral principles and lectures on flight safety were useless. Promises by the shippers meant nothing at all. The only remedy was to make attempted trickery unprofitable.

In a way it was refreshing to deal with men who were openly dishonest and would admit a willingness to sacrifice lives to make money. They admitted to being villains and were proud of it. Americans in the same position would have screened their evil deeds with an outward piety and extolled their actions as being for the good of someone else.

John Yim assessed the shippers more harshly than I did. He said that the group of Chinese we were dealing with controlled all business in Southeast Asia, and that they were the main instigators of war. They had loyalty to no country and belonged to no culture. They took Khmer names in Cambodia, Thai names in Thailand, and Lao names in Laos, but "their only home is where their gold is." He maintained that an American could never come out ahead in dealings with these businessmen, and that the bulk of the aid pouring into the Khmer Republic was quickly diverted into their pockets. He admitted that in most cases, he could not avoid being gypped himself.

Part of what he said rang true. The USAID and other State Department officials were cheated time and again on large contracts, and most of the time they did not even seem to realize it. Bureaucratic regulations prevented the management of the aid programs from running anything themselves, and the money had to be turned over to "local businessmen," supposedly natives of the countries being aided. The Chinese businessmen knew how to obtain any passport they wanted by bribery, and as "local citizens" they were then able to start filling their pockets with an almost unlimited supply of United States tax dollars. As far as the State Department personnel were concerned, these businessmen were strictly "local nationals." The class of Americans who monopolized the foreign service positions could never seem to tell one Asian from another, and they could not speak the local languages enough to know that the contractors they were choosing could not speak the language either.

Only the Vietnamese seem to display enough business acumen to compete successfully with the closely knit group of Chinese merchants, several generations removed from China, who control business throughout the rest of Southeast Asia. In fact, there were successful Chinese businessmen in Cholon near Saigon, but they speak a Fukien dialect and usually cannot even communicate with the Tae Chou Chinese who were predominant in the cities of Cambodia, Laos and Thailand and who were also influential in Malaysia and Singapore.

I mentioned to John Yim that the Chinese in Southeast Asia are not really a negative factor, even though some of these businessmen are totally corrupt. In Thailand, many Chinese are scarcely distinguishable from the Thai population. The Thais are notably tolerant and assimilate the Chinese after two or three generations, avoiding the racial strife common in Burma, Malaysia and Indonesia. The business sense that the Chinese brought with them helps the economy as a whole.

Burma presents a strong contrast. The country is definitely not a melting pot, and a diverse assortment of closed ethnic groups view each other with mutual hostility. The Chinese had dominated Burma's economy until they were slaughtered or driven out. After that, Burma ceased to have an economy at all.

The Khmers were well disposed toward their Chinese business community because it had displaced the strong Vietnamese influence. The Khmers generally consider the Vietnamese as their prime enemies after watching Vietnam expand at their expense for so many generations.

A point of disagreement with John Yim concerned American policy. As a naturalized American of Korean descent, he had a real respect for his new government. He was convinced that the American people were highly moral and willing to make every sacrifice to establish and preserve freedom and justice. He was sure that government representatives would never willfully lie or break their word. He did not say these things directly in a trite way, but he seemed to sincerely believe them. That was to cost him his life.

After serving five years in the Air Force and taking part in the war in Southeast Asia for so long, I had stopped expecting anything but the worst from my government. I felt that the people in charge were searching desperately for any excuse to leave Southeast Asia to the communists, and I did not expect any embassy official to do more than the minimum work unless there was something extra in it for him. John Yim maintained that

America would lose too much prestige by abandoning its allies, while I said that America was already in the process of "bugging out."

We also discussed the Khmer officials and their qualities of stupidity and arrogance. They treated their own countrymen like human refuse and would treat us the same way if we let them. Tri-9's Khmer troubleshooter Savouth was embittered by the greed of his country's civil servant class, and he commented that Khmers are different from all other people in their anatomical structure. He said that when a Khmer puts his hand out, it is impossible for him to face the palm downward. It always extends palm up.

In applying our theoretical considerations to the practical problems of running an efficient operation, some disagreements arose. John Yim still believed in the Korean business tactics built around courtesy and finding courses of mutual benefit for both parties. In spite of his strong condemnation of the Chinese businessmen in Southeast Asia, he was still not fully convinced that his customers were simply interested in an orgy of uninhibited greed. He still hoped to find some honor among them.

Bill Davis, our chief pilot, believed in taking a tough line with the shippers. No one who dealt with them every day could maintain really good relations with them. I disagreed with Bill on the proper treatment of the Khmer civil servants, however. He did favors for them because he still thought that they would be more cooperative if appeased. He had considerably more trouble with them than I did.

The next day, Tong Ky, John Yim's business assistant, met me at the office. He was a quiet, easy-going Chinese-Khmer who had worked for Tri-9 for a long time. He had the tough, thankless job of collecting debts owed by the customers. He told me that I was exactly right, and that he had been trying to tell John Yim to take a tough line with the shippers all along. Our customers were so persuasive and conciliatory when they talked to John Yim that they could lie to him again and again and still convince him of what they were saying. They would admit that they had lied before but swear that they were now telling the truth, and he would accept their latest excuses. Tong Ky was obliged to visit them again and again to try to settle the debts or settle contract disputes. If John Yim had taken a "letter of the law" approach, Tong Ky's job would have been much simpler. He agreed with my assessment of the people we were dealing with, and he was convinced that they would lease our aircraft no matter what our conditions. There were not enough airplanes in the country to meet the demand, and anyone who shipped air cargo could make fantastic profits. The shippers' threats to go to other companies were just bluffs to wheedle better terms for the charter contracts from John Yim.

The final result of our somewhat nebulous discussions was the formulation of a contract policy for Golden Eagle Airlines. Because of a very light basic weight, TFB's could legally haul more cargo than anyone else, so

TFB was the most expensive DC-3 to charter in the country. In spite of the advance payments required and the fines for overweights, we were swamped with customers. John Yim found that he could pick and choose the ones he wanted, and I recommended those that had been fairly honest.

During my next flights in the DC-3, Phil Schneider flew with me to familiarize himself with the country. He was a former Air America pilot who had been hired by Tri-9 to fly the Convairs. They had been grounded so long that John Yim wanted to give Phil something to do.

I started to take off with a cargo of government rice to show him Svay Rieng, where he had never been. As we reached about 40 knots, the aircraft began to pull to the left. The rudder failed to bring it back to runway heading. It continued to swerve so I applied the right brake and cut the power. It felt as if we had suddenly been hit by a very strong crosswind. I knew that something was wrong, so I told the tower that we were aborting our take-off and taxied back to the ramp.

Ernie Solares, our Filipino mechanic, met us. I told him that the aircraft had swerved to the left on take-off, suggesting that we had either lost power on the left engine or had a dragging left brake. He quickly opened the brake adjustment ports on the wheel and got out his feeler gauges.

"Take the parking brake off and I'll check the clearance," he said.

"The parking brake isn't on," I replied.

"Ohhhhhh!" said Ernie.

That incident was the start of a long and unpleasant series of maintenance problems. The reason for these could be traced to the Convairs.

Many companies purchased Convair 240s and 340s from various airlines to use in the Khmer Republic. I was absolutely convinced that they could never operate profitably there, but John Yim always tried to buy them when the price seemed right. I hated to see them arrive because they occupied all of our mechanics' time. With one exception, I am sure that all of the companies that tried to use them lost money on the Convairs. The Convair 240 was a very complicated machine and demanded a maintenance facility that did not exist in Cambodia.

The single company that made a profit with the Convair was Angkor Wat Airlines, and they were able to do so only because they never paid for the aircraft. By what seemed a stroke of luck, Tri-9 was able to sell one of its newly imported Convairs to this new local company for a handsome profit. The trouble started when John Yim tried to collect the money for it.

The second Convair to arrive brought real trouble with it. One of the engines needed some minor repairs. Joe Weaver set about repairing it. He made a small error with large consequences. The downdraft carburetor was removed, and the opening was left uncovered. A bolt fell in. No one noticed that a bolt was missing. The engine was reassembled and run, and the bolt tore the impeller apart.

In order to repair the damage, the entire engine had to be disassembled. This job is not supposed to be attempted outside of a fully equipped engine shop. It was done on the airport parking ramp. After the job was completed, the engine simply refused to start. After several days, Joe Weaver finally got it to run. It did not last long. It was put back on the aircraft, and several trips were attempted. All were aborted but not without some scary moments for the pilots.

The Angkor Wat management was smart enough to make a few small payments toward the agreed upon payment price in order to keep Tri-9 from starting repossession proceedings and to induce Tri-9 to fulfill its side of the maintenance contract. A suit in a Khmer court would have been an almost impossible undertaking anyway, so John Yim tried to induce Angkor Wat to pay small amounts of their enormous profits by threatening to withhold the necessary spare parts.

The managers of Angkor Wat rejected Tri-9's offer to supply pilots because they had found a Chinese pilot who was willing to work for very low wages. He was an ex-fighter pilot for the Nationalist Chinese Air Force with neither experience in nor a license to fly civilian aircraft. Consequently, if he wanted to work, he had to take whatever he was offered. He controlled the aircraft satisfactorily, but he did not know how to work any of the systems. His first landings were all very costly for Tri-9. Because the length of the runway is often critical for fighters, their pilots pride themselves in stopping in a minimum distance. This pilot liked to show his skill in stopping the Convair as quickly as possible after landing. Unfortunately, he did not know how to operate the prop reversal system, so he either blew or completely wore out a tire on each of his first four landings. This exhausted Tri-9's supply, which had been programmed to last two aircraft several months. The pilot was very proud of himself for being able to stop the aircraft by the first taxiway, leaving about 7000 feet of runway unused.

Because the mechanics' time was completely taken up changing tires and rebuilding engines for the Convairs, they no longer met the DC-3s when we returned from our flights. If we required minor maintenance, we had to search the field for a mechanic.

In spite of all the time invested by the mechanics, the Convairs spent most of their time parked on the ramp. The two DC-3s were flying almost every day and making all the profit for the company, but the Convairs possessed the potential for making much greater profits, if only they could be made to fly, so they received priority.

The Angkor Wat Airlines management terminated their Tri-9 maintenance contract in a spectacular fashion. After their fighter pilot blew another tire, they simply drove to the Tri-9 warehouse and took the last spare. It was needed right away so the Angkor Wat Convair could make one last trip to Battambang to spend the night. The tire was being saved for Tri-9's own Convair, and since the Angkor Wat managers had not paid for the other tires they had taken and refused even to pay for this last one, Joe Weaver told his mechanics to load the tire back on the Tri-9 truck and return it to the storage room. As the tire was being loaded aboard the truck, the president of Angkor Wat Airlines and a large number of his workmen, armed with tire irons, attacked Weaver. The Tri-9 mechanics grabbed their boss and tried to drag him away, but while they were holding him, the president of Angkor Wat kicked him in the ribs. The terrified Tri-9 mechanics then ran away. Weaver promptly punched the president of Angkor Wat, a big, corpulent man, knocking him cold, and began to battle with a large number of his entourage. Weaver described their fighting style as "the worst exhibition of kung fu I have ever seen."

While the mêlée was in progress, Bill Davis was walking along the parking ramp and noticed that something was going on. He walked over to see what was happening. As he neared the scene, the Chinese fighter pilot approached him from the Convair, pulled a knife, and slashed him across the chest, wounding him superficially.

The fight ended through mutual exhaustion. The last trip of Angkor Wat Airlines had to be cancelled, and the matter was quickly turned over to the civil authorities. The next day the entire staff of Angkor Wat Airlines were in the Tri-9 office apologizing profusely and offering to let bygones be bygones. They were afraid that Tri-9 might repossess the Convair, and they still needed spare parts.

My copilot on the day of the brawl had been Tony Pradith who had worked briefly for Angkor Wat as a ferry pilot. They had cheated him out of a month's pay. As a Thai who liked his national boxing sport, he was extremely sorry that we had gone home before the fight broke out. He was heartbroken to have missed the chance to settle the score with his former employer.

Tri-9 terminated the contract, and half of our Convair maintenance problem was eliminated. The other half of the problem still kept the DC-3s from getting their fair share of the maintenance effort, however.

Chapter 16

During a visit to Vientiane, Laos, John Yim had purchased some DC-3 spare parts. Among them were rubber oil pressure lines for installation between the cylinders. They had been sold from the stock of the Royal Lao Air Force and had apparently been in storage far beyond the allowable time. Although not externally apparent, the rubber was badly deteriorated from heat and moisture.

These oil lines and some rebuilt cylinders were to be the cause of six engine failures within five weeks. Some brakes purchased in Vientiane were the cause of still worse problems.

TFB had used the same expander tube brakes for years without any problems, but within two days in late April, two of the expander tubes blew out. The first tube blew at Kompong Chhnang. After parking and releasing the brakes on the aluminum planking that served as a ramp, I noticed that the aircraft slowly began to roll backwards. I therefore set the parking brake so that I could get out and look for some chocks. Before I could get out of my seat, the hydraulic system began to chatter, and the pressure gauge dropped quickly to zero. One of the workers ran in front of the window and pointed to the wheel. Hydraulic fluid was flowing out rapidly. The flow stopped when I released the parking brake. After a long search, I found a wrench to disconnect the hydraulic line to the broken expander tube. There were still a good brake on the wheel and two good ones on the other side, so we flew back to Phnom Penh and landed uneventfully. As I taxied to the parking place, Cary, the SEAAT Convair pilot, called me on the radio to tell me that it looked as if my wheel was on fire. I shut down the engines and hurried out to see what was wrong. It was really smoking badly, but there was no fire.

The mechanics removed the brake cover and found a thick mass of oily dirt in the compartment with the good brakes. This brake had apparently been out of adjustment for a long time. After the other brake was disconnected, the unused brake suddenly came into use again, and all of the accumulated oil began to vaporize to a thick white smoke.

The following day, the brake pedals felt spongy because some air had gotten into the system through the disconnected brake. I asked to have the system bled before our overnight trip to Battambang. Some of the mechanics' assistants, who knew almost nothing about what they were doing, attempted to bleed the system and just got more air into the brake system on the opposite wheel.

I was finally able to coax one of the real mechanics away from the Convair, and he set about bleeding the lines correctly. As soon as the parking brakes were set to begin the procedure, the expander tube on the opposite wheel blew, spraying strawberry red hydraulic fluid all over the ramp. A United States Navy lieutenant commander whom I had promised a ride to Battambang was on his way out to the aircraft. I just looked at the wheel and shook my head. There would be no trip to Battambang that day. I was particularly disappointed because the shipper had finally agreed to let us stay at the government motel, the only decent quarters in Battambang.

The next morning TFB had new brakes. They were not expander tubes but rather a very old style brake with semicircular shoes, similar to those on some automobiles. They were the very worst available for the DC-3. I learned later that the linings did not match the drums, which were designed for the expander tubes. That meant that they could never be adjusted exactly right.

On May 24, while climbing out on our third return trip from Kompong Chhnang, we noticed the smell of hot oil in the cockpit. We scanned the engines and saw thick gray smoke streaming from the left engine. We were only at about 3300 feet, climbing slowly toward Phnom Penh with our usual maximum load. I made my decision quickly and punched the feather button. After shutting down the engine, we were able to hold our altitude and maintain about 90 knots with climb power on the right engine. There was obviously no fire; the smoke had been a fine spray of oil. The outside of the left engine cowling was black. Kompong Chhnang is normally about 25 minutes flying time from Phnom Penh in a DC-3, so there was no sense in turning back.

The aircraft handled well in spite of the load, and it was not necessary to use METO (maximum continuous) power at all. We let Phnom Penh tower know that we were inbound on one engine. The only hazard was ground fire from the blockading communist forces. We succeeded in gaining some altitude, but we were still low enough to be hit by anti-aircraft fire. If we were shot at, the bullets did not come close enough for us to hear.

Our landing was uneventful. It was the first one I had made on one engine since leaving SEAAT. I taxied off the runway and shut down the good engine at the entrance to the parking ramp. The tower controllers were very annoyed that I did not taxi into a parking spot. They did not understand that a DC-3 cannot be taxied slowly on one engine. I ignored them because I did not think that they knew enough to understand any explanations.

We found out that the cause of the leak was a broken high pressure oil hose. It was replaced that afternoon by one that had been purchased in Vientiane.

On May 25 I was asked to check Joe Chan out as copilot for the DC-3 since he was not going to be getting much time in the Convair. He was used to large, comfortable cockpits and took an instant dislike to our old aircraft with its primitive systems. Our flight took us to Svay Rieng, where the crosswinds during the early part of the southwest monsoon had become strong and tricky. Since the wreck of the CACO DC-3, a Khmer Hansa machine had run off the runway near the middle. It had been claimed by the crosswind. The pilot had made himself unpopular by cutting other aircraft out of the traffic pattern and complaining on the radio if the tower sent him around, that is, told him to circle the field to let other aircraft land first. He had a rather nasty disposition on the ground as well as in the air.

He always made full-stall landings, which are pleasant to watch but give the pilot a less than desirable directional control near the touchdown point. As he made his usual full-stall touchdown at Svay Rieng, a strong gust of crosswind picked up one of his wings, and he lost directional control. As he strayed a few feet from the centerline of the narrow highway, one wheel sank into the mud. The aircraft spun around 270°, breaking off both main landing gear and destroying both propellors and engines. The wreckage remained a monument to "acrobatic landings," as Tony called them.

When I landed that day, I was surprised at the severity of the crosswind. The wind sock stood straight out almost 90° to the runway, occasionally making a sudden swing of up to 90° to briefly parallel the runway. Needless to say, landings were not much fun, and take-offs were even worse. That day I bounced a little on landing for the first time in about two months. I was not too upset about it though because the bounces were along the centerline. Averaging four to five landings per day for months at a time had brought my skill level quite high. I began to have the feeling of being a part of the aircraft. Under these circumstances, even a small bounce on landing can damage one's pride.

On May 29 I was to need all my skill. Joe Chan and I were scheduled for another trip to Svay Rieng. It was the first trip of the day, and we had been loaded with rice by the government authorities in charge of feeding the refugees. The brakes worked normally before departure, although I only had the chance to check them at taxi speed.

We arrived over the highway-runway just as a Khmer Airlines DC-3 landed. I decided to land in the same direction, toward the parking ramp. The wind that morning was a light crosswind but with some tailwind component in the direction I was landing. There was plenty of runway, so I expected no problem. I approached over the highway, heading southeast. Very tall palm trees lining the road passed beneath me until I had almost reached the part designated as the runway. At the end of the line of trees, I nosed the aircraft down slightly and reduced power, rounding out for landing slightly high on airspeed. As a result, the aircraft travelled about 100 feet beyond the line marking the start of the runway before we touched down.

As we rolled out, before the tail wheel touched down, a gust of crosswind swung the aircraft abruptly to the right. I touched the left brake to keep the aircraft on the center line, then applied both brakes. I could feel the wheels scraping along the loose gravel along the sides of the road. Aerodynamic braking is much more effective on loose stones, so I let up on the brakes and eased the tailwheel down. The aircraft slowed down nicely.

As we approached the parking ramp at the end of the runway on the right side, the Khmer Airlines pilot was just shutting down his engines. He had parked rather close to the runway to avoid getting blocked by later arrivals.

The ramp seemed to be approaching rather fast, so I decided to apply the brakes to bring the aircraft almost to a stop before turning onto the ramp. I would have to maneuver rather close to the two parked aircraft, so a high speed turn off would have been risky.

I applied the brakes, but the end of the runway continued approaching with undiminished speed. I depressed the brake pedals as far as I could, but the aircraft continued to roll forward. We were already at a fast taxi speed, and for a moment I had the sensation of being on ice, of just sliding forward. Several seconds passed, but the aircraft had not slowed down at all. As we reached the ramp, there was a sudden hope of turning onto the entrance extension of the ramp and whipping the aircraft around on one engine in a slow ground loop, avoiding the other aircraft as best I could. Joe sat beside me calmly, apparently not knowing that anything was wrong.

At the right moment, I released the left brake and put my full weight on the right one. Absolutely nothing happened. With full right brake and a crosswind to help me turn, I could only get the aircraft to drift slightly to the right. I was half on the ramp and half on the highway, but the aircraft was still on runway heading.

I had no more than several seconds to come up with another idea as we approached the holes and piles of debris in front of the site where the Cambodia Air Commercial DC-3 had demolished the house. Straight ahead on the highway was the morning rush hour traffic of bicycles and pedestrians halted by the military police while the aircraft landed. Even if I could prevent the wheels from going off the runway without brakes and at a speed too low for effective rudder control, I would still wipe out a whole mob of people. Straight ahead on the highway was therefore certain destruction.

To the left, high stone piles and dikes bordered the rice field. I saw one spot where the shoulders of the road were level before dropping off into the rice field. It was too narrow to ground loop the aircraft with power, so I had only one hope. If I could just miss the stone piles and get both main wheels to leave the road at about the same time, I might avoid disaster. We were going too slowly to nose over, but if one wheel dropped in before the other, the props and landing gear would certainly be badly damaged.

As I stamped the left brake to the stop, I felt the aircraft respond. The left brake was just a little bit effective, just enough. I was prepared to use power, but I did not need to. The brake and left rudder turned the aircraft slowly to the left. The highway was just wide enough to allow the plane to turn about 70° before the main gear left the highway with a leap. A shower of muddy water coated the outside of the aircraft and splashed on the wind screen. I yanked the control yoke all the way back to save the elevators as the tail wheel dropped in.

The fully loaded aircraft ploughed through a mud dike and came to a stop. The wheels were embedded in the soft mud. The first thing I was aware of was that both engines were idling nicely. I quickly shut them down. One of our cargo conveyors rushed up to ask what had happened. I told him that we had lost the brakes. Joe reacted phlegmatically, as if he had just realized that something was wrong. I pumped my brake pedals, and both went all the way to the stops. "No brakes!" I repeated, with a few expletives.

Joe tried his. "Mine work all right," he said.

"Well, I wish you'd used them back there," I replied.

We exited the aircraft. I stood on the ladder above the water and looked underneath. No damage to the antennas or the props, and probably none to the landing gear.

The workmen took off their shoes and socks and waded out to unload the rice. I gave a message to the copilot of the Khmer Airlines DC-3 to take back to Phnom Penh. He would tell the Tri-9 staff to send some mechanics with a tow bar. I also wanted the brakes repaired; I had no ambition to attempt a take-off from Svay Rieng with its tricky crosswinds without brakes for directional control.

The problem remained to find a vehicle to tow us back on the runway. It was very embarrassing to sit in my DC-3 in the middle of a rice paddy. I climbed back inside and decided to take a nap until our mechanics showed up. Bill Davis in 422 would be making a trip in the afternoon, and he would bring Prapas, our best DC-3 mechanic, with him.

There was a large tow truck in Svay Rieng, but it had no fuel in it, according to its driver. We negotiated a price for the gasoline, and for a modest sum, he agreed to tow us out. He seemed in no hurry, but he assured me confidently that he knew exactly what he was doing. He recounted proudly how he had pulled the Cambodia Air Commercial DC-3 out of the hole after it had smashed through the house.

While we were waiting, the commanding general of the Svay Rieng garrison arrived with his staff to view the latest mishap. He arrived with due ceremony, was introduced formally by one of his officers, and began to inquire how an aircraft came to be parked in a rice field. He was sure that it must be badly damaged, but I assured him that it was in excellent condition except for its lack of brakes and its need of a good washing.

The general was justifiably concerned about accidents. There had been so many recently that there might possibly be a boycott of his field by all of the commercial companies. The Khmer Air Force rarely landed at Svay Rieng because the town had nothing to export, and there was no chance for making money.

The military authorities were glad to learn that there was no damage to the aircraft and that the incident could not be attributed to the airport conditions. The general gave me a perfunctory compliment for not driving the aircraft into anything solid, got back in his jeep, and went back to town.

A few minutes later some police officials arrived and asked me to accompany them to the police station to give a report. They had a form that had to be filled out with blanks for the names of the dead and other sordid details. They wanted me to draw pictures and diagrams to satisfy their bureaucratic requirements for filing complete reports. I simply certified that there was no one hurt and no damage to the aircraft, and I gave the cost of the tow as the cost of the damage.

As we left the old French-colonial style house in the town and headed toward the airport, another DC-3 arrived overhead. It was Bill Davis in 422. I climbed into TFB and turned on the radio to tell him that we were fairly close to the runway and that he should exercise caution if he decided to land to the west. Because of the winds, he decided that it would be best to land to the west, anyway. About a minute later, 422 skimmed overhead and touched down on the highway.

Prapas was on board with some helpers and a tow bar. Bill was pleased to see that TFB had made it to the middle of a flooded rice field without sustaining any damage. After his rice was unloaded, he took off again. He told how he had once lost his brakes at Kampot, and at the last second, he had ground looped the aircraft using engine power to keep from going off the end of the runway.

A few minutes later the tow truck arrived. It was a very powerful crane-like tug. The tow bar reached the tail wheel only from the side at an angle, but Prapas was able to hook it up. I went to the cockpit to make sure that the tail wheel was unlocked. After I got out again, Prapas sent Joe Chan to the cockpit to make sure that the tail wheel did not lock. That was a mistake. I did not see him get in, but I noticed that he was in the cockpit during the towing operation. I signaled to him to keep the tail wheel locking lever back in the unlocked position. He gave me an OK signal, then hit the lever, releasing it forward. The tail wheel first swiveled to one side so it did not lock right away, but the locking pin fell into place as soon as the wheel straightened out.

The tug growled and the aircraft slowly unstuck itself from the mud dike. Slowly it rolled back toward the road. The tow bar then straightened out, just scratching the tail cone as it lined itself up with the aircraft. TFB climbed the embankment to the road and headed toward the parking ramp. It was a relief for me after a hot and embarrassing day to see the aircraft back in a place where an aircraft belongs.

Just after the tug came to a stop on the ramp, turning a little to avoid some equipment, we heard a loud crack. I knew right away what it was. I climbed into the aircraft just in time to see Joe fooling around with the tail wheel locking lever. I asked him where it had been, and he admitted that it had been forward. He said that he had become confused about which way it was supposed to be. He placed the lever in the unlocked position. I told him not to waste his time; the lever had lost its function since we no longer had a tail wheel lock. The pin had been sheared. It was the only damage sustained from the day's happenings, and it made me feel very irritated. It was not Joe's fault. The company should have left Convair copilots in Convairs and DC-3 copilots in DC-3s.

Prapas opened the brake adjustment ports on the left wheel. The first one revealed the top of the shoe against the drum. It was dragging, that is, it was always applied whether the brakes were engaged or not. The lower part of the shoe was about half an inch from the drum. The brake shoe was so crooked that no more than an inch of lining could have been applied. The inner brake on the same wheel was also crooked, but not quite as bad. The brakes on that wheel had allowed me to steer the aircraft into the rice field. The brakes on the right wheel were both adjusted at extreme angles to the drum. One had a corner worn off, and it was obvious that only a quarter inch of the shoe was being applied to the drum.

Prapas started adjusting the brakes. He said that he had not been around that morning and did not know who had adjusted them. After he finished, he washed them with gasoline, paid the tow truck driver, and we were on our way back to Phnom Penh. That was our last trip of the day. The maintenance crew met us for a change and set right to work replacing the brakes. One of the drums left over from the expander tubes was worn out, and two shoes were cracked from the lopsided application.

When I returned, some of the pilots expressed surprise at seeing TFB taxi onto the ramp. Rumors of its total destruction had spread around the airport restaurant. Gus Pang, one of the most experienced Chinese pilots in the country, told me about the rumors and said that he had told those spreading them that he did not believe I had lost TFB.

The next day TFB was ready to fly again. Joe and I made two trips to other fields. My next trip to Svay Rieng was on June 2, and when I arrived overhead, I spotted another DC-3 hulk not far from the Khmer Hansa wreckage. It was closer to the runway, close enough to make me a little nervous. Our left wing tip passed disturbingly close to the wreck's cockpit windows.

Surprisingly enough, the wreck belonged to the Khmer Air Force. On one of their rare visits to the place, they had hit a water buffalo that had decided to cross the runway as they landed. It surprised me that such an accident had not happened sooner because cows and water buffaloes crossed the highway without interference any time they wanted.

The buffalo had sheared one landing gear completely off the DC-3, as revealed by the deep scratches left in the highway surface. The aircraft then slid off into the rice field, winding up roughly between the Khmer Hansa hulk and the runway.

After this accident, guards were stationed along the runway to keep it clear of animals. The little shacks built by the guards beside the road added still another hazard, but the livestock was kept under control.

Chapter 17

On June 1, 1974, as Ben Crawford and I departed the Phnom Penh airport traffic, I began to smell hot oil. Su Koun, our steward, rushed forward to tell us the left engine was spewing white smoke. We were just a few miles from Phnom Penh, so we turned back and told the tower we were returning on one engine. It was only the second time that an oil line had blown, so I wasn't positive that there was no fire. I pushed the feather button and shut off the fuel to the engine.

As I reached the approach end of the runway, my airspeed was a little low. I added some power on the good engine and got a demonstration of the poor directional control of the DC-3 at low airspeed. The landing was not bad, but I learned a good lesson for the future, one that I was soon to need rather frequently.

This trip was in a way monumental. It marked the first time that I had taken off and not made it to my scheduled destination since arriving in the Khmer Republic over eight months and about 600 flying hours earlier.

On the ground, we learned that our replacement oil line had burst. The next replacement lasted until June 12. On that day, we had gotten a little farther from Phnom Penh before having to return. It was replaced, but too late for us to complete that mission.

Two days later Joe Chan and I left Phnom Penh for Svay Rieng. It was our first flight of the day. The cargo was government rice, but several sacks had been removed from the normal cargo to allow space for several passengers. They must have had an important reason to go because normally the authorities did not permit a shipment of less than 53 bags of rice weighing 60 kilos each.

It was very cloudy to the east, and I began looking for a clear path through the building cumulus clouds. We reached the big bend of the Mekong north of Banam, a city believed to be at or near the site of an ancient capital city mentioned in records from the first millennium, A.D. That was as far as we went. The familiar smell of hot oil filled the cockpit. Out of my side window I could see a wisp of white smoke trailing from the left engine. As I watched, a great puff of fine atomized engine oil signaled the disintegration of another oil line. I had already started to turn back toward Phnom Penh as I pushed the feather button. I knew that there was enough oil left to restart the engine in case further problems arose.

Joe called the tower, and the controllers displayed a surprising amount of competence that day as they informed us that fire trucks would be standing by. Fire trucks were a luxury that we normally could not count on. I asked for a left base leg entry to traffic and was told to call five miles out.

I made a gradual descent to maintain a reasonable air speed without using much more than climb power on the good engine, but I noticed that the aircraft was not holding airspeed and altitude as well as it had on earlier single engine flights. Perhaps I was noticing the lack of thermal currents early in the morning. When we reached 3000 feet, we were still east of the Bassac River looking across at the stretch of open land between Phnom Penh and the sprawling refugee camps to the south. The real estate under us had been left to the communists by default. I temporarily leveled off.

As we approached the Bassac, Joe suggested that we fly a little farther south to make sure we were clear of the restricted area over the city. I carefully checked the city streets to our right and determined that we would be well south of the restricted area border. I wanted to avoid a big detour that would cost us more altitude. With a full load of cargo and passengers and only half of the engines operating, altitude can be important. Looking out the lower right window, I could see the bridge to Chhabar Ampoe disappear behind the window's rear frame. Joe could see it from his seat. We were still at 3000 feet and a quarter to half a mile south of the bridge. As we reached the river, a sound with which I was very familiar from my Air Force days in Vietnam prompted me to throw the aircraft into a steep left turn. As I dove it toward the refugee camps, the clatter of the 37mm anti-aircraft fire rapidly diminished.

Each 37mm round is almost the size of a beer can and contains an explosive charge that can tear a very large hole in an aircraft. I have seen sections of wing and stabilizer blown off by these rounds. Fortunately, the guns are World War II vintage and not very accurate. The Khmer gunners were less than competent at using them, but for reasons I would find out later, they tried to substitute quantity for quality in firing the guns.

As the sound of the fire faded, I turned steeply back toward the airport. We had lost much altitude, so I had to increase the power almost to META. I began to hear the sound of other rounds passing by. The deep clatter of 12.7mm fire was interspersed with the crackling of small arms. I flew as erratic and irregular a course to the runway as a single-engine DC-3 is capable of. The last burst of fire that I heard passed us as we crossed the runway overrun, 100 feet above the ground.

When we got to the ramp, we were told that the tower commander wanted to see us. One of the tower employees had brought a map with him, and I checked to see how far the restricted area had been extended south of the Chhabar Ampoe bridge. To my surprise, the map showed that the official limit of the restricted area was still where it had always been, five miles from Sihanouk's old palace. The entire southern end of town was unrestricted airspace. An unofficial restricted area had been arbitrarily declared to include the American Embassy and Lon Nol's palace, however. Although no one ever bothered to change the navigation charts, all of the pilots knew that this area reached as far south as the Chhabar Ampoe bridge, which we had been south of.

I had thought that the aircraft had remained outside both the official and unofficial restricted area, and the map in the tower showed that I had been. It is not forbidden to fly close to a restricted area, and as I showed the tower commander our exact route, I explained that I had flown closer to the city than usual because one of our engines had failed, as we had reported over the radio more than 30 miles away.

The tower commander was very sympathetic to our problem because we were not the first aircraft to be fired on. Several days earlier, he told me, a French pilot had been shot at, and he too claimed not to have been over the city. After discussing the matter with the tower commander and filing a report, I went to the airport snack bar. Some of the pilots congregated there told me that they had heard plenty of shooting, and our mechanics had found a hole made by a 12.7mm round in the horizontal stabilizer of TFB. John Yim was at the airport, and he had gone to the aircraft with Joe Weaver to examine the damage.

As I sat in the snack bar, I watched a black American-made auto cross the field and stop beside TFB. A few minutes later, it left by the gate through which it had entered. I could not see clearly who was inside.

After finishing a soft drink, I walked out to the aircraft again. John Yim met me and asked, "Why did you fly into the restricted area?"

I told him that we flew close to it but not into it.

He said, "Oh, come on! The air attaché was just out here, and he said he saw you fly over it."

Beginning to feel angry, I said, "Then he's a liar."

Joe Weaver told me that the man reputed to be the air attaché had examined the bullet hole and oil soaked engine. Then he told the group around the aircraft that he had spotted us across the Bassac River as we were headed straight for the American Embassy. He said that we were headed right into the restricted area, and that he had remarked at the time that the anti-aircraft batteries would open up momentarily. They did, and when our engine was hit, we dropped off toward the south. He told in detail how he saw us feather the prop while the guns in the city were shooting at us. The batteries near Lon Nol's palace fired over 500 rounds, and the shooting continued for a long time. An air raid alert had been called at the

American Embassy, and the staff had spent some time in the gigantic concrete bomb shelter under the building.

Weaver said that the man in the black car had been told my side of the story, and he replied that if we actually weren't in the restricted airspace, we would have been in a few seconds. He then added something very elucidating about himself: "That's what I'd say if I were in his place."

Because his story was so blatantly false, I decided to write a letter to the ambassador and demand an apology. It was on the record that I had declared an emergency and reported an engine failure over 30 miles from the field. The cargo had not been delivered, and the fire trucks were in place before the first shot was fired.

The story told by the man in the black car was meant to detract from my veracity, and even my own copilot, who had been certain about our position south of the bridge, began to doubt his own senses. He suggested that maybe he had seen another bridge.

A few minutes later, a French pilot, who flew a DC-3 for Khemera Air Transport, stormed into the airport restaurant. He was in a fury. He had been flying about two miles south of the restricted area when all of the guns on the south side of the city had opened up on him. It was about 20 minutes after I had been fired on. Someone commented that once the soldiers are awake, they shoot at everything they can see.

Prior to writing the ambassador, I found out as much as I could about the activities of the anti-aircraft crews. The pilot of the United States Army courier aircraft told me that the embassy staff had instructed him to fly no closer than five miles south of the city, which kept him south of the refugee camps. These instructions were delivered because a United States Embassy liaison aircraft had been shot at about a week earlier. The embassy failed to inform the civilian pilots. It was not their job.

The incident with Lon Nol's anti-aircraft guns occurred at a time when some reporters from American newspapers were arriving in town to report on the airlift. There was much discussion with the reporters and among the pilots, and a few interesting facts came to light.

Several months earlier, a disgruntled Khmer Air Force T-28 pilot had bombed the Presidential Palace. Lon Nol was not hurt, but several other people were killed. A reporter for the *New York Times* who was visiting Phnom Penh and flying with Bill had interviewed the Khmer lieutenant in charge of the anti-aircraft batteries at the time. His soldiers had simply refused to shoot. Not a shot was fired as the single-engine trainer made repeated bombing passes. The pilot flew off, not to be heard from again until after the communist victory. The lieutenant was sent to jail. The official story distributed by government sources was that the soldiers had bravely manned their guns but found that the ammunition was the wrong caliber.

The leaders decided that the gun crews needed an incentive. The sum of 1500 riels per round was to be paid to the gunners as a reward for firing. One young American official admitted that the gun crews were paid this sum for firing but denied that it was paid by the United States Embassy. He said that it was Lon Nol's secret police who paid out the money. Someone asked him where the secret police get their money. The answer, of course, was from the United States.

For the princely sum of 1500 riels per round, it was very profitable to shoot at aircraft. It would be a shame to lose the chance for wealth for the sake of a few miles, so the gun crews shot at everything in the sky. If an aircraft was not in the restricted area, it must be headed there. They fired on the United States Embassy's own aircraft, on United States military aircraft, on many aircraft belonging to the local companies, on Khmer Air Force T-28s, and even on a DC-10 belonging to UTA and carrying over 200 passengers. The last incident prompted Air France to threaten suspension of service to Phnom Penh. A week after I was shot at, the gunners gained their greatest success. They shot down a Khmer lieutenant colonel in an L-19, who had made the mistake of flying along the Bassac River. It is interesting to note that the American taxpayers paid for the L-19, the parachute used by the lieutenant colonel, the ammunition, and 1500 riels per round for the gunners.

A few weeks after I sent the letter to Ambassador Dean, I received a letter from Colonel Oldfield, the air attaché. The colonel denied that he or any member of his staff had gone to the airport to inspect my aircraft. He claimed that his office had made no statements to anyone concerning the incident, but he wrote that he could not be held responsible for statements made by visitors who were not connected in any way with his command. He added that I should be careful flying in such a hazardous environment.

When I showed the letter to John Yim and Joe Weaver, both were furious. John Yim said, "He's a liar."

Joe Weaver added, "It was him at the airport."

As far as I was concerned, the case was closed. I was off the hook, and the accusation of lying was now directed by the embassy at John Yim and Joe Weaver. I suggested that, if they felt so strongly, they should write letters demanding a clarification of the matter. Neither wanted to. John Yim was more interested in business than in points of honor, and Weaver was afraid of reprisals. A hostile United States Embassy could easily have forced the company out of business, and blacklists are maintained for persons who have aroused displeasure. The power of the purse strings may not be used to eliminate corruption or inefficiency, but it is often used for personal reprisal.

Who was really lying never became clear. On the one hand, the air attaché had won himself the reputation for making foolish statements.

Several months before I arrived to work in Phnom Penh, the worst mistake of the air war in Southeast Asia had been made. The river town of Neak Long had been hit by a B-52 raid and wiped out. The death toll ran at least into the hundreds. Colonel Oldfield had made a quick trip to the scene of the tragedy and announced to assembled reporters, "It didn't look so bad to me."

The men of the fourth estate loved it. Many of the newspapers with strongly anti-Vietnam War editorial policies placed Oldfield's quote beneath photos of incredible carnage and destruction. The hospital, market, and houses of the townspeople were shown after their disintegration by scores of powerful explosions. The pictures were richly decorated with dead and wounded. No better words could have been chosen to portray official callousness toward human misery than, "It didn't look so bad to me."

In reality, however, the statement did not reflect a callous attitude. It was more a desperate wish, that in reality it had not been as bad as it seemed and that it would be quickly forgotten if it were so curtly dismissed. The statement was hasty and thoughtless and represented a judgment made without an examination of the facts. The implication of the words and what a hostile press could do with them were not considered.

A similar statement to dismiss a disagreeable situation would not have been out of character after the anti-aircraft firing. Because my engine was covered with oil, it would have been easy to assume that it had been hit, especially by an Air Force officer who had never seen combat during a long, successful career. Because TFB could be seen from within a restricted area, it might be concluded that it was heading toward it.

On the other hand, Joe Weaver was far from honest, as attested to by a $700 bad check he wrote. John Yim, however, had a reputation for truthfulness, and I never knew him to lie.

Weaver held American officials in awe. He recommended that I write no more letters. He told of the Federal courts refusing jurisdiction over the complaint of an American who had been assaulted by federal employees abroad, thrown into the hold of a United States Navy ship, and locked up until reaching the American three mile limit. Citing his own experience, Weaver told how the American Military Police had confiscated his motorcycle. His senator interceded for him, and because they had no grounds for doing it, the Army was ordered to pay him the value of the vehicle. They acknowledged the debt but refused to pay anything. That was Weaver's story, anyway.

His point was that agents of the United States will stop at nothing in their treatment of private American citizens overseas. The government of a small country living on American aid is not likely to displease those disbursing the funds by protecting an American from persecution, just or unjust. Without the protection of the foreign government, an American finds himself at the mercy of his own, but without the benefit of courts, juries and lawyers. Weaver's philosophy was, "If you want to work here, you better just keep quiet and stay out of people's way."

I was not earning enough to care if I stayed or not. I had spent several years in Southeast Asia hoping to contribute to a process bringing peace and freedom to the region. Instead, I was forced to witness an army of incompetents sent by the United States government horribly mismanaging an enormous fortune entrusted them by the American taxpayers. If they wanted to kick me out of the country, they could, but I would not be afraid of them and I could not respect them. Why should I have risked my life for the freedom of the Southeast Asians while losing my own to a small clique of self-proclaimed elite from Washington.

Chapter 18

Besides having some of us shot at, the United States Embassy staff managed to antagonize the American residents of Phnom Penh in more subtle ways. Their security officer, formerly employed by the armed forces in the same capacity, was the most adept at this. While veterans with useful skills who were used to working under demanding conditions remained unemployed, any arrogant, disagreeable, and officious individual who could show certification that he had been assigned in the field of military security could expect immediate employment by almost any government agency.

The man assigned to protect the United States Embassy in Phnom Penh put into practice systems he had learned in the service. Because of the war, the embassy personnel had some reason to be concerned with their own safety, but he carried matters to extremes. The building housing the United States Mission had been constructed as a huge reinforced concrete bunker, modeled after Hitler's final refuge in Berlin. It could have withstood heavy bombardment and was equipped with a wall and fence sufficient to stop an assault by suicide troops.

Max, a SEAAT first officer, and I had signed the access list for the free movies shown to personnel of American agencies. I never attended one but Max went often. At the beginning of 1974, the old list was thrown away and a new one was compiled. No announcement was made of this, and many pilots continued to attend without signing the new list.

One evening Max and some friends went to see a movie, and while they were waiting for it to start, the defender of American security made a surprise spot check of the audience to see it they were all on the new list. Max's name was absent, so he was asked to leave. As he was departing, the security chief shouted after him that if he wanted to see movies, he should come during duty hours to sign up. He couldn't sign Max up before the film because that would require him to work overtime.

Max was rather quiet. He was neither obnoxious nor a trouble-maker, but some of us could be if aroused. Daryl, who had also been hired as a first officer for SEAAT but quit and went to work for Stan Booker, was the type of person who liked to talk about his days playing football, and sometimes came on rather strong. He let it be known that he didn't like being pushed around.

One of the security procedures at the United States Embassy was signing people in who did not arrive in private cars. Everyone knew that the people planning to attack the American Mission never rode in cars, so those riding were just waved in, while pedestrians had to present identification, sign in, then be frisked by a Khmer security employee for weapons. In the hot climate, no one wore bulky clothing under which a weapon could be concealed, but the procedure apparently allayed the fears of consular employees who seemed to be in constant fear of attack by irate Americans.

The Khmer employee chosen to do the frisking had marked homosexual mannerisms. When he felt people, he didn't seem to be looking for weapons. I noted his behavior, so on the infrequent occasions that I had to visit the consulate, I just pushed past him. Some people played the game and stood with their hands raised while he pawed their bodies for a few minutes with a strange grin on his face.

Daryl noticed the guard's great pleasure in his work and became annoyed at the ambassador's choice of employees and procedures. His wife, who was staying with him in Phnom Penh, was also mishandled, so he wrote letters of protest to his congressman in California. Shortly thereafter, the frisking was discontinued.

Undaunted by his setback, the security officer went right to work instituting a new system of harassment for Americans trying to visit their consulate. All visitors were required to surrender their passports at the gate in exchange for a numbered metal tag which was to be worn around the neck at all times in the building. This game was a hot topic of discussion around Phnom Penh for a while. The personnel were also supposed to wear tags, but some did not. The American vice-consul, George G. McGonnigal, may or may not have worn his tag, but the love beads would have concealed it if it were there. The Vietnamese receptionist said that she was not an American's dog and flatly refused to wear it.

By the time the procedure went into effect, I had decided that it was a waste of time trying to get any services there. On one occasion, I had applied for extra passport pages. This normally takes about five minutes, but in Phnom Penh, it took two days. The reason for the delay was supposedly a shortage of extra pages. To remedy this, the seal had to be locked up to prevent the secretary from giving pages out without the knowledge of George McGonnigal. Although it was during duty hours, neither he nor the consul was anywhere to be found, so my passport was not ready until the following afternoon, almost two working days after I left it. The consular office workers were convinced that the pilots had nothing to do but take long walks back and forth across town for their convenience.

A retired Army man working for Tri-9 as a copilot told me I should have just taken my passport back and told them, "Never mind, I'll take it to Bangkok. They can do it in two minutes there."

On another occasion, I phoned the air attaché's office and asked one of the officers about the possibility of reserve participation. He promised to get me the information on his next visit to Udorn Air Base. When he returned to Phnom Penh, he told me that there were no such possibilities. I later found out that this was completely false, and I assume that he simply forgot to ask and made up a story to avoid any extra work. Like some other government employees, he felt no obligation to provide correct information. He simply said whatever sounded good at the time.

There were one or two exceptional Americans attached to the United States Mission who seemed to be working with competence and dedication. They were engineers working on various projects, such as the extension of the runway at Battambang. They were the only ones who ever asked the pilots for transportation to places outside the capital.

In contrast to the government employees, many representatives of private charitable organizations often flew with us to various provinces. Members of Catholic Charities visited outlying refugee camps such as the ones at Kompong Thom. Some Danish medical team members often asked me for transportation between Svay Rieng and Phnom Penh, and French relief organizations operated at locations distant from the capital.

American officials could not travel in secret since the only way out of the city was by air. The appearance of an Air America or United States Embassy aircraft at the provincial capitals was so infrequent that it was noteworthy. The very few visits by United States officials were invariably short, certainly not long enough for them to learn anything.

The men who bore the ultimate responsibility for the rapid spread of corruption and decay of the war effort died their thousand deaths in their giant concrete bunker, and I am sure that they knew no more about where the aid money was going than their superiors on the other side of the world in Washington.

Chapter 19

Besides the problems with the brakes and oil lines, other mechanical troubles were beginning to crop up. In late May, more smoke than usual started puffing out of the exhaust of TFB's left engine. It worsened rapidly day by day. Joe Weaver decided to change some of the cylinders, although the engine had logged only half of the time recommended before overhaul. Evidently, oil was leaking into the combustion chamber of at least one cylinder.

The replacement cylinders came from the stock of spare parts procured from the Lao Air Force in Vientiane. The cylinders suspected of leaking were changed in one afternoon, and the aircraft was ready to fly again the next day. On the first flight, there was just as much, if not more, smoke in the exhaust as there had been before the change.

For the next two weeks, Joe Weaver and a large number of pilots working for Tri-9 and other companies puzzled over possible causes of the problem. I asked whether the new cylinders might also be defective. Weaver said that they were new and in perfect condition. The Lao Air Force had received them as aid from the United States, and they had just been overhauled and reconditioned under a federal contract.

Assuming that the new cylinders were good, we began to list other possible causes of the exhaust smoke in logical sequence. If the supercharger was leaking oil, a major overhaul would be required. Perhaps other cylinders that had not been replaced were leaking. Bad valve guides had been suspected earlier, but the cylinder change would also have eliminated the problem.

No answer was found. Meanwhile, I was flying an aircraft that appeared to be using a steam engine. There was no power loss, and the engine operated very well. The spark plugs did not foul during normal operations, although at idle, they did. The most important thing at stake was Weaver's reputation as a mechanic. Several other pilots called me on the radio during ground operations to ask if I had an engine fire. I had to run the engine at higher than normal RPM while holding for take-off to keep the tower from calling me to say that my engine was smoking excessively, which I already knew. The coincidence of the series of single engine landings with the smoke problem greatly harmed the image of Golden Eagle Airlines, even though the two problems were mechanically unrelated.

Weaver was talking more and more of an engine change. I was sure that this was unnecessary. Its only purpose would have been to eliminate a source of embarrassment.

The smoking engine sometimes came in handy in unexpected ways. The Khmer government was continually increasing the number of mandatory rice and troop flights as the Air Force was increasing its commercial operations. Tri-9 was increasing its own efforts to avoid these flights since it was so hard to collect the money from the government. The smoking engine was used as an excuse to abort several such flights that were scheduled late in the day. I would have preferred to fly and earn more pay but I had to think of the company, too.

In June the government ruled that all companies were to make one flight for one of its agencies for every two commercial flights. The first flight of the day would transport rice, bullets or troops, and no other flight plans would be approved before this chore was accomplished.

A few companies owned by relatives of key government officials were not compelled to haul for the public good. For us, avoiding these flights was difficult. There was a huge backlog of cargo needed to keep the isolated bases in the provinces alive, and the Khmer Air Force had no time to haul it.

The Tri-9 management figured out a clever way to avoid some of the indirect taxation. We would file a flight plan for a triangular route, taking us first to the government's destination with rice or bullets, then directly to our first commercial destination to pick up the customer's goods. The record would show that we had flown only once for the government. Naturally, we couldn't do this without the knowledge of the authorities. Our Khmer station manager secured the cooperation of the appropriate officials in return for considerations, the nature of which I never learned. I did notice, however, that we were taking many more unauthorized passengers at the request of the tower staff. I balked at carrying people for any official who had given us trouble in the past, but several times our station manager convinced me that it was imperative for the future operations of our company.

One shipper was able to set up a cargo shuttle between Kompong Cham and Krakor. This enabled us to stay away from Phnom Penh for the whole day. Most of the time, however, we flew triangles to Svay Rieng and Kompong Chhnang, Svay Rieng and Kompong Thom, or Kompong Cham and Krakor. I enjoyed these flights because I had the chance to fly the DC-3 at cruise for a longer time than usual while looking at some new parts of the country. The usual routes we traversed were already so familiar that I could recognize individual houses.

The stretch of road ahead served as the landing strip of Kompong Thom (photo courtesy of Bill Ernst).

On June 16 we flew the route Phnom Penh–Svay Rieng–Kompong Thom–Phnom Penh. Kompong Thom was actually starting to export more to Phnom Penh than it imported, since the refugees were being forced to slaughter the cattle they could no longer feed and sell the meat. They had also set up an extensive fishery at the inlets to the Tonle Sap, and besides fresh and fermented beef, our cargoes included dried fish, palm butter and furniture. Volunteers from Catholic Charities and other private organizations had organized these self-help programs. The Khmer officials at Kompong Thom were far better than those I saw elsewhere, with a few exceptions.

After this flight we returned to Phnom Penh much earlier than we would have after two separate trips. We arrived after most other aircraft had already left on their second trip, and ramp congestion was minimal. We were able to make another long trip to Battambang and return early in the afternoon with 5 hours and 5 minutes flying time, block to block, for the day.

Suddenly, we were confronted by the demand to take troops and ammunition to Kompong Cham. Our station manager was furious at being double-crossed. We had made one official government trip and one of our own, so we should have been allowed to make one more commercial flight before the next one for Lon Nol. The mechanics pulled the cowling off the engines, and we went home. The Khmer troops just stayed in the airplane all afternoon waiting to go, even after I told them that the maintenance work would not be finished that day. The next morning the troops and ammunition were still waiting. The engines were run up by the mechanics, a custom that only Tri-9 followed. Normally, this is a good practice, but in Phnom Penh it was useless. The poor procedures used by the mechanics' helpers caused more harm than good. On my runup, I invariably found problems that the mechanics missed, or perhaps caused.

The oil that was leaking into the cylinders of the smoking engine was not fully vaporized at idle, and the morning runup was starting to result in fouled spark plugs. I noted excessive RPM drops on single magnetos only before the first flight of the day after the runup by the maintenance personnel, who were obviously running the engines too long at idle, contrary to good procedures. Unfortunately, our best mechanics were still fully occupied with the sick Convair 240s, and the DC-3s were in the least capable hands.

After the long wait, the troops were finally on their way to Kompong Cham. About halfway to the destination, the left engine began running roughly. I tried various adjustments of the automatic mixture control, then used the primer to unfoul the plugs. The engine ran smoothly for a while, but soon the roughness returned. As it increased, I pulled the power back, and suddenly the engine started to backfire. I turned back toward Phnom Penh. Kompong Cham was no place to be stuck.

For a few seconds, the vibration continued with an occasional backfire, then I shut the engine down. I thought that the problem was a dead cylinder, one in which neither spark plug is firing. I didn't want to hurt the engine by running it with unbalanced forces on the bearings, and we had plenty of altitude. I made a long straight-in approach and turned off the runway with enough speed to roll all the way into a parking space. The mechanics went right to work and found the cold cylinder. When they changed the spark plugs, it ran fine.

The soldiers had become very impatient. Some of them thought that we were just looking for excuses to stay away from Kompong Cham. Their ground for this suspicion was a recent boycott of Kompong Cham by most commercial companies after Don Douglas had flown one of Stan Booker's DC-3s to the field on one of his famous low-level runs and picked up ten small arms and 12.7mm bullet holes. I could only find seven in his airplane myself, but I could have overlooked the other three.

Kompong Cham was supposed to be safe again, and I had no objection to landing there, even with a load of ammunition. A greater problem than the ground fire was the bands of mutinous soldiers who tried to board the aircraft to go to Phnom Penh. While we were loading old furniture on one commercial flight, about 12 soldiers had boarded the aircraft and demanded to go to Phnom Penh. Even though they were obviously trying to desert, the military policemen at the airport were afraid to try to make them disembark. I told them flatly that I would not take them, but they were very scared and appeared desperately determined to go. One threatened to shoot the aircraft if I refused to take them, so I countered by telling him that if I did take him, I would throw him off over the city. They stopped making threats but refused to get off.

Finally, a Khmer Air Force colonel arrived and talked to the would-be deserters. One by one, they departed until only three were left. He told these three that he had exhausted his patience, and he was going to order the military police to take them off and shoot them on the spot. The three hold-outs left the aircraft with a leap. I was about to thank the colonel when he himself boarded the aircraft and sat down. He had talked the other deserters into leaving so that there would be room for him.

Late in the morning, we were ready to go again, and the soldiers and their ammunition finally made it to their destination. A large troop rotation was in progress, and we took some combat veterans back with us. They had heavy equipment so I had to calculate the weight, and I took as much as possible without dangerously overloading the DC-3.

Chapter 20

After our return from Kompong Cham, we learned that our next flight was scheduled for Kompong Thom. Sawai, the former Thai Air Force pilot, was my copilot. I had been there the day before, and while sitting in the "Rustic Inn," an enemy artillery round had splashed into the rice field across the road from TFB's parking spot.

Again I went into the "Rustic Inn," a picturesque open shack covered with a thatched roof that had been set up as a snack bar by Sam the FAC, a Khmer Air Force captain, who had learned his trade in the States. We didn't know it at the time, but we were about to spend a day drinking tea there and watching a battle from front row seats.

We landed and parked as usual, but as we left the aircraft we heard a loud hissing sound overhead. I flattened myself on the ground as the artillery shell exploded in the rice field where the round had hit the previous day. The impact site lay about 60 or 70 yards from our aircraft. The probability of shrapnel hitting TFB would have been very good if the rice field had not been full of water and soft mud in which the shell buried itself before detonating. The mud suppressed the flying bits of jagged metal but chunks of sod rained down after the explosion.

As I stood up, another hissed overhead. I dropped flat again as the second round hit in the same spot as the first. I thought to myself that it must be a 130mm artillery piece. They have a long range and are extremely accurate. If the gunners didn't adjust their fire, every round should fall almost in the same hole.

Sawai and I raced to the drainage ditch behind the parking ramp and crouched, listening for another round. Momentarily, another hissed overhead, but this time, there was no explosion—a dud!

Many bystanders and prospective passengers huddled in the ditch. Some lay flat on the ground. A few minutes passed without any more incoming rounds. The workmen got up and hurriedly started unloading the aircraft.

Our cargo was freshly killed and skinned cattle. The weight of the flies following the beef was considerable, but it was not counted as part of the

154

load. We stayed low, sitting on rocks and listening for more incoming shells.

After a while, we decided that the communist gunners had gotten tired, so we headed for the Rustic Inn. As we sat drinking some tea, we could hear the growl of a C-123 circling overhead. We saw it turn its final approach. In a moment, everyone was running toward the runway. A huge cloud of dust and smoke rose from the landing aircraft. It swayed crazily back and forth, coming to a stop about two thirds of the way from the stripe designating the beginning of the runway. When the smoke and dust cleared, we could see the remains of a disintegrated tire twisted tightly around one wheel. The aircraft listed, blocking the entire runway. We would not be able to take off, even empty, and we could not taxi around, under, or over the crippled C-123.

We strolled over to view the stricken Khmer Air Force transport and suggested that it be towed back toward the side of the runway so that the field could be used. There was a path wide enough for it between two rice paddies. The pilot declined. He was afraid of damaging the rim.

Soon two DC-3s were circling overhead. I turned on my radio and explained the problem. They returned to Phnom Penh, and the crews relayed the news of our predicament. A short time later, a Huey helicopter belonging to the Khmer Air Force landed beside the wounded transport. A large jack, tire and wheel assembly was deployed along with a team of mechanics.

The hiss of incoming artillery sent Sawai and me back into the ditch. We made it there just as the round exploded in the same spot as the others, spraying mud and sod over the airport.

Another round hissed overhead and exploded in the rice field. The Khmer civilians around us were very frightened, but I was impressed by the nerve of the mechanics who didn't stop work while the rounds were falling. The C-123 was about twice as far from the impact point as we were, but it was still pretty close. The helicopter did not wait around unnecessarily. It leaped into the air and made a bee-line for Phnom Penh.

Meanwhile, the thudding of mortars and rattle of machine-gun fire could be heard to the west. The Khmer Army dispatcher and Sam the FAC told us that the perimeter was being assaulted. Large communist units were moving toward Kompong Thom. We were told that over 100 Khmer Rouge had been killed during the first contacts about a week earlier, and now some large units were moving against the government defense perimeter.

There was nothing we could do, so we began speculating on where the artillery pieces were located. Sawai and I agreed that the gun must be to the northeast, and the gun-target line must have crossed over the C-123. If the gunners dropped about 100 meters in range, they would be able to destroy the transport. To get TFB, they would have to drop slightly and move a little to the left. As we talked, another round ripped into the rice field. The crackle of M-16s and rumble of machine-gun fire continued to get nearer.

A cargo agent who was lying in the ditch near the log where Sawai and I sat called to us. He offered us 50,000 riels for passage to Phnom Penh. I told him that we already had a full load of beef and referred him to the shipping agent who had chartered our aircraft. There were obviously many others willing to pay plenty to get to Phnom Penh.

Sawai and I began discussing the shortcomings of the Khmer pilots. They blew tires so often it was almost funny. They didn't seeem to like using reverse but tried to stop in the shortest possible distance using only the brakes. We speculated that it was the sideways skidding caused by poor directional control that really tore up the tires. The composite result of all their bad practices was my wish to own stock in some rubber companies.

As we talked, a flight of four T-28s circled lazily overhead. As we watched, they began diving and zooming over the fields to the northwest. They were close enough for us to see the bombs dropping off them and wiping out patches of tree and bush lines dividing the fallow rice fields. They dropped quite a few bombs and then strafed for a while. Finally they headed back toward the southeast.

Although they had stayed a little too high while bombing, they had been much lower than most of the T-28s I had seen bombing before. After they left, the machine-gun fire was not as intense as it had been. One hour and one more air strike later, it stopped entirely.

By sundown, the tire change was completed and the jack removed. The Air Force crew were busily engaged in loading cargo and selling passenger tickets for Phnom Penh. The man who had wanted to go with us bought a ticket from them. We asked how much the tickets cost and someone told us 7000 riels each. The aircraft was surrounded by a mob of jittery people who did not want to take the chance of falling into the hands of the Khmer Rouge. The flight was quickly sold out.

It annoyed me considerably to watch our beef spoiling in the heat while the Air Force completed its private business transactions. I suspected that there would soon be some cases of food poisoning in Phnom Penh, and I decided to subsist on pork or chicken for the next few days.

After an annoyingly slow passenger check-in, the crew boarded their aircraft and started their checklist. Their United States Air Force mentors had obviously convinced them of the great importance of never deviating from the checklist, so all of the navigation lights went on.

I remarked to Sawai that checklists don't eliminate stupidity. The lights should have stayed off until take-off, for obvious reasons. Sure enough, just as the engines started to turn, another round hissed overhead in the direction of the lights. Sawai and I hit the ground, but it was the second dud of the day. Of the seven rounds the communists had placed within 100 yards of us that day, only five had exploded.

Sawai and I climbed over the rank, stinking beef, brushed scores of sleepy flies from our cockpit seats, and started the engines. They were running as the C-123 lumbered past us toward the end of the runway.

I taxied TFB behind it, and as we turned around, a sea of pitch black stretched before us. The C-123, taxiing with all its lights on, turned around, giving the highway some illumination with its landing lights. I had already started my take-off roll, flipping our landing lights on as we started to roll.

With the heavy load of beef, we didn't lift off until nearly reaching the end of the runway. As we broke ground, I started a shallow turn to the right to avoid a tall tree. During the daytime, I usually climbed right over it, but at night, I wanted to allow plenty of room. As we broke ground, Sawai flipped our lights off so we wouldn't invite any anti-aircraft fire. We set our course toward Phnom Penh, remaining blacked out until reaching an altitude of 3000 feet. After that, I wanted plenty of lights on because I knew the C-123 would be overtaking us.

About halfway to Phnom Penh, the transport passed us on our left. The Khmer Air Force had passed the word to the tower to expect us, so as we circled overhead, the runway lights were turned on. The C-123 landed just before we did. I had flown in the dark for the first time since the Pakse pig runs.

The flight plan room under the tower was deserted. The airport gates were locked, and the shipper started to worry about his beef again. After some searching, the lieutenant acting as chief of security was found. He was the same one who had let us remove Hour Souk's overweight cargo. He told the shipper that he could not find the key to the main gate. The shipper discovered that the fee for finding the key was 40,000 riels. Fortunately, the truck had parked outside the gate before it was locked. The driver had learned of our problem and waited several hours after the airport closed. It was critical to get the beef to a refrigerator. The shipper paid the 40,000 riels, but he still had to wait for the chief of security to okay the release.

The security chief thought it would do us good to crawl under the tiny space beneath the large cyclone fence at the main gate. I simply climbed the fence, stepping gingerly over the barbed wire strands at the top and descended the other side. Sawai followed, thus spoiling the evening for the lieutenant, who was waiting to see our white shirts covered with mud. Only our Khmer steward, Narong, was too old to climb the 20 foot fence and had to squeeze underneath.

The shipper's partner had his car waiting outside the fence to drive us to town. On the way, he seemed so anxious about his beef that Sawai and I offered to get out and walk the rest of the way home. It was almost curfew, but aircrew members were not stopped on the street after hours. We often walked home from supper after curfew if our last flight was delayed or if we had business at the company office. The city became very quiet after 9 P.M., with only rats and dogs going about their business.

The next day we flew to Kompong Thom again and found another Khmer Air Force C-123 broken down. This one had gone off the hard surface at the end of the runway near the parking ramp, and its tire had buried itself deep in the mud. Fortunately, it had passed the end of the runway.

After the replacement of TFB's expander tubes with the old-fashioned brakes, it was no longer such a simple matter to stop the aircraft before the end of the runway at Kompong Thom. Landing toward the C-123 with a slight tailwind was not very pleasant, but it turned out to present no problem. Most of the parking ramp was blocked by the C-123, which was listing toward the rice field on the right. The wheel had sunken in so deep that the fuselage was resting on the mud.

The crew of mechanics from Phnom Penh seemed to know their business. When we landed there again the next day, the C-123 was gone.

Chapter 21

On June 22, 1974, we made our first visit to Koh Kong. It was a good flight, one hour each way. TFB was the first commercial aircraft to land there. Others quickly followed when word spread that the fields were usable.

The shipper told me that the landing field was still closed, but a temporary landing strip beside an army post was available. We made a low pass and saw that the runway was covered with sand and overgrown with grasses. It had been deeply rutted by the trucks that supplied the soldiers. A rain storm had left pools of water and a small, temporary stream crossing the runway which cut deeply enough into the surface to give the aircraft a good bounce.

The setting was idyllic. There was a bay with blue water and many islands. A large mangrove swamp bordered a wide river mouth, which spewed brown and black waters into the amethystine sea. A few fishing boats and some Khmer Navy patrol boats were tied up beside small docks near the little, scenic town.

Tall palm trees filled a wet, sandy plain in which houses were widely scattered. Beyond the plain to the north and east were ranges of high, jungle-covered mountains. To the north, the mountains dropped off steeply into the sea. Beyond the estuary on which the town was situated stretched a long, hilly peninsula, and beyond that was the sea.

Just north of the point where the peninsula joined the mainland was the Thai border. Thai territory included only a narrow stretch of seashore. The mountains just inland belonged to the Khmers.

After landing, we noticed many large rocks on the runway. Brakes were unnecessary. The wheels just sunk into the sand, and the aircraft slowed down by itself. The ground was soft, and there was no parking ramp, so we just left TFB right in the middle of the runway, knowing that nobody else would be landing.

The surroundings of the airport were unlike those anywhere else in the Khmer Republic. The air was cool and moist. The soil and vegetation were unusual. Large numbers of pitcher plants grew everywhere. Their large

159

fluid-filled leaves look like harmless green pitchers. But they are deadly traps for insects. Orchids and other epiphytic plants grew in the trees and bushes. Most of the varieties were found neither in the Mekong and Tonle Sap valleys nor near the coast at Kampot and Kompong Som.

We had no other trips scheduled, so we decided to accept the shipper's offer of a tour of the town. After a long wait for transportation, we took a small Lambretta taxi along the narrow, marshy trails through the countryside to the main road. From there, we proceeded to the center of town, where the cargo warehouse was located. Several Chinese companies operated there, dealing in seafood and goods imported by boat from Thailand.

We noticed many crates of fresh eggs, much fresh fruit, and baskets of crabs. In the central market, we saw an amazing variety of fishes, then had some refreshments in a small restaurant opposite the warehouse, while our cargo was loaded on wagons for transport to the aircraft.

One of the company representatives told us about his experiences when he had visited Baltimore as a crew member on a ship. The charterer told us about his operation and explained that several shippers were contributing cargo for our flights.

The weight of the load was correct, so we were ready to go shortly after our return to the aircraft. We taxied to the southwest end of the runway where a steady water flow across it had removed the sand, exposing firm laterite below. Although we rolled through water, we did not sink in as much as we had at the other end. We had almost reached V-2 take-off speed as we reached the soft sand. The first pockets caused the aircraft to yaw back and forth as one wheel or the other sank in. I thought that we would be better off flying, so I eased the DC-3 off the ground. The bumping and shaking abruptly ceased as the wheels left the ground. I saw some big rocks pass beneath us, and I was glad we weren't on the ground to hit them. We headed back over the wide muddy river mouth and turned back toward the east.

We saw the new airport about half a kilometer from the temporary strip we had landed on. It looked to be in good condition. It even had a wind sock and parking ramp. We never used the temporary strip again. The following day we observed trucks at the new airport and landed on signal from the shipper. The new field was paved with sharp rocks. Otherwise, it was in good condition. An occasional gash in the tires was the price we had to pay for doing business there.

Chapter 22

Just as the overload problem had finally been brought under control, John Yim decided to emulate SEAAT and most of the other companies and introduce a policy of charging the shippers for cargo in excess of the contract weight. The aircrews were to collect the money, which was later to be divided among the company, the chief mechanic, and the pilots.

The idea did not sound very good to me, but I hoped that the system could be used to control the greed of the shippers. By asking a price for the overweight cargo that was much more than the shipper's profit for sending it, we could eliminate his incentive for exceeding the contract weight. With many other companies, the incentive for both the shippers and the aircrews to carry all that the engines could drag off the ground had led to disaster. The pilots who indulged their greed on every flight invariably came to grief the first time even a minor mechanical problem arose, and most of the wrecks that littered the countryside would not have been there if the maximum safe gross weight had not been exceeded.

An advantage of the new system was that the shippers could no longer pester us to take a little extra as a favor. It was now strictly a business proposition. They would no longer go to John Yim and complain that we were being unnecessarily strict or say we did not understand their problems, nor would they plead, wheedle, whine and make preposterous excuses to keep from losing part of their deposit for getting caught overloading us. If they wanted to put on an extra pig weighing 30 kilos, they would simply be told to pay 3000 riels. This was about double the normal shipping price, so the shipper would remove the pig with a show of great indignation but with no arguing and no delays. If the pig was dying and had to be sold right away, the fee was paid, but the next time, the shipper would bring no extra pig.

An overload of about 100 kilos was of no concern to me. The DC-3 was capable of handling it, even on one engine. My greatest concern was the 400 or 500 kilo overweight that I didn't know about until take-off. The avoidance of this danger was still an everyday concern.

The new system sometimes led to great windfalls. We found that we could charge for cargo that we took returning from trips for the government. When local officials came to request us to take their sisters, brothers, aunts, and uncles, or other adoptive family members, we could simply charge them the fare and let them go. If the official had tried to make trouble for us in the past, I made sure to ask for several times the official price. He usually agreed because the people he was introducing as his relatives were no doubt paying him much more than we were asking. People who did not have an official escort were asked to pay the official price for a ticket, which was very low.

We never asked the volunteers who were helping the refugees or bona fide displaced persons to pay for transportation. The passengers we collected from were mostly members of a new kind of airborne merchant class who travelled around the country buying moderate amounts of sugar, meat, fish and fruit to sell in the capital. Their profits were considerably more than the air fares. This was an extremely inefficient way to supply Phnom Penh, but nobody made any effort to discourage it.

The passengers that the province authorities insisted that we carry from Krakor and Kompong Chhnang to Phnom Penh had been paying the military policemen at the airport for their tickets. Although the shippers were entitled to this money, they were afraid to ask for it. We weren't afraid to ask, and we enjoyed seeing the MPs squirm when they had to hand over the large wads of paper money to us. It was enlightening to see exactly how the airport MPs were able to afford new cars and motorcycles on their soldier's pay.

While our cargo was being unloaded at Kompong Thom or Svay Rieng, the military policeman on duty could often assemble a full load of passengers for us at our request. At these fields, the police did not do this as a matter of routine, so we let them keep the price of two or three tickets for their trouble. Takeo was a particularly good source of passengers, and we seldom had company cargo to carry from there. As it turned out, most of the money we were collecting under the new system was earned by finding passengers and cargo to carry when we otherwise would have flown empty.

One improvement introduced into the new contracts was a 20 minute limit placed on our waiting time for cargo delivery. One particularly obnoxious overload specialist had chartered TFB for trips to Kompong Chhnang. One day his agent in Phnom Penh, who had misunderstood his instructions, began demanding vehemently that we fly his cargo before making a previously scheduled trip to Krakor. His threats and demands were so animated that our station manager changed the schedule to appease him.

When we landed at Kompong Chhnang, there was no cargo truck waiting. Obviously, we were expected later, as originally scheduled. The agent, who had accompanied us from Phnom Penh, told us to wait and rushed to town. He returned to tell us that the cargo would be delivered to the airport in five minutes. His look of panic and desperation told us that he was lying, as usual. I knew that he planned to stall us for a few hours while his partners looked for something to ship. We waited the allotted 20 minutes plus an extra five, but there was no sign of a truck on the road from town.

Cargo belonging to other shippers was waiting, but they were the enemies of our shipping agents, so an exchange was out of the question. During the delay, I had discreetly told the military policeman that I expected no cargo to arrive and would be willing to take any passengers he could find. They filled every seat, and the money went into our fund.

The shipper went to the Tri-9 office the next day and asked John Yim for the money we had collected. He whined that he had lost money, and the passenger fares were needed to cut his losses. Of course, it was illegal for him to send passengers, so he had no legal right to claim the fares.

When John Yim told us of his request, we had a good laugh. That shipper had always been the champion time waster, delaying us on numerous occasions while trying to cheat on the weight or sneak extra cargo on board. He was the same one who had caused me trouble while I was working for SEAAT. He had finally cheated himself and was crying "foul."

After being refused the passenger fares, he reduced his request from all of the money to some of it. He never received anything from our fund, but he made a final request for a discount on the charter price. I never learned whether he got it or not.

Chapter 23

The Twin-Beeches were out of business, but there was still business to be done at Takeo. Tri-9 decided to get in on this business with the DC-3. I had had plenty of experience landing the Twin-Beech there, so why not TFB? Actually, I felt more confident landing a DC-3 on the short strip than I did landing the old AT-11 there. The only thing that made me uneasy was the weak brakes on TFB.

John Yim decided not to fully load the aircraft because the runway was too short. Our inaugural DC-3 flight was scheduled for June 25. After landing, the weak brakes caused no problems at all. The wheels sank into the sand, and the DC-3 came to a quick stop with hardly any need for braking. The shipper left for town to find the cargo, and the usual gawking mob of rural people closed in around the airplane. Each person seemed compelled to feel the fabric that covered the elevators. Curious fingers and sharp sticks punctured it in several places.

The process of ripping the fabric apart had become a sport at many of the fields where we landed, but nowhere was it so intensively practiced as at Takeo. Where holes in the fabric had been patched, the people took fiendish delight in peeling the patches off to see what was underneath.

At most of the stops, people standing under the wings liked to reach up and grab the ailerons. They sometimes shook them, which caused the control yoke in the cockpit to suddenly move. It was becoming dangerous to sit in the pilot's seat while the aircraft was parked. The wheel would suddenly spin, whacking a hand or catching an arm. Meanwhile, the hands pulling the cloth control surfaces outside were warping and blackening them.

In other Southeast Asian countries, people would have thought twice about making destructive modifications on someone else's aircraft. The Khmers seemed to take it for granted that the aircraft was parked at the airport to provide shade and give them something to play with. The child-like mentality they displayed made me very pessimistic about their chances in war against their highly intelligent neighbors.

Countermeasures had to be devised against the thoughtless mishandling of the aircraft. When outside, I constantly told the people that the controls were made of cloth and might tear if touched. The people always complied with my requests, but new people were constantly arriving who had not yet been told. It got very tiresome repeating my explanation continuously while the MPs assigned to guard the parking ramp just stood under the wings.

When I sat in the cockpit, I had a better way of making my point. If someone was fingering the ailerons, the control wheel moved. I watched for this telltale sign, then suddenly swung the control wheel full travel in each direction. From my window, I would observe the results. When the aileron moved upward, it was jerked out of the hands of the heedless manipulator. A movement the other way, if well timed, caused the trailing edge of the aileron to hit the head of the culprit. The offender was usually stunned when the control in his hand moved, as if by itself. Often he would grab it again, as if manifesting the age-old human desire to control a suddenly animate natural force. In this case, I would repeat the maneuver. Several aircraft vandals were hit on the head twice before they could figure out what was happening. The other bystanders would roar with laughter.

Word of the game got around fast, and no one wanted to be the goat. The system worked at all the airports where I encountered the problem, and soon the frequency of control surface snatching markedly decreased. Unfortunately, at Kompong Chhnang, one of the shipper's helpers came up with the idea of luring unsuspecting victims under the ailerons, then signalling me to smash them on the head. This tended to defeat my purpose by once again increasing the number of people fooling around with the controls.

Although I suspected that I might damage the control surfaces myself by slapping people with them, I never found any tears or cracks where the ailerons had hit a head. On the other hand, the holes made by fingers were numerous, and there was even a set of initials carved in the dope coating on the left elevator. Deliberate damage was obviously more of a threat than accidental damage I might do myself, and my method did keep people away from the parts of the aircraft that they could easily damage.

After we had shown that DC-3s could operate there, other companies began to land regularly at Takeo. Soon, a barbed wire fence was constructed around the parking ramp to keep the mob away. The money-making operation quickly ended, however, when the government rice shippers found out that DC-3s were operating there at their own volition. The officials had previously assumed that the 1800 feet of runway was too short for the DC-3, but now Takeo was suddenly added to the list of destinations for government rice. For us, this was a bad trip. The aircraft had to be loaded and unloaded just to log a total of 40 to 45 minutes for the round trip, for which the company could collect from the government only with great difficulty.

My personal relations with the Khmer military authorities at Takeo started off very poorly. Some of my annoyance stemmed from their lack of ability to provide security for the airport. Takeo had been the scene of heavy fighting, and the communists had only recently been driven away from the town. Bill told of being shot at on the ramp while his Twin-Beech was being loaded. He said that every two or three minutes, a shot would whiz by. He surmised that the sniper was sitting in a tree several miles away lobbing shots in the direction of the aircraft.

On our third trip there with the DC-3, we took off to the southwest. The landscape beneath us looked like a photo of the moon, it was so pocked with bomb craters and shell holes. As we made a turn over the remains of the railroad lines about 300 feet above the ground, I heard a volley of AK-47 fire. Out of the corner of my eye, I saw something fly through the back of the aircraft. I turned the aircraft sharply in a turn, pulling two to three Gs, and the sound of the firing faded away. As we circled over the city, I borrowed Tony's .38 caliber revolver. He had seen the men firing at us from the edge of a large bomb crater. We were already at 3000 feet as I flew back over the spot: high enough to be safe from anything but a wildly lucky shot. I emptied the revolver at the spot from which we had been shot at, aiming behind the target to allow for the speed of the aircraft. My chances of hitting one of the culprits was perhaps one in a million, but I was sure that they could hear some of my shots hitting near them. This was the only occasion I returned ground fire, and I think it was the right thing to do under the circumstances.

It was never clear whether the shots were fired by communist troops close to the airport or government soldiers shooting for sport. Bursts of fire sometimes were directed upward from "friendly" outposts at approaching or departing aircraft. I had seen this myself at Kompong Cham. At Takeo, the fire had been directed at us less than half a mile from the end of the runway, and firing from uncamouflaged positions in the open was not a usual practice of the communist units. Government soldiers often carried AK-47s, so the weapons used gave no clue to the identity of the culprits.

Other American civilian pilots had returned ground fire and were criticized for it. I disagree with critics who think that shooting back will encourage the enemy to take revenge and fire more. To my knowledge, we were never again fired on at Takeo, and no fire was ever again reported by the crews of any other commercial aircraft.

At Phnom Penh, we assessed the damage. One bullet had entered near the centerline of the fuselage only two feet from the spot where the steward had been standing. It tore a large splinter from the wooden floor and grazed the scale, knocking off some of the weights. It then exited through the ceiling. It was the flying splinter of wood that I had seen out of the corner of my eye.

Early in the morning a few days later, we waited on the ramp at Takeo for someone to unload our cargo of rice. One of the many MPs standing around told me that the workmen had to be brought from town in a bus. My next question was why the soldiers couldn't unload the cargo. The MP was stunned. He laughed at the idea of soldiers doing work. Although all enlisted men, the soldiers apparently thought that they had achieved some status which made physical labor a disgrace far beneath their dignity.

I grabbed some of the rice bags and started throwing them off the aircraft. The soldiers realized that they would have to be lifted from the ground into the truck, so they decided to back the truck to the cargo door. First the MP in charge, then some of the other soldiers joined me in throwing rice bags into the truck. In less than five minutes, we were unloaded and ready to go. As we took off, we could still see no sign of a bus with the laborers from town. After the precedent had been set, the soldiers never hesitated to unload TFB themselves if no workmen were at the airfield. In this way, our relations with the Army began to improve.

A different kind of problem was brought to Takeo by the Khmer Air Force. The frequency of their trips to the short field began increasing. The pilots claimed that the parking ramp was too soft for their C-123s, so they simply stopped to load at the end of the runway. If we landed over the very high vertical stabilizer of the C-123, we would have only the last, downhill third of the runway remaining after touchdown. During the southwest monsoon, landing toward them meant landing with a strong tailwind.

After landing, the aircrews began a long process of rounding up commercial cargo from town and finding passengers for Phnom Penh. Their pace was leisurely, and at least half the day went by before they were ready to go again. A huge crowd gathered, and the festive air of a county fair prevailed among the visitors.

The whole scene infuriated me. First of all, the cargo and passengers should have been carried by the commercial companies. Second, the government rice and ammunition should have been carried by the C-123s, which could have carried much more than the DC-3s and could have quickly supplied all of the necessary rice. Third, the C-123s could have backed onto the ramp rather than block the extremely short runway. If necessary, the ramp should have been reinforced before the C-123s began their operations. Finally, their ground time should have been kept to a minimum, and the festive crowd should have been kept far from the airport. The idle bystanders were so ignorant of operational hazards that they did not even get out of the way of landing aircraft. The C-123 has a rear ramp that facilitates much faster loading than does the side cargo door of the DC-3. Nevertheless, we could unload our rice and take on a full load of cargo in about 15 minutes, while the Air Force took many hours to do the same thing.

The organization of the airlift by the Khmers was so poor that large numbers of DC-3s were sent to Takeo with rice while the runway was fully blocked by the C-123. On one occasion, TFB and two DC-3s from other companies were sent there with rice. When we arrived, the C-123 was parked at the end of the runway. Landing toward it meant landing with a tailwind of about 10 knots. Cary landed his Khemera Air Transport aircraft first. As we watched from overhead, he approached into the wind on the right side of the military transport. The onlookers scattered like ants from a smashed nest as he touched down on the commercial ramp about 40 feet from the runway. He angled sharply toward the center line, getting the aircraft on the landing strip just before reaching the sand dunes beyond the end of the ramp. He taxied back and parked on the ramp, blocking his route of approach for the next aircraft. The pilot of the second DC-3 then duplicated the landing I had made in the Twin-Beech on the left side of the transport, making the mob of onlookers run for their lives in the opposite direction. These landings revealed new possibilities for aviation, making the airplane an instrument for the training of broken-field runners. The pilot swept past the obstacle and landed on the narrow runway, heading about 30° from the path he wanted to follow. He whipped the machine around just in time to keep from going off the side. Both landings were very impressive when viewed from overhead, particularly because of the thick clouds of sand that formed in their wakes. The wind carried the small particles toward the military aircraft, and they rained down on the festive throng.

I elected to land with a tailwind. Although less impressive to view, my landing required my best short-field technique. I had to acccurately estimate my ground speed as I passed over the tall palm trees on the short final approach. I then let TFB sink rapidly into the hollow just beyond the runway and rounded out in a slight climb to match the steep upslope of the first third of the runway. I touched down just on the end but with considerable ground speed because of the tail wind. It required full brakes all the way to the ramp, even with the help of the soft sand. We stopped well short of the military aircraft, but I could smell hot brakes as we parked. The crew of the C-123 just stood idly watching, seemingly unaware of the supreme hazard to aviation that they represented.

I casually walked over to the military crew and asked one of the pilots whether they would be able to park on the ramp. He answered that the ramp was only for civilian aircraft but that the government would soon build a military ramp on the other side of the runway. Sure enough, a few weeks later, a ramp was built on the other side, but the C-123s continued to park on the end of the runway because the crews claimed that the ramp was too small.

The Air Force did business under enviable conditions with free fuel and maintenance courtesy of the American taxpayer. Tony returned from home leave in Thailand with some stories from his Thai mechanic friends who were performing major maintenance on Khmer Air Force aircraft under a United States contract. They said that the accumulation of sugar under the fuselage floor was one of the biggest problems encountered during the overhauls. It caked on the metal and became rock hard. Even the Khmer Huey helicopters were full of the sticky remains of their black-market sugar cargoes.

Sugar, of course, was one of the most lucrative items for transport to Phnom Penh and for resale. On several occasions, we had seen T-28s take off from Kompong Chhnang with so many bags of sugar in the cockpits that the pilots' heads were barely visible.

After their commercial activities, the military crews had little time to support the war effort.

Chapter 24

Buon, who had been our best steward, was promoted to chief steward for Tri-9 after the new companies began operations. Narong, who was about 40 years old and had a large family, replaced him aboard TFB. Su Koun, the son of a Khmer colonel, was assigned to 422.

Narong learned very quickly to display the necessary toughness to handle the overbearing shippers and corrupt officials, who were always looking for "easy money" at someone else's expense. All the stewards were learning English, but their vocabularies were still limited, and we could communicate better in Khmer. I noted that I often had one of the only crews in the country that was one step ahead of our customers linguistically. The shippers usually spoke Tai Chou, a southern Chinese dialect, in order to keep their conversations private. However, two of my copilots, Tony Pradith and Joe Chan, understood Tai Chou and kept me informed of the latest expletives that the shippers were directing against me. We could keep our own conversations private by conversing either in English or Thai. Thai was Tony's native language, so we generally used Thai for our conversations. Joe was from Singapore, but carried a Thai passport. Interestingly, he could hardly speak Thai at all, and we conversed in English. The stewards and I could understand Khmer, which the workmen and most of the shippers were also able to speak. A few of the Chinese shippers could speak little Khmer however. The result was that we knew everything the shippers said regardless of the language they used, while we were able to communicate with each other in languages the shippers could not understand. The shippers learned this quickly, and their annoyance was so obvious that we often had to laugh about it.

John Yim had instructed all the Tri-9 pilots to keep a low profile. If the shippers were annoyed about something, at least the complaints would not be directed against the pilots. We still had to keep our eyes on the weighing, but the customers were supposed to haggle with the stewards and not with us.

Narong had learned to be a very good steward, and our loading times were becoming quite short. Unfortunately, some of our new customers at

Koh Kong did not care for the accuracy in weighing that we insisted upon. They became particularly annoyed because we refused to accept several extra crates of eggs after we were already fully loaded. Because the copilot and I had taken no part in checking the weights and had passed our refusal to take the overload through Narong, they blamed him.

After our trip to Koh Kong on June 25, the charterer went to John Yim to accuse Narong of trying to extort money in exchange for accepting overweight cargo. When we saw John Yim at the office in the evening, he told us that Narong had been fired. I was incredulous that the charges of the shippers had been accepted at face value. I told John Yim that I could detect overweights as small as 100 kilos by watching the climb performance of TFB, so it would have been impossible for Narong to sneak anything on without my knowledge. The shippers obviously wanted to get rid of Narong because he was doing his job too well.

John Yim was worried about losing business. I assured him that the shippers had no choice but to do business with him if they wanted to make money. I added that plane crashes would soon eliminate the companies that took huge overloads, and much competition would be eliminated. This prophecy was already in the process of coming true.

Hiring and firing were not my duties, so I could only express an opinion. The next day Su Koun was our steward. He tried hard, but he was not yet 20 years old. The shippers often tried to bully him, and a sheltered life in a well-to-do family did not prepare him for the variety of tricks in the shippers' repertory. The copilot and I always had to keep a close watch on the loading.

On his first day with us, Su Koun failed to see that the foreman of the loading crew at Krakor had his foot under the scale platform and was pushing it upwards from underneath with his toes each time something was weighed. I saw it from outside of the aircraft and swung myself up through the door in a way that I could land hard on the offending foot. I shoved the foreman out of the airplane and onto his truck, telling the shipper that in the future that man would be barred from the aircraft. I reacted strongly to tactics which could be interpreted as attempted murder in light of all the plane crashes that had been occurring due to improper loading.

Su Koun added 100 kilos to the weight to make up for what might have already been sneaked aboard. The shipper accepted this fine with the usual protestations of innocence. He loudly berated his foreman, although I was sure he himself had devised this method of cheating.

On June 27 Phil was scheduled to fly as my copilot. The Convair 240 he was supposed to be piloting was still out of order, and he had not flown for a long time. He was naturally becoming restless and talking about taking a job with Royal Air Lao.

After a flight to Kompong Cham for the government, we took off for

Koh Kong. The shipper was waiting for us at the new airport. I noticed that it was the same overload artist who had insisted that Narong be fired. I decided to let Su Koun handle everything and weigh the cargo at Phnom Penh if it seemed too heavy. That was exactly the procedure the Tri-9 management was recommending. During the loading, I sat in the cockpit and read.

The shipper had some passengers, including children, to send with the cargo. He argued that children should be considered to weigh less than half an adult's weight. However, most of the youngsters carried baggage, and some were as old as 16, so I insisted that two children should equal one adult in weight unless he wanted to put them on the scale. He realized that weighing the passengers would be to his disadvantage, so he made the calculations the way I wanted them, at least on paper.

His next request was for me to take 200 kilos more than the contract weight for the legal freight price. I insisted in receiving 150 percent of the official rate. Phil was shocked that I would agree to take so much, but I told him not to worry. I knew that the shipper would balk at the price. Finally, the shipper did agree to pay the price I asked for 100 kilos of eggs that might spoil if they didn't go.

Before the passengers boarded, I noticed the tires looked flatter than they should have. This meant the shipper had cheated on the weight. Normally, I would have thrown some cargo off, but I wanted to get the proof against the shipper for John Yim. As we prepared for take-off, I told Su Koun that no cargo was to be released at Phnom Penh until it was weighed.

With the 10 passengers, including children, who were supposed to be flying with us, I estimated our overload to total 300 to 400 kilos. While the passengers were boarding, however, I noticed the shipper loading three large crates of eggs. I knew from experience that these crates weighed almost 100 kilos each. I told Su Koun to kick two of them off. Some arguing ensued, and the shipper exhorted me to honor our agreement. Of course, I insisted that the two be taken off because he was trying to put on about three times as much weight as we had agreed upon. The shipper hotly denied that they were so heavy, but he took them off with a great show of indignation and threats to talk to John Yim.

Phil and I were already sitting in the cockpit when the passengers were loaded. I then made the big mistake of closing the cockpit door behind us, making it impossible to see how many passengers were getting on. I told Phil to monitor the take-off acceleration very carefully because the load was surely far heavier than the shipper claimed.

Our take-off and climb performances were very sluggish, so I reminded Su Koun to keep the cargo on board until the scales were available. I contemplated landing again and throwing off some cargo, but then the evidence for our management would have been gone.

Our rate of climb was much slower than normal but acceptable at normal climb power. We made a wide, shallow turn over the estuary and across the peninsula, then swung around lazily toward the towering mountains that stretched beneath our route to Phnom Penh.

The Elephant Mountains are one of the largest ranges in a predominantly flat country. Almost completely uninhabited, they are covered by a dense, lush jungle. They are beautiful to look at from the air, especially when they are covered by rain clouds interspersed with clear, sunny areas. Viewing the scenic landscape made flights to and from Koh Kong very pleasurable. There were tall cliffs with waterfalls, deep ravines cut by streams, and misty mountain peaks almost reaching our altitude. These features of Southeast Asia were rarely seen by anyone except the cockpit crews of the reciprocating-engine aircraft that are forced to operate among or below the clouds.

After we passed the edges of a few light afternoon rain storms on the seaward side of the range, the air became absolutely clear. The sky ahead was punctuated with many large isolated cumulus clouds in the process of condensing rainfall for later in the day, but the flight path ahead was unimpeded.

We struggled slowly to altitude and finally leveled off at 7000 feet. The aircraft cruised more slowly than usual, a sign that we were indeed very heavy.

After only five minutes or so at cruise, we were suddenly aware of a problem. The now familiar smell of hot oil filled the cockpit. I immediately looked out at the left engine. As I expected, a wisp of white smoke was trailing from beneath the cowling. Phil stretched over to look, and we knew that we were in for some trouble. As I watched, the wisp became a thick white trail. My decision was immediate. I pushed the feather button and pulled the mixture control to cut-off. I watched the propeller slow quickly to a stop. After completing the checklist items, I told Phil my plans.

Even if we could not hold our altitude, the situation was not too bad. We surely did not have enough oil to run the engine all the way to Phnom Penh, but we had enough to restart it and run it for a while in case of a real emergency. I instructed Su Koun to move all the passengers far away from the cargo door and position the cargo so that it could quickly be jettisoned, if necessary. We ran through the checklist restart procedure up to the point where the engine is motorized by the starter. With these precautions completed, we could lighten the aircraft or restart the engine in minimum time. We were not yet halfway to Phnom Penh, but it would have been foolish to turn back. We had already cleared the highest mountains on the route, and the terrain elevation ahead was gradually decreasing. We had a tail wind, and maintenance awaited us at home.

After the engine was shut down, our airspeed had died off rapidly. As it reached 80 knots, I advanced the power on the right engine from climb to METO. Although we could maintain altitude and slightly more than 80 knots at that power setting, I decided against operating the good engine at high power and low airspeed. TFB did not have adjustable cowl flaps, and the cooling airflow at 80 knots might not have been satisfactory. I decided to slowly sacrifice altitude for a little extra airspeed and better cooling of the good engine.

As an aircraft descends, the air becomes denser, allowing more efficient engine operation, better propeller efficiency, and more lift from the airfoils. We couldn't maintain 7000 feet at climb power, but maybe we could maintain 3000 feet.

We were still over the mountains, and some of them were of considerable height, their peaks rising above us as we descended. Fortunately, we could maintain visual flight. If there had been thunderstorms ahead of us, we would have been in real trouble.

Su Koun was busy preparing the cargo for jettison. The passengers had moved forward, and the cargo was being pushed rearward toward the door. Getting weight to the rear also helps get more lift efficiency. I glanced back through the cockpit door that Su Koun had forgotten to close and was horrified by what I saw. Instead of the ten passengers on the manifest, a huge multitude of people were sitting all over the cargo. Most of them were children. I had been a little too careless in letting Su Koun handle everything. The overload was obviously much more than I anticipated, and it consisted mainly of people.

Several companies were noted for overloading their aircraft with passengers. Pilots had compared the people disembarking from their DC-3s to the crowds leaving the stadium after the weekend football game. I called Su Koun to the cockpit to ask him how many people had gotten on. He just shrugged and said that he had forgotten to count them. I told him not to do anything else with the cargo since I knew I might have to throw it out myself. Obviously, if Su Koun did the job, either he or some of the passengers would join the cargo on the long trip down. Losing stewards while dropping cargo had been the common experience of most companies that operated in Southeast Asia for a while. Some pilots have also been lost while closing partly opened doors.

Phil was prepared to take over the controls while I dumped the eggs, but there was a complication. The pins in the cargo door hinges had never been too secure, and several days earlier, a truck at Kompong Chhnang had backed into the door during loading operations. The hinges were bent, making the fit of the pins even worse. To eliminate the danger of the pins slipping out and the door flying open in the air, an adjustable tie-down strap had been rigged from the handle of the door insert to a tie-down ring. If the insert was removed to dump cargo, the pins might slip out of the locks, and we would be flying with an open door. I had heard too many stories about DC-3s operating without doors in China during World War II, and about how they lost two or three passengers on almost every flight. I decided it would be preferable to restart the engine if things got worse.

We were still over the mountains and losing altitude at a worrisome rate. I kept the airspeed between 85 and 95 knots to insure proper engine cooling. If not overheated or run at excessive power settings, there is no more chance of one engine on a twin failing than there is of the engine on a single-engine aircraft quitting. Nevertheless, after one engine on a twin has failed, pilots are generally more concerned about the operation of the other than they would have been if they had only had one to begin with.

To slow my rate of descent, I advanced the prop control 100 RPM and the throttle a few inches above climb power. We normally held no more than 36 inches of manifold pressure to climb, but we were holding between 37 and 38 inches. This considerably slowed our rate of descent. At METO power, we would have been holding 42.5 inches.

On this very long glide to Phnom Penh, we called the tower and informed the controllers of our problems. As we descended, we had to retard the throttle regularly. The manifold pressure increases as the air becomes denser at lower altitude. As we passed through 5000 feet, the end of the mountain range came into view. Beyond the mountains was the great plain of the lower Mekong Valley. Far off to our right sparkled the bay of Kompong Som. Normally a good emergency airport, Kompong Som was not available to us at this time because of heavy fighting nearby.

The air over the mountains had been calm. As we began passing over the cultivated fields on the foothills, we were bumped by strong thermal currents. The children began crying in unison. They were already aware of the engine failure and frightened by the movement of the cargo. Now they were sure the end had come. The adults were apprehensive, and the rough air brought on an epidemic of air sickness. We closed our door to keep out the strong smell of vomit.

The thermals were actually a great blessing. I had hoped that they would be strong, and on that hot sunny day, they were. Many pilots do not realize how strong these currents can be. I had flown gliders long enough to pass my test for a license and had discovered that even a rather heavy training glider can stay up all day using only the energy obtained from these upward currents of air.

To minimize altitude loss, I had to be extremely light on the controls. The least deflection of the control surfaces caused the vertical velocity indicator to register a distinct increase in our rate of descent. I tried to let the aircraft fly itself, using only gentle pressure to coax it along the flight path. Any use of the rudders caused particularly large increases in our rate of descent.

As we dropped below the level of the cloud bases at about 3500 feet, I began to steer the aircraft under every cumulus cloud near our route. Under each one, there was a strong thermal, and some particularly strong ones caused the vertical velocity indicator to momentarily register climbs as much as 500 feet per minute. On two or three occasions, we gained almost 100 feet without losing any airspeed.

As we left the mountains behind us, I could see the runway under construction at Kompong Speu. With two engines running, this field would have been 15 minutes flying time from Phnom Penh. This airport being built would be a monument to the ineffectiveness of the Khmer Army since it showed their inability to keep the road open. To require aircraft to fly cargo and passengers such a short distance along one of the nation's major highways was a disgrace.

Seeing the new airfield was a very encouraging sign of our progress. After reaching about 3500 feet a long way from Phnom Penh, our descent had become negligible. As the city came into view in the distance, I began a slow descent to gain some airspeed. We were cleared for a straight in approach.

As we neared the field, the crying in the cabin increased in intensity. If we restarted the left engine, our oil would now last to the field. We had plenty of altitude, however, so it did not seem necessary.

We watched the distant runway come closer and closer. I planned to land past the newly extended part of the runway in order to have enough momentum to roll into the parking area. As we approached the end of the runway, I called for the landing gear. We were already close enough to glide in. In fact, we were a little too high.

Cutting the power to 21 inches and adjusting the RPM, I pointed the nose down to gain airspeed. Over the end of the runway, I called for full flaps to lose altitude faster. The extra altitude had been my safety margin, but in this case, too much safety margin is as dangerous as too little. Many people have overshot runways when making forced or single engine landings.

The DC-3 descends quite fast with full flaps, and the altitude I had been nursing so long was quickly lost. We rounded out, and I made the best single engine touchdown of the six I had made during the past 37 days. When Phil laughed and commented how proficient I was in single engine landings, I said that it was just the result of all my recent practice.

We were rolling with plenty of speed, so I was able to make it all the way to the parking ramp and part of the way into a parking place. Adding power on the right engine would have made the aircraft turn the wrong way, so I had to shut the engine down and let the ground crew shove it into the correct position.

The passengers were wiping their tears and cleaning up their belongings.

DC-3 engine maintenance on the parking ramp at Pochentong Airport (photo courtesy of Bill Ernst).

I thought that it might have taught the ones who had sneaked aboard a lesson. I stopped the shipper's truck from backing up to the aircraft. Everything had to be weighed.

Phil told me he had had enough. He returned to the Tri-9 office and resigned. Then he booked a seat on the next available flight back to Laos.

The station manager for Golden Eagle Airlines found Tony at the airport and recruited him for the next flight.

We had blown two oil lines, but this time I was assured that the spare parts from the Lao Air Force had been discarded, and new lines would replace the defective ones. We never again blew an oil line, and that flight turned out to be my last single engine landing in the Khmer Republic.

The passengers were counted, and their weight was determined. There were 44 in all. The cargo alone almost reached the maximum allowable load. We had carried over 4400 kilos, more than 800 kilos over the legal weight for the DC-3. To my knowledge, that was the most weight I had ever carried in a DC-3, and it had to be that trip on which we lost an engine!

Many skeptics have disparaged the performance of the DC-3. Pilots who have never flown one sometimes doubt what the old "gooney bird" can do. Three years earlier, we had tested the performance of a DC-3 at full gross weight in Laos, simulating single engine operation. The maximum gross weight was considerably heavier than that approved by the Federal Aviation Administration because, under the Lao rules, the weights for the C-47 established by the United States Army Air Force were in force. At 6000 feet above sea level, we could turn in either direction without altitude loss using climb power on the good engine. The performance of TFB with the extreme overload that day left me with an even greater respect for the designers who produced the DC-3 during the Great Depression. One remarkable phenomenon for which I have no explanation was our high fuel consumption for only about 45 minutes flying time at only slightly more than climb power.

We made one more trip to Krakor that day. Tony and I landed, and this time we supervised the loading ourselves. We both knew the shipper and experienced no problems with him. As we started our take-off that late afternoon, a herd of cows and water buffaloes decided to cross the runway. I aborted the take-off and taxied back. The livestock at Krakor were becoming an irritating problem. They had the habit of suddenly running out on the runway from behind clumps of low bushes on the side. After the herd had moved far enough down the runway, we took off. We broke ground and climbed a few feet, then I leveled off. I wanted to see what the cattle would do when approached by an aircraft. Exactly as expected, they ran from the approaching machine, right down the middle of the runway. I was sure that sooner or later someone would hit one.

Back at the offices, I presented the facts. It was plain that Narong had been fired unjustly on the word of a lying crook. I had kept out of the weighing arguments according to instructions from the company, and the result was disastrous. It was obvious that we could not trust the shippers, something I had been saying all along.

When the shippers arrived, the first thing John Yim said was, "Thank you! I asked you to come here so I could thank you. Thank you for putting only 1000 kilos overload on. If you had put a few hundred more on, we wouldn't have an airplane anymore."

They all went into his office. I never saw those shippers again, although their contract for ten trips was still not nearly fulfilled. On subsequent trips to Koh Kong, we dealt with another shipper, although the cargo was the same type. I assumed that Tri-9 fined the culprit at least the price of one trip.

Chapter 25

The incredible crowding of the parked aircraft on the parking ramp at Pochentong Airport precluded taxiing at more than a minimum speed. Checking the brakes satisfactorily was therefore out of the question unless special arrangements were made for a high speed taxi check. The brakes on TFB had been functioning fairly well for a while, so I had no special reason to check them on July 4.

The day before, a DC-3 belonging to Sorya (Khmer for "sunrise") Airlines had landed short at Kompong Cham. The pilot, Captain Chang, was famous for "acrobatic landings." He liked to make low, steep turns to final approach, rolling out and touching down simultaneously. At Kompong Cham, the northern end of the runway is at the edge of a steep cliff. As Captain Chang rolled out of his turn, he saw to his dismay that the aircraft was below the runway. He tried to climb, but the right main wheel hit the edge of the drop-off. The plane skidded sideways across the runway, turning almost 270°, and came to a stop in the grass several feet from the edge of the concrete. A deep gash had been cut in the runway by the stump of the landing gear. No one was hurt, but Sorya Airlines' only aircraft was irreparably damaged, putting them out of business.

The next day Tony and I surveyed the damage from the air as we approached for our landing. The assorted aircraft parts strewn on the northern end of the runway induced me to land from the opposite direction. The wind was about 110° to my flight path, so we had a slight tail wind.

Luckily, Kompong Cham had a good, wide runway. We had flown a very tight traffic pattern to avoid the ground fire reported from the vicinity of the field. We touched down a little long, but we had so much runway left that I eased the tail wheel down before applying the brakes to take full advantage of aerodynamic braking. As we reached the taxiway to the parking ramp, I depressed the brake pedals. The sensation was the same as braking an automobile on ice. I held the pedals down and heard the hydraulic fluid hissing through the lines, but the aircraft just slid forward at the same speed.

I yelled to Tony, "No brakes!"

Tony was a sharp copilot. He knew what had happened at Svay Rieng,

180

An aerial view of the overcrowded parking ramp at Pochentong Airport, Phnom Penh, during the height of the airlift in 1974 (photo by Bill Ernst, courtesy of Charley Pennington).

and he jumped right on his brake pedals. With both of us on the brakes, there was still no appreciable rate of deceleration.

To take advantage of the wide runway, I began using the rudder and whatever brakes I had to make S-turns back and forth. The side-loads on the wheels during the turns provided some braking action but I could not turn as sharply as I would have liked. We had been slowed to a fast taxi speed by the aerodynamic braking, and at that speed, the rudders were not very effective. I could have made a ground loop with power, but I kept this maneuver as a last resort. As we reached the Sorya wreckage, we were already at a very slow taxi speed. We would stop in time.

I headed the aircraft toward the left side of the runway. It was rolling very slowly, and the brakes were very slightly effective at the speed. I held both brakes as hard as I could and just let it roll. We stopped about six feet from the edge of the concrete. If we had gone off, the grass would have stopped us. About 50 feet farther down to our right was the end of the runway. Beyond that was the steep downslope that had removed the landing gear of the Sorya DC-3. In any case, I felt thankful that Kompong Cham was not some highway runway.

Looking through the brake adjustment windows that I had opened with the steward's screwdriver, I could see that the shoes had been adjusted at an extremely crooked angle again. There was less than a square inch of braking surface on each of the eight brake linings. I adjusted them all myself. The passengers helped to push the aircraft backwards to give me room to turn around. Then we all got in and taxied back to the parking ramp.

Our next scheduled destination was Kompong Chhnang, but I decided to return to Phnom Penh so that the mechanics could check the shoes for damage and adjust the brakes as well as possible, considering that the linings did not fit the drums. The chief pilot suggested that since my adjustments were good, I should have gone on to Kompong Chhnang, but I doubted whether the time lost for a little extra security would cause us to miss a scheduled trip.

At Kompong Chhnang, we encountered a garrulous shipper who complained loudly about our refusal to take a huge overload at less than the normal cargo price. He shouted that the other companies were taking overloads all the time. He ranted and raved in Tae Chou to Tony and in broken Khmer to me, curtly informing us that he would look for another airline to do business with after his contract with Tri-9 was finished.

I answered him calmly, suggesting that he hold his cargo for Sorya Airlines. They would gladly carry more than 4000 kilos for him at a very low rate. Sorya had been known to take large overloads, and word of its mishap had not yet reached Kompong Chhnang. The shipper started to listen with genuine interest. Tony had overheard my recommendation to the shipper, and was laughing uproariously in the back of the aircraft. As soon as he was able to keep a straight face again, he jumped out of the aircraft and started explaining about Sorya's liberal overweight policy to the spellbound shipper, who walked off loudly vowing to his friends that he would try to get a contract with Sorya. Tony shouted after him, "Just keep your cargo here and wait, Sorya will be here soon and take it."

John Yim's worry about losing shippers to other companies turned out to be ill-founded. As I had expected, the ranks of the competitors were rapidly thinning. Many customers who had left Tri-9 in the hopes of shipping heavier cargoes with other companies were beating on the office door, pleading for us to take the cargoes stranded by the collapse of our competitors.

Besides the wreck of Sorya, one Samakki Peanich, two Khmer Airlines, one Khmer Hansa, one Cambodia Air International, and two Cambodia Air Commercial DC-3s were out of the flying business. All but two of these had been eliminated by crashes, and the DC-3 population was rapidly declining.

The most bizarre of the crashes had involved Cambodia Air Commercial. A French captain was en route from Battambang to Phnom Penh when the throttle cable to one of the engines disengaged. Vibration caused the throttle to slowly close. As the power agonizingly bled off, the captain compensated by advancing the throttle on the "good" engine. Unfortunately, that engine was not as good as it was supposed to be. In fact, so much time had been logged on it that it was practically a piece of junk. After a short time at a high power setting, it failed. The pilot had almost reached Phnom Penh when he suddenly found himself in command of an overweight glider. He made a very nice forced landing in a rice field, and no one was hurt. On board as cargo was a Honda motorcycle, which he calmly mounted to finish his trip to Pochentong Airport.

The other Cambodia Air Commercial DC-3 was one of the two not eliminated by a crash. It made it to Vientiane for its airworthiness inspection, after which it was grounded on the spot. The fish water and pig manure had caused so much corrosion that it was no longer airworthy. The mechanics who inspected it were astounded that the wings hadn't fallen off already.

One aircraft belonging to Samakki Peanich Airlines blew a very low time engine. The aircraft had been imported from Taiwan with brand new engines and a beautiful interior. It was grounded for a long time before a replacement engine could be found. The pilot, Captain Shu, was a very agreeable type of person who flew his aircraft competently. His was one of the few new companies that did not deserve to be out of business.

Some unusual aircraft models were also showing up in the country. Several new DC-4s, two C-46s, and a Lockheed LodeStar arrived, along with a Viscount that had been the mainstay of Lao Airlines. Royal Air Lao had recently gone back into business, and the Lao government decided that this company should take over all the international routes from Lao Airlines. The fact that the Lao prime minister's son, Prince Panya, was the new manager of Royal Air Lao may have had some bearing on the decision.

This Viscount, which had been used on the Vientiane–Hong Kong route, was now to run regularly between Phnom Penh and Battambang under the colors of Khemera Air Transport. It could go nowhere else because these two runways were the only usable ones in the country long enough for it. A great problem was encountered obtaining Viscount spare parts, and it did remain grounded for several rather long periods. Otherwise, it had good business. Battambang was the only large city in the country with operational overland links with the outside world. Goods shipped by train from Thailand were loaded on aircraft at Battambang for further transportation. This route was so attractive to the many larger aircraft operating in the country that there was little need for DC-3s to make the trip.

Much of the time, Highway 4 was open from Battambang to Krakor. Cargo was sometimes shipped by truck from Thailand to Krakor via Battambang. Occasionally, truck traffic could make it as far as Kompong Chhnang. Only near the capital were the highways perpetually closed. Highway 4 had been cut by deep trenches to the east of Kompong Chhnang. The tracks of bulldozers that had cut the trenches could be seen from the air. As a forward air controller in Vietnam, I had learned how easy it is to find bulldozers by following the tracks, and I speculated where the camouflaged machines were hidden during the day. The Khmer Air Force had nobody willing or able to find them, and foreign pilots were forbidden to take part in the war effort for political reasons, so the vehicles were left to do their demolition work unmolested.

On several occasions, Highway 5 from Kompong Som was opened for truck convoys. Several hundred trucks generally made the run in one long line. Although the amount of supplies brought into the capital this way was enormous, there was no appreciable abatement in the air traffic.

The pilots joked that Air Cambodge and the other companies should pay people to dress up like Khmer Rouge to close the roads. It was well known that opening the highways would immediately put almost all of the aircraft out of business.

The needs of the population in the capital, swollen by so many refugees, were greater than the transport potential of both the trucks and the aircraft. The most vital line of supply was the shipping lane up the Mekong. Enormous tonnage was carried by the ship convoys that fought their way through.

One morning a representative of the American aid mission asked to fly with one of the DC-3s bound for Svay Rieng. A ship convoy was on its way from Saigon and he wanted to check on its progress. His flight passed the convoy, and two of his ships were already belly up in the water. They had been sunk by heavy weapons and rocket fire from the shore in spite of their armed escort.

By the summer of 1974, the river traffic had become extremely hazardous, and truck convoys from Kompong Som could no longer make it through the blockade. The noose was tightening.

Not all of the damage to the shipping industry was caused by the enemy. The fuel that had been withheld from the airlift for bureaucratic reasons was still taking up most of the storage capacity in the harbor, preventing the arriving tankers from promptly unloading. One oil tanker waiting to unload had caught fire, apparently accidentally, and burned right at the Phnom Penh docks. A pall of heavy black smoke billowed over the city for more than two days, adding to the gloom.

Fewer and fewer ship captains were willing to make the run up the Mekong. The convoys were made up mainly of older vessels with inexperienced crews. Their losses cost the United States plenty.

One "bad" news item brought considerable cheer to some of the pilots who were harassed daily by the incredibly greedy Khmer officials. A Khmer Navy PT boat had taken a load of fresh food that had been flown into the capital at great expense down the river to sell for a fine profit in Saigon, where food was not subsidized by American tax dollars and brought a much better price. On the way, it was blown apart by rocket fire from the shore.

Chapter 26

The most amazing company history belongs to SEAAT. I had resigned from that organization believing that it would not survive, or if it did, I would be working and not getting paid.

In order to take over the Air Cambodge contracts from their former employer, Tri-9, the SEAAT executives had needed financial support. Their sources of funds were reputed to be two California medical doctors. Although there had been many rumors that the executives were misappropriating company funds, these circulated only in Phnom Penh. Whenever the doctors would arrive in Bangkok to inspect their company's operation, Jack and Cedric would rush to intercept them and tell them that Phnom Penh was far too dangerous for men as important as themselves to visit.

After some of the pilots who had quit began showing up in California to demand their back pay, however, the doctors began to hear about what was going on. The stories of their disgruntled pilots so troubled the two major stockholders that they finally insisted on seeing the operation first hand. They had been told that their company owned many aircraft and employed many pilots, but they had not been informed that the airplanes did not fly and the pilots weren't paid.

When it became evident in early 1974 that Phnom Penh was not going to fall right away, Jack and Cedric decided that it was time for some reinvestment in the company. As already mentioned, they returned together with Donny Slugger as a bodyguard, who became another "leak in the payroll" as "chief of security."

When the two doctors arrived, they turned out to be very dissimilar types of individuals. One spent his time on his company's business, while the other quickly gained himself a very unwholesome reputation.

The not-so-serious doctor gave medical examinations to the SEAAT pilots when he arrived, and he issued them medical certificates recognized by the Federal Aviation Agency (FAA). These examinations became a hot topic of gossip among the SEAAT pilots. The doctor tested his examinees for prostate cancer. This test is not called for by the FAA, or at least it was

186

never performed during any FAA examinations that I took. Only military pilots are so examined after they reach a certain age.

The test involves feeling the prostate gland through the rectum. The SEAAT pilots concluded that the doctor performed this examination because he liked to.

When I first started working in the Khmer Republic, Pete had been the SEAAT "chief of supply." He and his wife, both Australian, had been nightclub entertainers for a while in Vietnam. Pete sometimes wondered out loud why he had been hired. He had no previous experience in either aviation or supply, and he knew he was simply excess baggage at SEAAT.

Pete's salary was relatively good, and he rented a beautiful house before his wife joined him. It was owned by a Khmer general who had been appointed ambassador to a European country. The rent amounted to about half of Pete's salary, but his employer agreed to pay a large part of it in exchange for the use of the garage as a supply depot.

SEAAT's Australian mechanic, Tom, never ceased his loud denunciations of his countryman. While Tom sweated at the airport from early morning until after dark, Pete went his merry way looking after his own affairs. The Khmer employees supervised by Pete were thoroughly demoralized. He treated them as a British colonial official might have treated an Indian orderly in 1912. The best Khmer employees responded to this treatment by going to work for other companies.

When Pete's wife finally arrived, it turned out that she was very attractive. She had already met all of the SEAAT executives when they were buying the airplanes in Australia, and rumor had it that some of them were interested in her future well-being.

Shortly after the arrival of Pete's wife, the doctors showed up. The prostate doctor took an immediate interest in her and invited her to his room so that he could help her get rid of some serious inhibitions that were troubling her. When she declined his kind offer, the doctor looked very troubled. He told her that she was exhibiting symptoms of deep emotional conflict, but that together, they might be able to overcome some of her serious psychological problems.

She persisted in her refusal to follow the doctor's course of therapy. A few days later, Pete was terminated by SEAAT. Pete and his wife talked bitterly about the matter before returning to Australia. Pete said that he finally understood why he had been hired. Although the SEAAT executives had made half-hearted attempts to seduce his wife in Australia, he had not considered these efforts sufficient reason for a serious businessman to pay out such a good salary for so long.

Pete's wife confessed to having severe feelings of insecurity as a result of these experiences. Although she understood all along that the doctor was trying to proposition her, his line of talk was so smooth and professional that she felt almost convinced of her own mental and emotional illness.

After his rebuff, the prostate doctor returned to his practice in California. The more business-like partner stayed on, resolving to get rid of the management that had almost ruined his company.

Rumor had it that Jack and Cedric had received their salaries for five years in advance. Nevertheless, the doctor dismissed them and managed his own company for about a month. During that time, Cedric arrived back in the country with his own DC-4, purchasd with the savings accumulated during his tenure as vice-president of SEAAT. This aircraft was leased to Hanuman Airlines, a new company with the monkey king of the Ramayana as its symbol. It naturally came to be known as "Monkey Airlines."

Since the doctor had previously turned over all of his liquid assets to SEAAT, he could not pay the pilots or meet other company obligations until Air Cambodge paid him for the previous month's operation. To his dismay, he found out that the officials of Air Cambodge refused to turn the money over to anyone but Cedric. The doctor was now placed in the embarrassing position of having to ask the vice-president he had fired to come back to work for one more month and to put up some money for the pilots' salaries. Cedric agreed to the doctor's request.

One month later, Cedric was thanked and told that his services were no longer required. This time he refused to leave. Although the airplanes were registered in the names of the doctors, the Air Cambodge hierarchy let it be known that they would deal with nobody but Cedric.

At this point, none of the pilots were sure who was giving the orders. Each of the rival bosses threatened any aircrew members who followed the instructions of the other with instant termination. Because the Khmer officials were working with Cedric, the doctor was effectively squeezed out. He returned to California to sue Jack and Cedric.

The doctor could naturally win in court. He and the prostate doctor had invested all of the money, and the aircraft were registered in their names. Unfortunately, court cases take a couple of years. In that time, rocket attacks and constant flying without adequate maintenance or spare parts would certainly have reduced the aircraft to junk. The good doctor might even be left with the bill for carting the scrap metal away.

If some California judge had issued an order grounding the aircraft, the Khmer authorities would have just ignored it. Cedric had plenty of time and money to see to that. The arm of the California law does not reach across the Pacific, and nobody was thinking about bringing any of the property back to California.

Jack and Cedric had never been popular with their pilot employees, but that didn't make the doctors objects of sympathy. The consensus of opinion was that SEAAT would make a good tax write-off for them and that it would only take them a year or two to recoup the losses at the expense of their patients. Doctors, like pilots, are noted for making poor investments. The two in California had not realized that the nice, respectable retired military officers were swindling them until it was too late.

The SEAAT executives were also good at swindling their employees. The chief pilot and several other pilots and mechanics quit after long payless periods. Those who quit received nothing more. Even the Thai mechanics, whose salaries were very low, worked for months in the hopes of receiving the pay they had earned. They all finally quit and received nothing.

One pilot succeeded in beating the SEAAT management at their own game. Bart Tanner, a Carvair and DC-4 captain, had fallen off the ladder while exiting his aircraft. The DC-4 cockpit is very high above the ground, and his fall was almost the equivalent of a fall from a two story building. His leg was badly broken, and anything but qualified medical treatment would have left him crippled for life. He wouldn't let the doctors in Phnom Penh touch him, so he had to be flown out of the country.

When he returned, he was told that he would have to wait for the pay he had accrued while he was hospitalized. The pilots who were working were not receiving any wages at the time, either.

Bart took a truck to the SEAAT warehouse and removed about $11,000 worth of supplies and spare parts. He hid them and told Cedric that they would be returned after he received his pay and benefits in full.

Because he was shrewd enough to take parts essential for the operation of some of SEAAT's aircraft, Cedric paid the money. It was quite a bit. Bart was one of the few people who worked for SEAAT without being cheated.

Chapter 27

Two of the most interesting aircraft to arrive in Phnom Penh were the Boeing 307s flown in from Laos to fly for Cambodia Air Commercial (CACO). They were combinations of B-17 wings and huge fuselages. Like the DC-3, they had conventional landing gear: two main wheels and a tail-wheel. Many years earlier, they had been used by Royal Air Lao. More recently, they had been flown by the International Control Commission between Vientiane and Hanoi.

The aircraft were real museum pieces, but they were in good condition. They went into active service in the Khmer Republic, but after a short period of regular operation, a pilot lost control of one and damaged it. The fleet was reduced to one. Tommy Ling himself, the owner and manager of CACO, began flying it.

CACO was one of the first companies to open for business in the Khmer Republic, and Tommy had more direct control of his company's finances than the managers of the companies that arrived later. His company had been chartered in the country before there was a requirement to share the profits just to use the name of a Khmer organization. He did not have to charter out his aircraft and could keep everything he took in for hauling cargo and passengers. Because his equipment and maintenance were not the best, he contributed a great deal of aircraft wreckage to the Cambodian landscape.

One morning during take-off from Battambang, one of his four engines quit. It reportedly started burning. The story of exactly what happened next was never clarified. Some reports stated that three of the engines had stopped running before the plane crashed, but no one is quite sure. There was some speculation that the wrong engine or engines were shut down, but even the pilots did not seem to be sure themselves.

The aircraft came down in some rice fields not too far from the airport. The damage was not extensive, but Tommy suffered a blow on the head. The copilot jumped out of the window, but when Tommy did not follow him, he returned to pull his captain from the cockpit. Tommy was groggy, and in the fall from the window to the ground, he broke his leg.

On board the aircraft was a huge overload of oranges in burlap bags and about 40 passengers, including the Khmer president of CACO. It was thought that everyone aboard had survived the crash, but nobody in the cargo compartment was able to get out. Piles of oranges blocked all exits, including the doorway leading to the cockpit. As the pilots watched from outside, the fire from the wings gradually began to engulf the aircraft. Everyone inside was slowly roasted to death. They perished because of the enormous overload and because they were carried with cargo in a way that is contrary to normal safety procedures.

CACO was permanently closed down by the Khmer authorities. Tommy went into hiding to escape arrest. He stayed at a small clinic where the authorities were unable to find him; then, after having recovered sufficiently, he slipped out of the country.

The other Boeing 307 was repaired and flown to Laos. The representative of an aviation museum offered to buy it, but Tommy still had plans for it. On a flight from Vientiane to Hong Kong, Tommy had to make an emergency landing on a sand bar in the Mekong River, where the 307 probably remains today.

Everyone aboard the aircraft was captured by the Pathet Lao, who were still members of a coalition government at the time. Tommy did not return to Vientiane for quite a while. When he was finally released, he told everyone of his plans to stay in Laos and gave glowing reports of the wonderful treatment he had received from the Pathet Lao, stating how much better the country would be under the communists. He quietly set his affairs in order, then suddenly fled the country. Apparently he succeeded in securing much of the fortune he had made operating his company in the Khmer Republic from 1971 to 1974, while many other businessmen lost their life savings when the communists took power in Laos or lost their lives trying to smuggle some of their belongings across the Mekong.

The loss of so many people in the accident at Battambang was enough to create a stir, even in the callous Khmer society. For a while, inspectors from the DCA made spot checks to see if unauthorized aircraft were carrying passengers. On one spot check of 422, the inspector told our chief pilot, "I know how it is, Captain, but you have to stop carrying passengers for a while. I know how it is!"

I was delighted by the stricter procedures. It gave me an excuse to stop carrying the passengers that I had been trying not to carry for so long. Even at the fields where the provincial governors insisted that passengers be picked up on every flight, I adamantly refused to take passengers without a signed authorization from the governor, in which he agreed to take full responsibility for placing the passengers on board.

For a few days, I was successful, and I left Krakor and Kompong Chhnang with nothing but cargo. It took lengthy arguments with the military police at the airport, but they gave in rather than go to the provincial governor for a letter. The cargo shippers were also delighted. Without passengers, they could send much more of their goods.

Finally, the furor died down, and we were told to take passengers again. I assumed that the DCA officials had been looking for bribes, and they had apparently gotten them.

Captain Sangob was one of the only ones to suffer from the sudden enforcement of the regulations. He had carried two badly wounded soldiers from Kompong Thom for emergency treatment at Phnom Penh. One had a stomach wound, and both were in danger of death if they did not receive immediate medical treatment. When Sangob arrived, the DCA inspector met his aircraft and charged him with carrying passengers in an unauthorized aircraft.

Incredibly, the DCA grounded him for two weeks. At the same time, a few companies that had made reasonable settlements with the DCA were carrying large loads of passengers in unauthorized aircraft without interference. The DCA needed to make an example of someone, and Sangob was selected.

The inspectors never approached me. I had the reputation of being someone the officials should avoid. My repertory of insults and wisecracks in the Khmer language had grown formidably, and the martinets and arrogant bureaucrats feared few things more than being made the objects of derisive laughter by crowds of workmen, who were already coming to resent the affluence of those whose only activities were to disrupt the airlift in the search for bribes.

Our chief pilot made it a practice to be as polite as possible to the authorities, but even he was pushed to the limit of endurance at times. The limit was almost reached when one of the tower officials sat down at a table in the airport restaurant with him and several other pilots, and said very unctuously: "It certainly was very nice of Captain Sangob to give up his flying authorization for two weeks to save the lives of some wounded soldiers."

The pilots could not find the words to reply, but they later expressed their contempt for this official in private. I knew him to be one of the very few Khmers whose English was excellent, an attribute particularly rare among the tower staff. I also had good reason to believe he was one of the driving forces behind the graft at the airport, and the tower commander had once let me know that he thought so too.

The callous treatment of wounded soldiers evacuated from the outlying outposts was a sore point with the pilots. Ford, the Carvair captain for SEAAT, told of flying several soldiers with very serious wounds from Kompong Som. He requested an ambulance to meet the aircraft about 20 minutes before landing, but none showed up. Several hours later, the wounded were still lying on their stretchers in the shade of the Carvair's wing. Other pilots told of similar occurrences. In at least one case, a patient died unattended during the long wait for transportation.

An ambulance was always assigned to stand by at the airport. Either nobody in the tower bothered to inform the driver that wounded were inbound or the ambulance was employed for someone's private business.

When wounded were on board TFB, I made it a point to tell the tower very forcefully that I expected to see an ambulance standing by when I landed. If I saw none while taxiing to the ramp, I always called the tower again. After shutting down the engines and quickly exiting the aircraft, my final recourse was to find the nearest government official and berate him loudly for the delay the wounded soldiers were forced to endure. I made it clear that I expected him to show up with a vehicle at my aircraft right away. My efforts were always rewarded, and the wounded that I brought in were always picked up within a few minutes after I landed, although not always in the official ambulance.

The treatment of soldiers who suffer wounds is generally regarded as an important factor in maintaining morale. Soldiers may be more reluctant to fight if they know that being wounded guarantees them a slow death. The story of the events at Kampot had already spread throughout the country, and the Khmer soldiers knew that the helicopters sent to pick up wounded had evacuated rich businessmen instead. The wounded could not afford the fare.

The troops at Kompong Cham were rotated in early July. The returning soldiers were dirty, exhausted, and seemed badly shaken by their experiences. We continued to fly government property from the wreckage of the city on the Mekong to Phnom Penh. The agent in charge was a very small man who commuted between the town and the airport in his truck, carrying a variety of odds and ends.

After one trip there, I was kept busy preventing loitering soldiers from draining the aircraft's fuel tanks. I saw about 20 passengers waiting to board, but when I looked inside TFB, I saw that a multitude of metal cans had been piled along the sides of the cargo compartment where the passenger seats were usually set up. I asked the agent where the people were supposed to sit, and he replied, "On the cans," as if I were some kind of an idiot.

I looked at one of the labels. There were two large international symbols, one meaning "poisonous" and the other, "flammable." The flash point was given as 30°C, or about 10 degrees cooler than the temperature in the aircraft at the time. The label also stated that the substance in the cans may be deadly if it comes into contact with the skin. The fine print gave recommendations on what to do if a victim of the brew stops breathing. The active substance was dieldrin, a poison that functions something like nerve gas. I noticed that the solution was seeping out of a few of the cans.

Calmly, I told the agent that I would carry his cargo of all-purpose biocide under no circumstances, and I recommended that it not be shipped by air at all, and certainly not with passengers.

The agent reacted with horror and disbelief. "The Chinese pilots took it," he quickly pointed out. The agent assumed the attitude that as a representative of a sovereign state, he had the right to order anyone to carry any cargo he chose. Pointing out that some passengers might arrive dead at Phnom Penh or that a bullet, or even a cigarette, could turn the cabin into an inferno made no impact. The argument was finally won when I stated that I would taxi to the runway and throw the cargo out at the edge before taking off. Since the agent could not fly the aircraft himself, there was no way he could assure himself that the brew would ever reach Phnom Penh aboard TFB. The poison finally came off, and another kind of cargo was loaded in its place.

There is a good possibility that I was listed as an uncooperative pilot in the official Khmer Republic records, and perhaps even the United States Embassy put in a bad report about me, but no passengers I ever carried were killed or injured during the trip, and I still believe that it pays to read labels.

Several years later, the World Health Organization and Consumers Union looked into the routine use of such biocides around the world and conservatively estimated that the number of deaths from exposure to such chemicals ranges from 5,000 to over 13,000 each year.

Except for this one flight, my experiences carrying government cargo had been good because of the short loading times. Although he lost money on them, John Yim regarded flights for the government as necessary annoyances. He often related how military officers in his native country had commandeered privately owned aircraft at the point of a gun during the Korean War.

Not one to withhold my opinion, I pointed out that there were some differences between the situation in Korea at that time and that in the Khmer Republic. In Korea, black marketeers and corrupt government officials had been shot. The Air Force had not engaged in private commercial operations, and as much was done for the wounded as possible. I could not visualize a Khmer officer commandeering a civilian airliner at the point of a gun while the Air Force C-123s were steadily arriving and departing loaded down with sugar, oranges, fish and paying passengers. John Yim had to admit that there were some fundamental differences between the two situations being discussed.

In the meantime, the Air Force commercial operations were finally starting to cause casualties. One of the C-123 pilots regularly took his sister along to sell tickets and buy cargo during the festive loading operations at Kompong Thom. While the engines idled, the pilot's sister ran forward

To the right of the runway at Kompong Thom were ponds, fallow rice fields, and the remains of a house (photo courtesy of Bill Ernst).

between the fuselage and propeller to shout something to her brother in the cockpit. Some crewmen screamed at her to turn back, and just as she had passed through the propeller arc once, she obeyed and ran back through it again. By some miracle, she made it through unscathed each way.

The next day the same C-123 was again at Kompong Thom with the pilot's sister again running the loading operation. As the engines were being started, the woman rushed forward to shout something to the pilot. Again, she chose the same route. Unfortunately, miracles cannot be expected two days in a row. David Chester witnessed the accident. He heard a sound like a watermelon being smashed, and a second later, the woman's twitching, headless body was lying on the ground under the propeller. David said that he had never before witnessed anything so horrible.

The most disturbing aspect of the situation was the attitude of the American officials assigned to the country. On one occasion, several pilots were sitting in the airport restaurant discussing some of the latest dirty tricks the civil servants had invented to accumulate graft. By this sort of information exchange, we helped each other avoid trouble. Sitting at the next table was a United States Navy commander assigned to the American Aid Mission. Overhearing the conversation, he interjected, "You'd take money too, if you were only making $60 a month."

The remark expressed an attitude that had been common among American officials for at least ten years. The right of a civil servant to steal or extort bribes if he feels he is underpaid seemed to have been accepted by American government employees in Asia, and probably elsewhere. The corruption they had nurtured by this attitude may very well be the primary reason for the nearly complete expulsion of American institutions from the Asian continent since the Second World War.

My response to this comment was to relate a story in a sarcastic way that I hoped would be a particularly vexing reply to such an idiotic statement.

"An American would starve on such a small salary," I admitted cheerfully, "but the Khmer government employees are so thrifty that they can live very well on $60 a month. One of the deputy ministers of commerce just bought a new Mercedes here in Phnom Penh, shipped it by air to Kompong Som, then put it on a ship bound for France for his sons to use while they go to school in Paris. The car, the shipping expenses, and the tuition for his sons are all paid for on only $60 a month."

The story is true, and I think the commander already knew about the case. The point was, the dishonest Khmer officials would have been willing to work for nothing or even to pay for their jobs just to get in on the action. I wonder what the commander's reaction would have been if an American seaman recruit used his small salary as an excuse after he was caught stealing a few hundred thousand dollars of government property.

The reason for the steady decline of American influence in the world and the repeated failure of United States foreign policy in Southeast Asia should certainly have been sought in the persons the government placed in positions of responsibility.

Chapter 28

On July 11 TFB was scheduled for only two trips so we finished early. Sam, the pilot of the C-46 belonging to Hang Meas Airlines, had not been able to find a copilot, so I offered to fly with him. Both Sam and the C-46, N9760Z, had been employed by Continental Air Services in Vientiane, Laos, for several years. The aircraft had been purchased from Continental by Tri-9 for resale to Hang Meas Airlines. Tri-9 supplied the maintenance temporarily, and Sam was hired as the pilot to replace another ex–Continental pilot who had returned to Laos.

Sam had originally arrived in Phnom Penh with his own DC-4, which he leased to Khemera Air Transport for several months with himself as the pilot. His relations with the Khmer shipping executives rapidly deteriorated, and he had to put his aircraft up for sale for want of customers. Even though he had married a Khmer girl, supposedly with relatives in high places, Sam could not break into the operations bringing in the big profits. He found to his dismay that the corruption was decentralized, and his wife's influence with one of the government ministries did not guarantee the cooperation of the others.

The shippers did not like to do business with Sam because they did not know what to expect from him. At times, he weighed each piece of cargo and strictly refused to carry any overweight, but on other occasions, he carried huge overloads. Once, one of the cargo conveyors smuggled about ten bags of sugar on Sam's DC-4 at Krakor. While my DC-3 was being loaded, I watched Sam drop the bags, one by one, from the flight station door. As bags of sugar were exploding on contact with the ground, the laborers were hurrying to the scene to scrape up every grain and hamster the precious powder in their pockets, shirts and hats. The conveyor could have made a small fortune with so much sugar in Phnom Penh.

Edgar, one of SEAAT's DC-4 pilots, had confiscated all smuggled sugar he found in his aircraft and gave it to his wife to sell. They accumulated several thousand dollars in a few months, but I understand that the money was later stolen from them.

Another incident that did not endear Sam to the shippers occurred when a fork-lift operator had damaged the door frame of his DC-4 while loading a Renault auto. After hitting the frame with the loading pallet, the man tried to ram it into the aircraft instead of backing up and trying to put it on at a different angle. The entire door frame was dislodged. Sam was furious, but the shipper and his crew just laughed with glee at their handiwork. Sam calmly told the shipper, "Go ahead and laugh, the damage will cost as much to repair as that car is worth, so I'm taking your car."

The shipper ranted and raved, but Sam did what he said. He had to make a temporary modification so that he could close the door because there were no facilities at Phnom Penh for repairing the door frame properly.

The problem of damage by loading equipment could often be serious. The truck drivers, who collected dents and other kinds of damage to their own vehicles with disturbing facility, thought nothing of treating the aircraft with the same cavalier wrecklessness. Trying to explain about aerodynamic streamlining and the stresses placed on a door latched in flight was just a waste of breath. To save money, the shippers hired the most incompetent people they could find because they would demand less pay.

Whenever my aircraft was damaged, I took the name of the driver and shipper, reported the incident to the military policeman, and gave a report to Tri-9. I never learned whether the shippers were charged for the damage.

Bill Ernst, while flying as a copilot, went a step further. He carried a hammer with him, and any time a truck dented the aircraft, he put a bigger dent in the truck. That did not prevent the damage, but it suppressed the culprits' laughter.

My flight in the C-46 was enjoyable after flying only DC-3s seven days a week from May 21 to July 18 with only one day off. The cockpit of the C-46 was enormous compared to that of the DC-3, and I had the feeling of sitting in an easy chair instead of on a seat in a crowded bus. The systems, arrangement of the instruments, and feel of the controls were quite different. Sam let me make two landings, which were not very beautiful but got the aircraft on the ground without scaring the passengers.

John Yim was not happy about me flying with Sam, even though he was theoretically taking care of the aircraft on behalf of Hang Meas Airlines. He never learned that his other DC-3 captain, Sawai, flew fairly regularly as copilot for Colonel SaNguon, a Lao Air Force officer who had brought his C-46 to fly in the Khmer Republic.

Some weeks after my flight in 60Z, Sam and his copilot, the unfortunate pilot of Indhandu's Twin-Beech on its last flight, took off with an overload from Kompong Som. As they began their climb over the bay, they entered a heavy coastal rain storm. Large rain drops battered the windshield and light turbulence shook them. The noise of the rain was so loud that Sam did not realize one of his engines had failed. The heavy drag caused by the windmilling propeller caused the C-46 to lose precious altitude.

After Sam realized he was descending, checked his instruments, and feathered the prop on the dead engine, they were already dangerously low — too low to make it back to Kompong Som. He set the aircraft up in ditching configuration — gear up and flaps down — and in a few seconds, they entered the water.

The aircraft floated, buoyed up by the fuel in the wings and trapped air. The crew assembled on one wing, and in about 20 minutes, they were rescued by a Khmer Navy patrol boat. Luckily, the aircraft was insured. Later on, another pilot contributed a DC-4 to the briny deep, but the insurance company refused to pay the claim.

Chapter 29

After our enormous overload and long glide into Phnom Penh, we did not return to Koh Kong for a while. Finally, the new shipper was able to convince John Yim of his good intentions, and we again placed that airfield on our schedule. The shipper ran into a run of bad luck, however.

On our trip for him, we landed at the deserted airport to wait for the cargo truck. I measured the width of the runway at the request of an acquaintance in Phnom Penh, and as I was walking back toward TFB, everyone suddenly started calling and waving to me. I ran back to the aircraft and was told by some soldiers and the shipper that rockets were being fired by the communists, and they would be impacting on the field momentarily. We were told not to load the cargo but to take off immediately. We leaped into the aircraft, started the engines that were still warm, and were in the air within one minute.

Beneath us, the people at the field and the cargo agent's truck were racing away from the airport at which they had just arrived. As we circled to climb, no rockets impacted. Nevertheless, the soldiers were busying themselves closing the airport. I thought about returning to load the cargo, but everyone on the ground was in such a panic, I did not think it would be possible. We returned to Phnom Penh with nothing aboard but a few of the shipping agent's employees.

Although we never learned about any fighting taking place near Koh Kong, no trips were scheduled there for two weeks. Finally, on July 14, our first trip was scheduled to fly government rice to Takeo; then, we were to proceed directly to Koh Kong. I was not happy about the planning. First, we would be unusually heavy for landing on Takeo's short, sandy runway with the large load of fuel needed for the round trip to Cambodia's west coast. Second, weather information about our destination was not available, and early morning storms along the coast were common during the southwest monsoon. Third, the charterers would protest that we could not carry any cargo from Phnom Penh to Koh Kong for them.

Joe Chan was my copilot again. For some reason, he always seemed to be with me whenever things went wrong. This was not his fault in any way; it was rather an unexplainable coincidence. As copilot of the Convairs, he also experienced a great many emergencies, and I am sure that he had more hair-raising experiences than most of the pilots in Phnom Penh.

In spite of the heavy fuel load, we had an uneventful landing at Takeo, and we were quickly on our way again. As we crossed the Elephant Mountains, the weather began to worsen. Towering cumulus clouds surrounded us. Finally, it was no longer possible to maintain visual flight, so we proceeded on instruments. As we flew deeper into the murky gray gloom, sheets of water began to envelop the aircraft. It created the illusion of flying underwater, and a steady flow of rain leaked through the tiny cracks in our ancient DC-3. Within minutes, our clothing was completely soaked. These typical coastal rain storms rarely penetrated very far inland. Their characteristics were very heavy rain, little turbulence, and coverage of a large area.

There were no radio navigation aids in the vicinity of Koh Kong. I planned to fly our heading until we reached the seacoast. Sometimes there are breaks in the rain and cloud cover where the land meets the sea. I hoped to descend over the ocean to an altitude below the cloud bases, pick my way between the hills on the coast, and land.

We were about 15 minutes from our destination when we entered the clouds. Premature descent would have been foolhardy because of the very high mountains right beside the sea a few miles north of Koh Kong. We had no radio contact with anyone on the ground, and it was impossible to get a weather report. I was sure that in 20 minutes, we would be safely over the open sea, and I planned beginning a gradual descent at that time.

At the appropriate time, we started to descend from 8500 feet. We could lose 2000 feet and still be above the highest mountain peak. As we reached 7000 feet, Joe called out that he could see down. We quickly reentered the storm, but after passing through a thin layer of clouds, we broke out into a large open area below the clouds. The rain was still heavy, but visibility straight down was good. Below us was the sea, with great whitecaps spewing foam over the usually calm Gulf of Siam. For these to be visible over 6000 feet through the gloomy mist meant that the sea must be very rough. I estimated the surface winds to be 25 to 35 knots. I began circling down through layer after layer of clouds.

As we reached 2000 feet, I could see the ragged bases of the clouds around us. Below us were some light, scattered puffs only a few hundred feet above the water. We headed back toward the land, but the rain on the windshield was so heavy that we could barely see ahead.

After three or four minutes, I spotted an arm of land with a small hill on it just below us. Beside it was an island. Between the two was a bay. As soon as we passed the coastline, the clouds closed in below us and the rain suddenly became very heavy, sending sheets of water across the windshield.

Any attempts at landing would have been foolhardy because of the many high mountains around the field. I estimated our chances of making it at about 90 percent, but people who like to take chances should not fly airplanes. I added power, and the unloaded airplane climbed rapidly back to a safe altitude. We were still in heavy rain as we leveled off, but suddenly the sky ahead of us was crystal clear. We had just passed over the ridge of the Elephant Mountains, and the storm line ended there. That was the only mission that I failed to complete because of weather while in the Khmer Republic.

It was the shipper himself who had been foolish enough to insist that the flight be made early in the morning. His cargo consisted of about three tons of live crabs. He not only had to pay for the flight, he also had to watch his crabs spoil. Although he claimed the dead crabs were dumped into the sea, I made sure not to eat any crabs in Phnom Penh for about a week.

The next day we flew to Koh Kong again, and I was able to ask about the weather on the previous day. We had been overhead at about 9 A.M., and the heavy rain had continued until about 10. We would not have had enough fuel to hold until that time. If we had come later, we would have had clear weather.

The small peninsula with the hill I had spotted was just at the mouth of the estuary, so we had passed within about two miles of the airport in the rain. Our navigation had been nearly perfect. If the airport had had an approach system, we could easily have landed. I knew too many pilots in Laos who flew into mountains to attempt it without radios. Mountains and bad weather must still be regarded as a fatal combination.

TFB was due its 100 hour inspection and needed plenty of repairs. The engine was still smoking, and the door hinges needed to be replaced. My Lao pilot license was also in need of renewal, so I took a few days off to travel to Vientiane.

The Lao director of civil aviation required a medical certificate from an authorized Lao doctor, which the American FAA refused to recognize. The Lao authorities did not accept the FAA medical certificate, either. I therefore had to have a medical examination at least every three months. The Lao examination cost less than $3 at the going rate of exchange, and because TFB was Lao registered, my medical exam in Vientiane was more important to me than the American one.

The FAA medical exam, which I had to have to fly 422 occasionally, was not actually recognized by the FAA. The Khmer doctor who administered it had no authorization from the FAA, but supposedly he had approval from the American Embassy which accepted his qualifications in the absence of an FAA approved physician closer than Bangkok. That the ambassador had the right to give such an authorization is very doubtful, but anyone working for any length of time in remote parts of the world quickly learns that there are often few things less important to American officials than the letter of the law.

The FAA-authorized doctor in Bangkok knew he had a monopoly, so he exploited it to the fullest and charged $30 for the examination. The Khmer doctor charged $20 and issued no certificate. In the United States, many doctors charged $15 or less at the time.

Such bureaucratic duplication may seem nonsensical until one remembers that a number of people were making plenty of money from it. That the medical examination system had anything to do with improving flight safety is questionable, but that doctors should make lots of money is beyond debate. The first medical examination I had taken in Phnom Penh while working for SEAAT was dangerous to the health due to an overdose of radiation from the huge, old-fashioned fluoroscope that was used. The doctor had no idea what he was supposed to look for, so he checked the nose, ears, and joints of the arm. He made sure that the test took a long time, most of which I spent waiting in the hall. He had gotten better organized when I returned for the next examination six months later. He simply collected the $20 and handed me the signed forms required by the director of civil aviation.

The tests in Laos concerned only the eyes and general physical condition and were accomplished quickly. The tests prescribed by the FAA were generally performed by the authorized American doctors, but one pilot received his first class medical certificates through the mail. While in the United States, he had once signed a stack of blank forms and paid in advance.

Even many of the doctors who went through the motions of performing the tests failed to do anything but take the pilots' hard-earned money. One retired B-52 pilot from the Strategic Air Command had trouble holding a job in the Khmer Republic because he had brought his Air Force drinking habits with him. While briefly employed with Continental Air Services, he passed out on final approach with at least a second class medical certificate issued by an FAA-approved doctor in his pocket. Before long, he found a job flying with another company. While many young men are kept out of aviation by the strict medical standards they have to meet, pilots with many years of employment with an airline have to deteriorate pretty badly before they would be refused a medical certificate. Many pilots were addicted to alcohol to the extent that they would have been unsafe behind the wheel of an automobile, but their medical records do not reflect their addiction at all. Civilians, however, are far better in this respect than military pilots, who are examined only by flight surgeons under the control of the armed forces.

After flying to Battambang with one of the other companies, I went to the market and boarded a Pugeot taxi bound for Poipet. The holes in the road had become noticeably deeper, and with 11 people plus baggage in the station wagon, the five hour trip was anything but comfortable. The fare in riels increased steadily with the inflation, but it always seemed to remain the equivalent of about one United States dollar.

There was a new officer in charge of the Poipet immigration station. He was a chubby, officious type who immediately spotted *"aerienne"* (by air) on my exit visa. He informed me cheerfully that the exit visa was not valid, and I would have to return to Phnom Penh to have the wording changed to *"routière"* (by road). After waiting some time, I asked him to let me exit one time as a special favor. He may have been expecting a little money, but I did not offer him any. Finally, he decided to make one exception and gave me the exit chop. While I was in his office, an American woman entered and tried to speak with him, so I found out that he spoke very little English. If I had not been able to speak Khmer, I am sure that I would not have been able to leave the country.

After I returned to Phnom Penh, I found out that one of our mechanics, a Korean, had encountered the same official. He was refused permission to leave the country and had to ride another five hours in the taxi to return to Battambang.

After crossing the border, I found that the last bus west had already departed, so I spent the night in Aranya Prathet. Early the next morning, I took the bus to Kabinburi, and from there I crossed the mountains to Nakorn Ratchasima, where I transferred again to the Nongkhai bus. Late that afternoon, I was on the ferry across the Mekong to Laos.

After renewing my license and submitting some papers for Tri-9, I returned by the same route I had come. I arrived before the mechanics had finished their work on TFB. The cause of the smoking engine had been found. Like the rubber oil lines, the rebuilt cylinders purchased from the Lao Air Force had been defective, and they were replaced, only a few weeks after they had been installed. The new set of cylinders had been purchased from a reputable firm, and no more white smoke poured from TFB's exhaust. How many of the products delivered by Federal contractors to USAID and the military aid missions for use in developing countries are similarly defective?

During July fuel was again becoming scarce. The companies had already found ways of accumulating a supply of avgas off the record, however. The Khmer authorities could have found out easily what was being done, but they were glad to accept a few donations in return for not investigating the situation too closely.

Besides all of the registration papers and airworthiness certificates, pilot licenses, Khmer pilot authorizations, and other assorted forms that we were required to possess in order to fly, a separate permit was necessary for each flight. These had to be referred to a vast number of bureaucrats, and each had to affix his own signature. Needless to say, the applications had to be filed several days in advance, long before the shippers knew exactly when their cargo would be ready for shipment. Therefore, we often had to fly to airports different from the ones we had approval for. For a long time, the Khmer authorities at the Pochentong Airport did not realize what a gold mine these permits could be, but when they did, they quickly learned to take full advantage of it. If a load of fresh fish was waiting in Kompong Chhnang and our permit listed only Krakor as a destination that day, the shipper could be made to pay almost any price so that an "exception" could be made to allow us to transport his fish before it spoiled. After a hectic round of bargaining took place beside the shipper's truck, the smiling official would come to us and say grandly that he had been generous enough to give us his special dispensation to make an "unauthorized flight," just this one time.

Very soon many junior officers were driving brand new cars. One day our crew car was not at the airport, and an airport policeman gave me a ride to town on the back of his motorcycle. In his driveway was a brand new Volkswagen. He told me he could not use his car until he learned to drive, but it looked nice in his driveway. The higher ranking officials at the airport naturally had more expensive cars than Volkswagens.

After the officials learned to get rich by reading the fine print on the flight permits, they became even more sophisticated. Not to let any opportunities be lost, they began looking at the time of day that the aircraft was authorized to take off. If a flight to Krakor was authorized to depart at 2 P.M. and it was ready to go at 1:15, the official would threaten to hold the flight 45 minutes unless the passengers would take up a collection for his benefit or unless the shipper would agree to carry some of his "relatives" free of charge. If the flight was late, it could be cancelled altogether. A Khmer Air Force officer actually cancelled a flight of another company because it was authorized to take off at noon but was not ready to go until 12:15.

The effects of these tactics on the airlift were devastating. Many flights never got off the ground because the shippers and the officials could not agree on a price. Soon, food prices in Phnom Penh began to rise again, and much spoiled food started turning up in the restaurants. Complaints to the American Embassy fell on deaf ears because the corruption was simply regarded as a reaction of the civil servants to their low salaries, and was therefore of no concern.

A more dangerous form of corruption was the theft of fuel by the security guards during the night. After spending one night at Battambang, we found that a considerable amount of fuel had been drained from one tank. The brother of the company owner, an army lieutenant, was angered when he found out because he had already paid the security officer a large sum of money not to steal from our aircraft. Later he told us that an airman had taken the fuel without asking his officer whether our company was "protected."

Because of the theft, we did not have enough reserve fuel on arrival at Phnom Penh. That happened to be one of the only mornings of the year that an overcast prevented visual operations. I flew an ADF (radio compass) approach, and we broke into the clear just at the minimum altitude. I noted that there were scattered rain showers and fog banks nearby, and if we had not been able to land immediately, holding would have been out of the question. Our only choice would have been to fly directly to Kompong Chhnang, where we could expect difficulties from the local officials for landing without authorization. Tri-9 then would have had to fly fuel there so that we could return home.

Occasionally, I had the chance to strike back. An airman was once imprudent enough to try to drain gasoline from TFB into several bottles during the day. I approached quietly from behind and suddenly snatched a half-filled bottle from his hand. Within a fraction of a second, he was sprinting away. I threw the bottle and hit him in the back. As he reached his motorcycle, I retrieved the bottle. I threw it again, and it smashed between his feet, sending broken glass flying all around him. He did a little hopping and skipping dance as the gasoline and glass slivers showered his trousers and boots. He did not stop running or look back until he had crossed the runway and reached the Air Force side.

The small amount of fuel stolen for the motorcycle was insignificant, but the damage that was being done to the aircraft sump drains was not. The thieves knew that if the drain cock was pressed, gasoline came out. Unfortunately, they did not know how to close it again. They invariably pulled down until the locking mechanisms were broken. One thief had actually pulled the whole drain out of a SEAAT aircraft. After filling his bottles, he made no attempt to plug the hole, and about 50 gallons of avgas poured out on the ramp. On both TFB and 422, the drains had been so badly damaged that fuel continuously trickled out. The sumps finally had to be wired and plugged shut.

During the wet southwest monsoon, there was often much condensation in the tanks. The broken drains prevented the water from being removed in the morning, creating another hazard. There were no spare sump drain plugs in supply, so occasionally I had to remove the whole fitting with a wrench to let the accumulated water out.

TFB had been used to transport automobile fuel in Laos, so gate valves had been installed in place of the sump drains in the rear tanks, which served as safe containers for flammable liquid. The large gate valves were so convenient for the thieves that they were very quickly broken. We were no longer able to use the rear tanks for reserve fuel. This was another example of how the massive corruption made our work more dangerous.

All crimes were not committed with impunity, however. The Air Force lieutenant who served as chief of airport security was arrested and tried by court martial for stealing aviation fuel. We remembered him best as the one who charged our shipper 40,000 riels for finding the key to the main airport gate at night to allow him to remove his cargo of beef before it completely spoiled. The consensus of opinion among the pilots was that his arrest was not for stealing aircraft fuel but rather for stealing it without cutting his superiors in on the profit. I heard that he went to prison, and I never saw him again.

Sokony, a Khmer Air Force lieutenant assigned to oversee operations on the civilian ramp, had rather good manners and spoke English much better than the usual English-speaking Khmer. He was also corrupt. He carefully examined each official form to make sure every authorization was exactly correct. If he found the slightest discrepancy, he grounded the aircraft and collected a rich payoff before allowing it to operate again.

Before or since, I don't think that I've treated anyone with as much studied contempt as Sokony. If he asked to send some passengers with us, I insisted that the company charge them the highest black market price for the tickets, while all other passengers paid the low official price. When he came close to my aircraft, I would loudly announce that the "air thief" was coming, which in Khmer is a play on the word "airman." The pun never failed to provoke peals of raucous laughter from the Khmer workmen standing nearby. The result was that Sokony usually stayed far away from me while continuing to carefully study the authorization permits of those who were nicer to him in the hopes of being able to find grounds for cancelling their flights.

One day I saw him standing beside his new Renault which he had parked a few steps from TFB. Under the aircraft was a very tall airman draining fuel into an ammunition can. Although the airman was much bigger than me, I walked up and grabbed the can out of his hands and threw the fuel at him. He retreated with a look of terror on his face. Our aircraft cleaners were standing around watching so I berated them sharply for allowing someone to steal fuel. Of course, I knew that they were afraid of the Air Force mob, but I wanted Sokony to know that if he tried to steal fuel again, I would be told about it. Sokony and the airman just drove away in the car, leaving their can behind.

Sokony once made a half-hearted attempt at reprisal by trying to cancel an "unauthorized flight." Unfortunately for him, he came to check the permit after a team of armed combat soldiers had already boarded to fly to Kompong Cham. I refused to speak English with him so that the soldiers would understand exactly what was going on, and they began to look very angry because of the delay. Sokony decided that discretion was the better part of valor and let Suvut, our station manager, talk him out of making any trouble before I had the chance to get out of the aircraft and make him the laughing stock of the whole airport.

Later, while Sokony was within earshot, Savouth told me that Sakony had decided to make trouble because he did not like me and claimed that I did not respect Khmer customs. I laughed and said in a loud voice, "Which of his Khmer customs don't I respect? Bribery? Theft?"

Some workmen loading the aircraft broke into laughter to Sokony's chagrin, and he never again bothered me about an authorization.

Bill, our chief pilot, warned me that some day Sokony would try to get even. I answered that I was not worried because Sokony's mind did not work in a way that made him capable of taking revenge. He was too dumb to hatch any plots, and he certainly must have felt insecure knowing that the hundreds of people who had to work long hours at the airport just to have a little bit to eat each day knew the source of his ill-gotten gains.

As it turned out, I was right not to be concerned. About three weeks after our last conflict, Sokony was arrested, tried and convicted by court martial for corruption. By that time, however, the country was so short of manpower that he was placed on disciplinary probation and kept on duty at the airport. His power and influence, however, were greatly reduced, and his open solicitation of bribes was curtailed. If he made a false step, he would be thrown into prison to serve his sentence. Slowly, the system was purging itself of its most harmful elements.

Chapter 30

I had spent ten months flying in the Khmer Republic without seeing Angkor Wat, one of the wonders of the world. This enormous temple building and the nearby Angkor Thom had been built by King Jayavarman VII for his capital city. Very shortly after their completion, they were captured and sacked by the troops of the Thai king, Boromoraja II. The city remained abandoned from 1430 until its rediscovery by a French explorer in the middle of the 19th century. Until that time, the Khmers had no idea that such a city existed in their country.

In 1970 communist troops had occupied this famous tourist attraction and a nearby luxury hotel. The international communist propaganda machine was ready to go to work any time the Khmer Army should attempt to recapture their national monument, which in the course of any ensuing combat was sure to be destroyed or badly damaged. Of course, there was no international outcry against the communists for using such a great work of art as a hostage.

From their safe haven, the communist troops were able to effectively interdict transport and communications on the northern side of the Tonle Sap and reduce the government positions to isolated enclaves. Of course, part of the fault lay with the Khmer Army, which failed to make any serious attempt to clear the enemy from such unhistorical spots as Siemriep Airport.

On July 26, I was finally scheduled for a flight to Siemriep. My copilot, Tony Pradith, and I crossed the great lake of the Tonle Sap and spotted the town along Highway 6. Just to the northwest was the beautiful concrete runway of the international airport, which was either in the hands of the enemy or in nobody's hands and therefore made unusable for us. Our runway was a section of road in the middle of the town itself, which had been covered with a layer of dirt to make it wider. The flying time for the leg was almost exactly as long as that for Battambang, making it one of the longest that we flew.

We both wanted to see Angkor Wat, but as we scanned the terrain to the north of the town, we could see nothing but jungle. Finally, as we were on the downwind leg for landing to the south, I spotted the ruins. As I looked north from 800 feet over the town, a great mass of black rock carved with intricate designs loomed out of the jungle in front of us. It was only about two kilometers from the town, and a large pool of water filled with floating plants surrounded it. The color of the rock produced by a thick coating of lichens and algae was so much like that of the thick jungle around it that it was extremely difficult to spot from the air. It was very impressive, but unfortunately, the craftsmen who built it were not capable of preventing someone else from taking it away from them by force. I thought that these people could not have been so different from the Khmers I was seeing every day. Some of them were very talented craftsmen and could do difficult jobs well, but their leaders were not able to put selfish interests aside, and they were gradually losing the last remains of their homeland.

It was amazing that a communist base could exist so close to a town in government hands. Whenever the communist forces had advanced so close to the defense perimeter of Phnom Penh, there had been heavy fighting.

We landed in a cloud of dust on the rough runway. We turned around and taxied back to the parking ramp at the north end of the field. Waiting for us was an official from the Khmer Directorate of Civil Aviation (DCA), about whom our chief pilot had told some amusing stories. Siemriep was the only field we visited where the DCA was represented. He was apparently one of the few officials who was not a grafter, but he was extremely officious. This explains his exile to the farthest point from the capital.

He rushed to the cockpit and asked to see our authorization. The steward produced it along with the cargo manifest. After satisfying himself that these papers were in order, he began asking to see more documents: the airworthiness certificate, the cargo lists, etc. I was getting annoyed, but I tried to ignore the proceedings as much as possible. Finally, he approached me with a copy of our manifest and asked me to sign it where it said "Captain's signature."

I decided to be uncooperative, so I told him that I could not sign it and certify the cargo weight because I had not weighed the cargo myself. I told him that the shipper would have to sign it. He then began assuring me that he was not trying to make any trouble for us, but he insisted that the document called for the captain's signature and only that would be acceptable. I told him that it was impossible for me to certify the weight unless he produced a scale and let me watch the weighing.

My experience in the country had taught me the Khmer style of making difficulties for people, and I was determined to turn the tables on a Khmer official. I questioned everything he said on legal grounds, and he was taken aback when I asked to see his authorization to take copies of my manifest.

Finally, he began to show signs of frustration. He declared that we could not take off unless we provided the signatures on the documents required. I asked him for the name of the hotel we should stay in. He began to understand that his power was limited. He might request the help of the Army to back him up, but it is doubtful whether the soldiers would have taken much interest in his problem. He had no power over the cargo agents who were busy loading the cargo. Soon, he began to show signs of desperation. I flatly refused to sign anything before he produced a scale, and I did want to weigh the cargo anyway because I did not trust these new shippers. This also surprised him because he expected pilots to be eagerly seeking overloads for profit.

In his desperation, he turned to Tony who told him brusquely, "I'm just the dumb copilot. I can't do anything for you."

Next, the DCA representative went to the steward. He told him, "I think your captain must be very stupid. He can't seem to understand what I want. There will be no trouble if he signs this. I'm not trying to create any difficulties for him."

My plan for the next round was to question the man if he'd checked the papers of the Viet Cong, who were camped on the international airport. I didn't get the chance to ask and see his reaction, however, because he gave up. He announced in a grand manner that he had decided to sign the manifest for me. If we came to Siemriep again, I knew he would certainly leave us alone.

Chapter 31

During July, 1974, the pilots formed an association. It was aptly called the Phnom Penh Pig Pilot's Association. Ben Crawford handled all of the adminstrative details during June before the first meeting was held in July. The interest was enormous. The American and Thai pilots joined at the start, and as soon as the Chinese pilots found out about it, Ben was inundated with their $5 membership fees, as well. Identification cards were provided to the members.

Bill Davis, our chief pilot, refused to join. He said that our organization would turn into a union, and he was management. Personally, I hoped that the pilots could work together enough to combat the corruption that was harassing our operations. Most of the members, however, professed the desire to keep the organization strictly social. I did not make any suggestions to the contrary because I was planning to leave for New York in August to get married, and I would not return until late September or October.

The first president of the PPPPA was David Chester, a long-time copilot for SEAAT. Ben, who had done most of the work organizing the association, remained the secretary.

The first meeting was held in an empty hall owned by Shane, an Indian businessman. It had once been the Tropicana Night Club, which had been closed for several weeks. In earlier days, this had been the scene of wild battles. In spite of the government rules closing the nightclubs, the Tropicana had been allowed to stay open thanks to the influence of its clientele of wealthy and powerful Khmer officials. As time went on, the social *niveau* of the patrons declined, and penniless Khmer soldiers often fought over the dancing girls, sometimes with automatic weapons. Finally, it became too dangerous to keep this "wild west with machine guns" open.

When I attended the meeting, I saw the inside of the building for the first time. It was on the second floor at the head of a rather dark staircase. The hall seemed very spacious, perhaps because it was completely empty. Ed, who had often flown as my copilot while I was with SEAAT, had retired from the flying business and was planning to take the building over

212

for use as a USO-type club for the local pilots. Pool and ping-pong tables as well as other facilities were to be installed, and some of the former night club girls were to be hired as waitresses. The deterioration of the military situation in the country precluded the success of this project.

The pilots were naturally a varied lot with a variety of different backgrounds. I was one of the only former American military pilots who had flown in combat in Vietnam. One American pilot had flown as a volunteer during the Battle of Britain, and several other American and many of the Chinese pilots had flown in World War II. Most of the Thai and Chinese pilots had spent many years in their countries' armed forces and had a great deal of flying experience. Many of the Americans flying as copilots had backgrounds in "general aviation." A few were former servicemen who had learned to fly using their veterans' education entitlements.

Two of Tri-9's copilots had received their training from Air America. Tony had been selected for flight training after he had returned a large sum of money that the management had lost. Other American and Thai pilots had also come to work in Phnom Penh after being laid off by Air America or Continental Air Services in Laos, but the majority of the pilots released by these companies would not work in the Khmer Republic because the salaries being offered were far too low.

Very often, I walked around Phnom Penh, which was undergoing a process of progressive deterioration. The contrasts between the rich officials and war profiteers in their villas and the poor refugees living in the tents and packing crates along the sidewalks were becoming stronger. The emigration of the rich was continuing, and magnificent houses could be rented for less than one would pay for small apartments in the United States or Europe.

Along the sidewalks, peddlers sold everything from canned food to gold teeth. One street near the Royal Palace was the dentists' street. Squatting on the sidewalk were a large group of elderly Khmer dentists with small display racks filled with gold teeth. Almost every man of means had gold teeth, generally in the front. They were a kind of status symbol. As I passed by, there were usually patients picking out attractive looking crowns from the assortment or having them installed. The drills were hand-driven, and it was the patient's job to squat on the sidewalk and turn the crank that powered the machinery while the dentist drilled. After the treatment was finished, the proud owner of the new gold tooth left smiling to show off his new piece of "jewelry."

After the food shortages became worse, due mainly to the chicanery at the airport, the government decided to reduce luxuries. Unfortunately, the Khmers considered restaurants luxuries. As a result, all eating places were closed on Mondays and Thursdays. For us, that meant that canned food would be our sole source of nourishment on those days. My meals

A meeting of shippers and executives of some of the Khmer air transport companies at the Pochentong Airport restaurant (photo courtesy of Bill Ernst).

consisted of sardines, lunch meat, and other assorted items purchased from the small shops or street vendors.

The canned food from France and Morocco was overpriced as were most European goods. A store that specialized in foods imported from Europe had the highest prices in town. For the French living in the city, however, some of the delicacies sold there were apparently everyday necessities. The products from Japan were the cheapest and also the best, at least to my taste. Much food from communist China was also on the market. It was ironic that a country with hardly enough food for its own people was exporting some of it to a country with a tiny population and an enormous potential for food production. There was also a scarcity of food in the cans from China. A few pieces of meat or fish were packed in great quantities of water. A can of sardines from China did not contain even half as much fish as a can of the same size from Japan. The canned poultry contained as much bone as meat, and the "pork leg" was nothing more than a bone in a can. The sale of these items was nothing more than a swindle. The Yunnan ham was the only product of Communist China worth buying.

Shortly after the rules closing the restaurants on Mondays and Thursdays went into effect, complaints started to reach the Khmer government. Permission was granted to a few eating places to open again on those days, but only foreigners could be served. In the evenings, I had been eating regularly at the Korean House, where I was able to get fresh food, tastily prepared. Because the clientele was mostly Korean, the restaurant remained open every day. The restaurant was also secure.

Some of the Khmer soldiers in the city were famous for terrorizing restaurants, movie houses and other public establishments. They ate and drank in the restaurants without paying, sometimes demanded money from the owners, beat or threatened the personnel with guns, and sometimes threw hand grenades into establishments they felt had not met their demands satisfactorily. Americans were not targets of the attacks of the drunken, rampaging deserters, but stray bullets don't ask a person's nationality.

I had seen soldiers shooting up the town from a motorcycle in the downtown section of Phnom Penh. One drove while the other fired his .38 caliber, army issue revolver, apparently to scare some merchant. The soldiers responsible for the periodic shooting were either deserters or were acting as "enforcers" for one of the local big shots. The military police never bothered them. They were afraid, not only of the physical danger but also of offending some high-ranking officer who was engaged in extorting money from the local merchants. Stopping passing motorcycles to check registrations and ID cards, as they did every day on a street corner near my apartment, was a much safer and more agreeable way to spend the day than chasing armed bandits, and there was always the chance of collecting a little bribe money if one of the documents had expired.

Once, a drunken Khmer soldier had demanded either free food or free drinks at the Korean House. The owner did not agree to his demands, so the soldier became belligerent. He pulled his .45 caliber automatic out of its holster. Before he could use it effectively, he was grabbed by several of the customers. He got off one shot that put a hole in the ceiling before he was knocked cold. His head bounced on each of the cement steps leading from the restaurant as his unconscious body was dragged out and around the corner to the police station. The word got around that the Korean House was no place to start trouble. Too many regular customers were Tae Kwon Do instructors.

Needless to say, the discipline in the Army was in terrible shape and getting worse. This was beginning to show at the outposts far from the capital, where the soldiers with absentee officers often had to fight with knives after exhausting their ammunition. For their efforts, they had never received thanks, and they were now seldom getting any pay.

The American Aid Mission, with its hands-off policy, made no attempt at reform. From deep inside their concrete bunker, these officials were pumping large amounts of money into a rotten system without making any effort to find out where it was going. They would have done better

A Sunday street scene in downtown Phnom Penh, ca. 1974 (photo courtesy of Bill Ernst).

throwing the money down a hole. America spends millions on public relations abroad, but the policy makers always seem to forget one important fact. Even in countries with primitive or backward forms of government, most of the ordinary people can distinguish between words and actions, appearances and substance, fiction and truth. Observations of the military and civilian representatives of the United States make a much more profound impression on people than the published words of the United States Information Service.

On a rather windy day in July, the Helio Courier belonging to the American Embassy crashed again, this time at Phnom Penh. I had just landed TFB and parked. As I departed the aircraft, a great cloud of dust arose from the grassy infield beside the runway. Under it sat the beautiful-looking Helio with "United States of America" written on the side, which had just become a crumpled heap of twisted metal. The pilot extricated himself from the wreckage. He was the same Army major who had gone into the flooded field at Kompong Thom. This time he had been trying to take off.

Some of the Khmer workmen on the ramp emitted peals of derisive laughter. One of them asked me if that was the American Army. I said it was. The laughter continued. It was obvious that the American forces were not held in any higher regard by the Khmers than they were by the American pilots, some of whom were also making derogatory comments.

I felt a little sorry for the pilot. The Helio Courier is notoriously

The parking ramp at Pochentong Airport with the tower in the background (photo courtesy of Bill Ernst).

difficult to control during crosswind landings and take-offs, and the pilot badly lacked practice because the bunker rats he was supposed to fly so seldom wanted to go anywhere. Furthermore, since the accident occurred in Phnom Penh, he could not lie his way out of the responsibility as he had after his accident at Kompong Thom.

The United States Army was so unpopular with the Americans and Khmers at Pochentong Airport because the personnel there were such a crude lot. Obviously, the Khmer Republic was the place the Army sent its misfits.

A large part of the parking ramp was set aside for loading and unloading of the C-130s bringing in ammunition and other supplies. That part of the ramp was under the sole supervision of the United States Army.

Occasionally, while waiting to take off, we would hold on the edge of this territory at the entrance to the taxiway so that the landing aircraft could pass by on their way to the ramp. If we held there for more than a minute, we could expect a visit from some surly private, who would ask how long we were going to be there. This happened even when there were no C-130s within an hour of landing.

One day Sam was trying to park his DC-4 on the crowded ramp. There was no space available, but another DC-4 was on its way out. One of the Khmer ground crewmen directed him to turn around on the empty military side of the ramp and hold long enough for the other DC-4 to taxi by. One of the American GIs walked out and kicked the Khmer crewman who was directing the aircraft. After Sam parked and left his aircraft, he walked over to the military office and asked why his man had been kicked. The NCO in charge called his band of noncombatant soldiers together and tried to start a fight with Sam. Sam simply left.

Such was the behavior of the United States government's representatives. They had diplomatic immunity and were subject to no laws. Though they were a quarrelsome lot, arrogant, and quick to start trouble, they fled like rabbits when the communists started to close in. In contrast, some of the civilian pilots were still in the country after it fell.

Chapter 32

In mid–August I left on an extended leave to New York. One of my last duties was to check Ben out as the DC-3 captain who would take my place. After the last flight on August 13, I presented him with his captain's bars. He had waited a long time for this promotion because the company had only two DC-3s.

I left Phnom Penh with Bill Davis in the Tri-9 Convair 240, which was finally flying. From Battambang, I took the taxi to Poipet and crossed the border into Thailand. My visa read "routière," so I had no trouble getting my exit chop. After a brief visit to Vientiane, Laos, to pick up some personal possessions, I left for New York.

After the wedding, my wife and I went to Europe, where I learned I had been admitted to a university. My doctoral research would be conducted in Southeast Asia. I returned to Phnom Penh early in October ready to fly for a few weeks and give Tri-9 a chance to find a replacement for me. I found that things had changed quite a bit. Bill, the chief pilot, had quit after working for the company since 1971. Joe Weaver, the chief mechanic, and Tony Pradith, another pilot, had also quit. A check Joe had given me before he departed for parts unknown bounced. He also reportedly left other bad debts. Captain Sawai, still bitter about receiving $2 less than the other pilots per hour, had also quit.

Captain Sangob, who had finally quit SEAAT after the company had dissolved in a confused fit or wrangling among the management, was now flying the DC-3 for Tri-9, whenever it had fuel to fly. The self-inflicted fuel problem had returned. John Yim told me that he would have another aircraft for me to fly in about a week, but I told him that I would return to Europe if I was not absolutely needed by the company. John Yim then offered me the job of ferrying two DC-3s from Paris in December. I accepted his offer, and the next day, I visited various offices to get an exit visa. I then took a flight to Battambang and left the country by road.

In December I received a telegram informing me that the purchase of the DC-3s had been delayed. Finally, in late January, another telegram arrived to say that the aircraft would be ferried in two weeks. I was to meet

John Yim in Paris after he contacted me. The message never came. Ben Crawford wrote me that rockets were falling on Pochentong Airport daily, and most of the companies had moved their equipment out. Some diehards were still operating out of Kompong Som, but Tri-9 had evacuated its aircraft to Singapore to avoid having them slowly shredded to pieces by shrapnel.

The Khmer Republic was in its death agonies. The train between Battambang and the Thai border had been blown up. The Mekong River lifeline had been made so unsafe that few captains would risk their ships on the hazardous journey.

Vern Pickup, a former Continental Air Services pilot, raised money to buy an aircraft to fly into the stricken capital. Very high prices were being paid for each trip. Vern did not check his cargo tie-downs very well. He was used to flying in Laos with expert loadmasters. His load shifted on take-off, causing his aircraft to pitch suddenly. It lost flying speed and crashed, killing Vern. He left a widow and a small daughter.

A very bizarre episode involved David, the president of the Phnom Penh Pig Pilot Association. While on approach to Phnom Penh, SEAAT's Convair with David in the copilot's seat, flew through the zone of "friendly" artillery fire that we always had to cross. I had always tried to minimize this hazard by watching for impacting rounds and calculating the gun-target line, which I carefully avoided. As the Convair descended toward the airport, a 105mm howitzer round from a Khmer Army battery suddenly crashed through his cockpit from below, ripping a giant hole in the floor right beside David's seat and another one in the roof as it departed. It could not have missed David by more than an inch or two. It then exploded just above the aircraft, spraying the passenger compartment with shrapnel. Several passengers were killed or badly wounded. David was badly shaken up but unscratched.

While I waited in Europe for word to start ferrying the DC-3s, I saw pictures in the newspaper of Ambassador Dean rushing to the helicopter that was evacuating him from Phnom Penh. Although the airlift was still in progress and Phnom Penh was not in imminent danger of falling, the ambassador and his staff had packed their suitcases, abandoned their concrete bunker, and dashed for helicopters waiting at the airport. They were under heavy guard, not to protect them from the Khmer Rouge, but rather because they feared reprisal from the Khmers for what must seem an act of betrayal and cowardice. The vegetable that remained of Lon Nol after his strokes was also carried out of the country.

The fears of reprisal were unfounded and perhaps stemmed from the consciences of the American officials. I myself could sense the great disappointment of the Khmers, whose fighting spirit must have been replaced by hopelessness, being dealt this psychological blow at a time that they were

The author's last flight in Southeast Asia was a ferry flight of the above DC-3 formerly owned by the French Embassy in Laos to Singapore in 1976.

most threatened. Long after the ambassador fled, American pilots were still landing at and taking off from the Phnom Penh airport.

In contrast to the "official representatives" of the United States, the airlift pilots worked for low salaries with no "combat pay," no medals, no elaborate search and rescue efforts if they went down, no guarantee of another job after the airlift, and no pension. The service was performed mainly to achieve a sense of accomplishment and for love of flying. In a little less than a year, I had flown over 800 hours and carried well over 15,000 metric tons of cargo and passengers. I had the satisfaction of knowing that my work had helped to keep a small country alive, at least for a while. At the end of the airlift came unspeakable horror.

The manager of Tri-9, John Yim, had worked tirelessly to keep our small company operating. He worked honestly and did not forget about the safety of his crews. As the communists closed in on the capital, he was apparently shot and killed by Khmer Rouge soldiers on the road to the airport, but his fate is not known with certainty. He had stayed in Phnom Penh after the aircraft were evacuated, stubbornly believing that the United States would not abandon its allies. I had done my best to argue him out of this opinion, but he always expected a rescue force to be sent in to save the country.

Some of the pilots were still in the country after the Khmer Rouge took over. Phil Schneider had the misfortune of having to land at Kompong Som with a bad engine at the time the communists were moving in. He was captured and loaded aboard a truck which was to take him to Thailand. He rode part of the way and walked the rest until he reached the border. He was married to a Khmer girl whom he never saw again. He worked for a while in Singapore hoping to receive some news about her from the refugees who were crossing the Thai border in a steady stream. He was bitter and disappointed at the refusal of the United States Department of State to give him any help at all after he had worked so many years in support of American foreign policy.

The Convair with the bad engine had remained at Kompong Som Airport until it was bombed and destroyed by the United States Navy during its operation to free a captured American ship. The loss was borne by the company alone, since the Navy refused to pay for an "enemy" plane that the pilots wanted to take credit for destroying.

The military and diplomatic careerists went on from Phnom Penh to better things. Their performance while in Southeast Asia was never questioned because they had been doing what was expected of them. Washington was only looking for a way to get out of its commitments without losing face, and the corruption of the Khmer government certainly made the desired end come faster. The bloodbath that had long been predicted by experts actually took place, but this little "embarrassment" to the United States was successfully played down for a long time. "Peace" was officially declared by the press, but the war in Cambodia has kept on to this day.

During nearly six years of war in Cambodia, it is estimated that 200,000 people, mostly combat soldiers, were killed. In the first year of peace, perhaps a million and a half people were executed or systematically starved to death in forced labor camps, but perhaps the estimates as high as two million are correct. Then the Khmer Rouge started to make rules for themselves and began being a little too friendly with China, and a new round in the war began.

In the meantime, the press praised the Vietnamese communists for not killing massive numbers of South Vietnamese right away. The concentration camps for the soldiers of the Saigon government were well hidden in the Mekong Delta, where the press wasn't allowed to go, and the drowning of thousands of refugees forced to leave to escape the elimination programs directed against various minorities, such as the Cholon Chinese, could also be ignored. "Peaceful" Laos was supposed to be free of bloodletting, but the Thai fishermen along the Mekong kept finding corpses in their fish traps. Nothing was mentioned about the fate of the Meos who had worked so many years with the American CIA. They could simply be forgotten.

In 1975 and 1976, I was again in Southeast Asia, this time continuing biological research I had begun in Laos in 1971 and working toward my doctorate. I heard many stories of the refugees and learned the fate of many people I had known in Laos and Cambodia. The United States had spent billions to win the "hearts and minds of the people," and now it didn't want to hear anything more from the people whose hearts and minds had been won and who had to live in misery in refugee camps rather than face internment in communist re-education camps in their homelands. It did not even want to know about the many children of American servicemen who had a legal claim to American citizenship at birth, not to mention the military pilots who had been captured over Laos and were therefore not released with the other POWs.

In Bangkok and Singapore, I saw most of the aircraft that had been evacuated before the Khmer Rouge arrived in Phnom Penh. Some had been seized by creditors, while others just stayed on the ground for lack of business. The pilots had dispersed to all parts of the world in search of employment.

When I returned to Southeast Asia after the fall of Phnom Penh, I found some of the aircraft from the airlift parked forlornly in Bangkok and Singapore accruing tie-down fees that will never be paid. The pilots who stayed with SEAAT until the bitter end never received their pay for the last two or three months.

Several American pilots actually went to find the president of SEAAT in Singapore, where he was living in seclusion. When confronted by a destitute former employee who hoped to collect some of the thousands of dollars in back pay that he was owed, this tycoon of the air followed a standard routine. He would first tell the pilot about a wonderful deal that was about to be closed and predict enormous profits would be made. Next, he would tell the pilot to go to Bangkok and wait for a week or two until he arrived with all the money he needed to pay off his former employees. Then, he would reach into his pocket and pull out two or three dollars, saying, "If you need money now, I'll give you all I have. It's not much, but maybe this one or two dollars will help."

The pilot usually went to Bangkok to wait, and wait, and wait. The pilot wanted to believe, and the former SEAAT president was a practiced con man.

Donny Slugger, the former bodyguard of the SEAAT management and security chief, was left in Phnom Penh when the communists arrived. He made the trip to Poipet in a truck with other foreigners, guarded by communist troops. He claimed to have stayed behind to protect SEAAT personnel and property, but one former SEAAT pilot told me that he stayed because no pilot was willing to fly him out.

Donny sold his story to the *Bangkok Post*, and he let the word spread that he was working for the CIA. He actually convinced Sangob that he was a secret agent, but some of the American pilots said that if he kept making that claim, a real CIA agent might hear about it and make him depart Southeast Asia in one way or another. He had been promised an enormous salary which the SEAAT management failed to pay him. He claimed that he was owed about $10,000 in back wages. This was a fate deserving of the man hired to intimidate others who were seeking their own unpaid salaries.

Unspeakable horrors awaited the Khmers. In 1974 the population of their country was probably between five and seven million. Approximately 20 to 40 percent of this total were killed in the cruelest ways, generally with knives, clubs, or strangling cords in order to "save bullets." The red Khmers themselves were then decimated by the Vietnamese who drove out Pol Pot and put their own man in power. The fighting, which is still going on, may not end before the Khmers are eliminated as an ethnic group.

The most corrupt of the government leaders escaped the country to live in splendid exile in other parts of the world. One of the honest government ministers, Long Boret, showed his patriotism by choosing to be executed in the marketplace by the victorious Khmer Rouge rather than deserting his countrymen in their darkest hours. While some of the minor grafters might have also perished in the bloodbath, the great majority of the victims of the Khmer Rouge were ordinary hard-working people who had never enriched themselves at the expense of their countrymen or contributed in any way to the downfall of their nation. Their only crimes were being literate, having lived in a city, or just being present when one of the communists went into a murderous rage. The American Embassy staff members, who let their aid program sink into a swamp of corruption, were assigned to better positions in the government service elsewhere in the world.

It is the misfortune of the pilots, who are living in all parts of the world today, that their cause was a lost one. Their efforts gave over a million people one extra year of life, but the tragedy of Indochina will always remain particularly close to them. I will always be very proud to have been a Phnom Penh pig pilot.

Index